Feathers from the Green Crow

Sean O'Casey, 1905-1925

O'CASEY IN LONDON

CONTENTS

Introduction

SEAN O'Casey had his first play, *The Shadow of a Gunman*, presented at the Abbey Theatre in Dublin on April 12, 1923. In the next year *Juno and the Paycock* appeared, and early in 1926 *The Plough and the Stars* was heralded in by the Abbey's most celebrated riot since Dublin playgoers erupted over John Synge's *Playboy of the Western World*. W. B. Yeats stormed onto the stage amid flying shoes and flying punches and shouted into the uproar:

> You have disgraced yourselves again. Is this to be an ever-recurring celebration of the arrival of Irish genius? Synge first and then O'Casey. The news of the happenings of the past few minutes will go from country to country. Dublin has once more rocked the cradle of genius. From such a scene in this theatre went forth the fame of Synge. Equally the fame of O'Casey is born here tonight. This is his apotheosis.

His words were prophetic. O'Casey's three early plays are among the greatest in the modern repertoire; his later phantasies, like *Cock-a-doodle Dandy* and *The Drums of Father Ned,* are beginning to be valued for their true worth; his massive autobiography is in its third edition. Surely when the Allardyce Nicolls and John Gassners of the twenty-first century have sifted through Ibsen, Strindberg, and Chekhov, they must turn to Shaw and O'Casey and O'Neill.

The reading public pretty well knows what O'Casey is like. Like Shaw and Hemingway and Dylan Thomas—and unlike Eliot or Foster or Joyce Cary—he presents a picturesque public image. The Aran sweater; the unlighted pipe tucked in the corner of a broad and firm mouth; the thick-lensed glasses perched bravely on the bridge of a notable nose; the skull cap with some few wisps of white hair escaping from under it: this is the memorable picture that O'Casey presents to the public.

Attached to this image are two inconsistent sets of public characteristics. Many Irishmen think him waspish, vindictive, and misanthropic; some Americans think him suspiciously red. On the other hand, he has been lately more regarded as a benevolent grand oul' man given to charming, elder-statesman blather about life, love, and God. Such a lovable old cod couldn't *really* be a Communist—just a mite eccentric.

Of course, O'Casey is neither of these caricatures, nor is he both of them combined. What he is and what he thinks appear with force and clarity in his writing, and anyone who wants to meet that wise and witty man has only to hie himself to the nearest library or bookstore.

This collection is not concerned with that O'Casey, but with a much younger one. O'Casey is now in his eighty-second year, but when *The Shadow of a Gunman* appeared he was already forty-three years old. He has been a public figure for so long that we forget that by normal standards—though not by his own—he was middle-aged when he made his first success.

What was he doing before 1923? What was he like? What did his contemporaries think of him? For readers of Irish there are a few glimpses of O'Casey in Ernest Blyth's *Trasna na Bóinne,*[1] or in an article by Michael Mullen, the original of Seumas Shields, in *Feasta,* Bealtaine, 1955.[2] In 1914 Thomas Clarke, one of the leaders of the 1916 Rising, wrote to the old patriot John Devoy of "a disgruntled fellow named O'Casey." But perhaps the best portrait of all is in Desmond Ryan's *Remembering Sion:*[3]

> Once Seamus and I left Mount Street and found ourselves in a Drumcondra Sinn Fein club. . . . On the back benches sat Sean O'Casey, then much swayed by memories of Wolfe Tone, Robert Emmet, and especially Shane the Proud's head spiked on Dublin Castle in the days of Good Queen Bess, this last event in those days a burning and personal grief of his; it jostled bitter phrases from Mitchel and Lalor's most urgent calls to revolt on the eve of Forty-Eight in all Sean's speeches.
>
> Sean O'Casey sits in silence at the back of the hall during the lecture, a dour and fiery figure swathed in labourer's garb, for he works on the railways just then. His neck and throat are bound in the coils of a thick white muffler, and he looks like a Jacobin of Jacobins as his small, sharp and red-rimmed eyes stab all the beauty and sorrow of the world. He speaks first, and very fluently and eloquently in Irish, then launches out into a violent Republican oration in English, stark and forceful, Biblical in diction with gorgeous tints of rhetoric and bursts of anti-English Nationalism of the most

---

[1] Ernest Blyth, *Trasna na Bóinne* (Across the Boyne) (Dublin: Sáirséal and Dill, 1957).

[2] Michael Mullen, "An Ruathar Ud Agus A nDeachaigh" (The Raid and What Went With It), *Feasta,* Bealtaine, 1955.

[3] Desmond Ryan, *Remembering Sion* (London: Arthur Barker, Ltd., 1934).

uncompromising style. He will have none of the Socialists who have turned in to heckle the lecturer and he rends them savagely and brushes their materialism aside. Yes, he reminds them, when roused by his sharp words they murmur interruptions taunting him with the poverty and degradation of the Dublin workers, there is all that in life. Half to himself he speaks, lowering his voice to an intense whisper, but there is something else: joy. He speaks the word, and his tone gives a meaning to it even as he sinks down into silence on the bench, his fierce small head an angry star over all the others in the rear. Walter Carpenter rises and would argue with him, serious anger a-gleam in two grey bespectacled eyes. Walter is a leading Socialist propagandist, a most humourless and self-sacrificing man who walks in from Dunleary each night from home to his meetings in the city; he has ruined his worldly prospects for his beloved Red Flag and all but lost his business on the head of it. He is to be heard at the Socialist Party of Ireland, announcing solemnly that there will be a social followed by a supper, a cold supper, comrades, and you are all earnestly invited to attend and see 'ow Socialists be'ave themselves. His voice moans a reproach and an argument to Sean O'Casey. The fierce star at the rear becomes a soaring and hissing comet: O'Casey rises in fury and growls in Irish like a thunderstorm that he wishes no Englishman to teach him. Sean strides through the door with flames in his eyes and his fists clenched. A translation of his farewell reaches Walter, whose accents grow more and more suited to a wake. With a sob in his keen, he wails: "I 'ope some one will go out after that misguided individual who 'as rushed out eaten up with racial 'atred, and tell him for Gawd's sike, that I am not an Englishman but a Scotchman, and that I 'ad the honour to drop a tear in the grive of Charles Stewart Parnell!" Soon Sean O'Casey fell under the spell of Larkin and became as fierce a Labourist as he had been a physical-force Republican, still suspicious of the Socialists, and perhaps finding models for his Covey in his *Plough and the Stars*. The pages of Larkin's *Irish Worker* carried articles from his pen, all remarkable in their style and power with an independent outlook struggling through the over-fine writing and exotic wordiness. Yet that night in Drumcondra who could suspect he would yet voice the darkest depths of slumland and the agony of unsuspected years of turmoil and terror? As O'Casey strode beside his pipers' band or spoke in the clubs there was a force and character about him even if you thought he was a crank, a fanatic, a man whose mind had room for only one idea at a time. In private he had a courtesy and simplicity.

Unfortunately there are few glimpses like this of the young O'Casey, and if we want to know more we must turn to his autobiographies. However, a chief merit of those dazzling books is their fantastic manner. At any moment our clear and realistic vision of O'Connell Street is liable to dissolve into a gaudy vision of St. Patrick haranguing Lord Nelson on his pillar. We come away from the six volumes knowing a lot about the character of O'Casey, but little about what he actually did.

Was there, for instance, any preparation for his brilliant early plays? Did he do much writing before? If so, what kind of writing? In the 2,156 pages of the autobiographies there are sketchy allusions to early work on perhaps ten pages. In *Windfalls* of 1934 he printed a few early verses. Beyond that, nothing.

Yet an apprenticeship preceded *The Shadow of a Gunman*. Its author did not erupt into literature without much hard work and sometimes bitter disappointment. This selection from old newspapers, magazines, pamphlets, and manuscripts is a testament to struggle and to courage, for every bit of it was composed under conditions which most writers would find impossible—not to write in, but to survive in.

Although there was a long apprenticeship, it was not a conscious one. Unlike Joyce, O'Casey did not consider himself dedicated to literature; and most of this early work was written for some immediate, nonliterary purpose. At one time or another, the young O'Casey was intensely identified with all of the major issues of his time and country. Many of the following pages are only in a broad sense literature. Much of the material deals with dead issues, but little of it is itself dead. Through all of it strides the spirit of an alive and engaged individual, and through all of it, I think, a pattern can be seen.

Desmond Ryan called O'Casey a fanatic. If by "fanatic" we mean a man who wants something with fierce determination, then O'Casey was a fanatic. He took up many causes with high hopes and a fervency for the ideal which few people have. He had little patience for half-hearted measures, and he was too honest to tolerate compromise. He was forever pointing out faults and suggesting improvements. He was, in effect, a critic; and criticism, harnessed to imagination, eloquence, and a scornful contempt for folly, can be a most unpopular trait. Time and again,

O'Casey was blocked. His proposals came to nothing, and when he saw that he could accomplish nothing, he retired from the field.

Only after he had tried many avenues of practical action did O'Casey seriously begin to write plays. As an artist he is interested in writing the best plays that he can, but he is an artist like Shaw was. He writes plays packed with opinions, plays that exist to teach and persuade as much as they do to amuse, to move, and to grip. His plays preach the full and free human life that his early struggles had taught him to value. The lyricism of his plays extolls that life; the comedy of his plays laughs at the follies that would hinder it from coming into being.

In this selection from his early work, we see O'Casey forming his opinions. The period of this selection is from 1905, when he was just beginning to write, to 1925, a few months before his departure for England; from the unpublished poem, "The Soul of Man," to the unpublished one-act tragi-comedy, "Nannie's Night Out"; from awkwardness to mastery.

In a sense, this book may be taken as documentation for an autobiography. The opinions in the stories and songs and essays were all O'Casey's; some of them he would disagree with today, for this period was one of growth. The opinions in the connecting notes are all mine; if I have misread his growth, the work is there to correct me.

I have wondered if I am doing the playwright a disservice by resurrecting some of this material. This problem I have pondered for some months, because I would wittingly do no disservice to a man whose work I have as strongly admired as I have ineptly discussed.

For myself, I have answered the problem in this way: if James Joyce had written "Trees," the worth of *Ulysses* would yet be undiminished. In fact, almost anything written by a Joyce would be of value to scholarship and perhaps ultimately to humanity. There is no "Trees" in this selection from O'Casey's early work, but there is, to my mind, one masterpiece.

One last defence. Of his early works O'Casey once wrote, "all . . . have gone down into the limbo of forgotten things. But I often wish that they were alive again, for buried in them are a wild joy and a savage bitterness that I shall never know again."

The world may be too full of savage bitterness; it cannot afford to lose one jot of wild joy.

* * *

If I knew how to avoid the conventional language of acknowledgement, I would, for my rather thorough ignorance of Ireland's history, language, and music has made the editing of this book, in a real sense, a collaboration with many people.

In particular, I received much help from the researches of Mr. Ronald Ayling, Dr. Robert Caswell, and Professor David Krause. For information about various Irish airs, I am indebted to Mrs. Rae Korson of the Library of Congress, Mr. Peader Nunan, Mr. Colm O'Lochlainn, Professor Donal O'Sullivan, Mrs. Raney Stanford, Professor Walter Starkie, Professor Mabel Worthington, and to my colleagues at Purdue University, Professors Ray Browne and Merle W. Tillson. For transcribing most of the music, I am greatly indebted to Constance Hunting. I am able to include the tune for "Twenty-Four Strings to My Bow" because Miss Ria Mooney graciously consented to sing it for me and Dr. A. J. Potter, L.R.A.M., transcribed her tape recording. The song, "That Old Fashioned Mother of Mine," in "Nannie's Night Out" is copyright 1919 by Lawrence Wright Music Company and used by permission of Harms, Incorporated. The songs, "Sergeant William Baily" and "The Soldier's Song," were written by Peadar Kearney. Selections from *Inishfallen, Fare Thee Well,* by Sean O'Casey, copyright 1949, 1950, by Sean O'Casey, are used by permission of The Macmillan Company. I am indebted to the estate of Mr. Lennox Robinson for permission to quote from *Lady Gregory's Journals,* and to the Public Trustee and The Society of Authors for permission to quote from the prefaces to *Immaturity* and *Man and Superman* by Bernard Shaw.

I must thank also Chancellor Franklin Murphy of the University of California at Los Angeles for lending me a manuscript; Mr. Cathal O'Shannon of Dublin for much information about the early days of the Irish Transport and General Workers' Union and for permission to quote from *Fifty Years of Liberty Hall;* Dr. Seán Ó hÉideáin, Consul General of Ireland at Chicago and Messrs. Barry Gray and Alf Mac Lochlainn for help in translating from the Irish; Professor Vivian Mercier for various helpful hints; and Mr. David Ransom for his guidance in matters of orthogrify, and, punctuation.

A special debt I owe to Mr. Gabriel Fallon of the Abbey Theatre for his invaluable help, and to him and his wife for much kindness and warm hospitality.

To librarians at the National Library of Ireland, at Trinity College, Dublin, and at Purdue University, I owe thanks for affording me every facility and courtesy; and to the Purdue Research Foundation I owe thanks for a grant which enabled me to spend a summer in Dublin collecting this material. A portion of my introductory notes has appeared in slightly different form in *Modern Drama*.

And finally I thank my wife for shepherding our many children and keeping the home fires smouldering while I caroused about Dublin's fair city.

R. H.

Lafayette, Indiana
June, 1961

Opinions

O'CASEY wrote between 1907 and 1925 dozens of articles for newspapers and magazines, for he was passionately engaged in the public issues of his time and of his country. So, although these essays are specifically about Irish Republicanism, Irish Labour, the Irish language, and Irish education and culture, through all of them runs one central theme, one ultimate issue, the explosive condemnation of what Shaw called "the greatest of our evils, and the worst of our crimes," poverty.

O'Casey was not writing belles-lettres. Some of his pieces, particularly for Jim Larkin's *Irish Worker*, were unsigned. Some, like "By the Campfire," his weekly column of notices and news about the Irish Citizen Army, record only items of interest for the historian. Many others lack "literary polish," and some are downright awkward. Yet even in the early essays, where O'Casey is fighting syntax or half strangling in gorgeous rhetoric, he makes his point forcefully. He was not greatly interested in beauty of expression, even though he sometimes grew intoxicated with words. But he was burningly interested in what he had to say, so he learned to use language as a weapon. His admired friend, Larkin, was a masterly orator; and O'Casey, like Shaw, became a frequent and fluent public speaker before he became a writer. The style of these essays sprang from oratory, from the immediacy of fluent, excited, and exciting speech. If these opinions are sometimes awkward, they also reveal an engaged, impassioned, and subtle man hammering out a weapon of expression and emerging ultimately as a master of English prose.

I have arranged these opinions topically, rather than chronologically, so that it would be easier to note the progression of O'Casey's thought. Rather than encumber the page with perhaps unnecessary footnotes, I have included at the end of the book a short biographical index to identify the principal public figures of O'Casey's Dublin.

Education and Culture

How I enjoyed the glory that was mine when something I had written first appeared in print! It was an article criticising the educational policy in Ireland sponsored by Mr. Augustine Birrell. . . . I remember sending the paper in which the article appeared to a Protestant pastor for whom I had a deep fondness, and from whom I expected great praise and many words of encouragement, but the comment he made was a dead silence. Venturing, some weeks later, to ask him what he thought of it, he placed a hand gently on my shoulder and shocked me, saying, "The man who wrote that article, John, is a traitor, and ought to be in jail."

Windfalls

Sound the Loud Trumpet

The Englishman, in the shape of the British Government, has lifted up his hands to bless us; yea, and we shall be blessed.

Now shall the winter of our discontent be made glorious summer by this illustrious son of Britain, the most eminent and right honourable authority on Irish Education—Augustine Birrell. Now can the Irish shout with a loud voice; now can they seriously break into solemn and joyous anthem of victory; now can they cast their caps into the air and cry with a deep and unanimous shout—hallelujah, hallelujah! And, why? Augustine Birrell, Chief Secretary for Ireland, the English Government's strongest man is for us; crowns us with his most sincere and most fulsome sympathy, and tells us that all, aye all, shall at length be well—listen to the voice of one who speaks—not as the nondescript leaders of Irish thought and intellect speak—but as one

2

having authority: listen to the voice of Mr. Birrell: "I have spent a few weeks in the study of Primary Education in Ireland, and I agree with the words that fell from the honourable member for Louth." Some weeks! Dear Augustine, how could you now? What a semi-sublime and delightful spirit of self-sacrifice you must have to devote some weeks to the careful consideration of such a trifling subject as *Irish* education.

We bend our rugged Irish heads in sweet acknowledgment of your wondrous and most pleasing condescension! Worthy Mr. Birrell. Yourself's the authority on Irish Primary Education. But hark! Mr. Birrell speaks again—"The schools of Ireland in their present state and condition are something like a scandal and a disgrace. I could entertain the House by reading to the House words of condemnation, but I am quite content with the extracts given by my honorary friend, Mr. J. O'Connor, in his most clever and persuasive speech. . . . For years quarrels have been going on betwen the Board and the Treasury with regard to the money to be granted for building; the late Chief Secretary, Mr. Bryce, as did the other secretaries, did his best, and I am anxious to do my best." Arrah! to be sure they did their best, and, you, too, Mr. Birrell, are anxious to do your best for poor old Ireland's sake. You are not the first Englishman that did his best. Praise be to God! England has raised up many true champions of Ireland's imperishable freedom; Birrell is one of them. It is all we ask, humbly and most respectfully, your best—sure, no man can do more. And if you fail—well sure, that is the sad lot of many and it can't be helped. You see there is going on an eternal quarrel between the Board and the Treasury, and what can a poor man do?

O foolish Irish people! Why do ye clamour and make unseemly noises? For goodness sake hold your peace and do not make the ears of your best friend tingle with your unhappy and discordant cries. Go on dear Board and dearer Treasury, take your time, and settle your disputes in a temperate and orderly way, and we, the Irish people, sons and daughters of Banba,[1] the historic Irish race, will be content with calm decay, and pray fervently to be allowed to die in peace and charity with all men and every nation. Again, hark to the voice that is like to the sound of a running brook: —"I am authorised by the Treasury to say that . . . they are prepared to consider any scheme for the teaching of Irish without regard to the question whether the result may be to restore the fees to the amount they stood at in 1905. We want Irish taught educationally, as a discipline and enrichment of the mind. In the meantime we desire that the Gaelic League should not be interfered with in the good work which it is doing. . . . I am glad to be able to make this announcement. I hope the House will consider it satisfactory. From what I have heard I believe that movement to be a great and permanent one, and one which will do much good to the mental calibre of the Irish people."

So do we, Mr. Birrell—our soul's within you! It is a great movement—permanent and renewing—outlasting Mr. Long, the Board, the Treasury, or even you, Mr. Birrell. Want Irish taught educationally, as an enrichment of the mind: Agreed again! Isn't it wonderful now how much we have in common with our British Government. So do we, Mr. Birrell; we want it taught so, and we'll have it taught so, too. As an "enrichment of the mind," why, yes! And more!—an enrichment of the Irish heart and soul as well, by infusing into them, through the language, the true and living force of patriotism.

"I hope the Gaelic League will not be interfered with." We hope not, Mr. Birrell. There are even still a few fiery souls in that body that might imprudently resent interference. But have no fears, Mr. Birrell; the great majority of Leaguers are men and women of common-sense, and welcome and fully appreciate your most sincere encomium and sagacious counsel. People of Ireland, what think ye? Sound the trumpet, beat the drum,

[1]A poetic name for Ireland.

sing and be glad, for is not Birrell our friend, our ally, our buckler, and our shield? Truly, it is a blessed thing that we have lived to see this happy and auspicious day. All is well now! Birrell will give us everything, and if he cannot give us anything, he promises us everything, and it's all the same! Good intentions are everything, and we will take the will for the deed. And though our poor children—the Hope of the Nation—will have to herd together in dismal places, which a short-sighted, yet well-meaning Government calls schools—though their tender and quick-witted minds be de-Irished and stupefied by a system which a paternal Government calls education; though they are taught to admire and revere the things of Europe, Asia, Africa, America, Australia, and especially England; while their own country is to them bare of all useful and inspiring memories— her history unknown, her language unspoken, her music unheard, her achievements despised, and her character unloved; though the nation's teachers live in humble splendour, on a small but regular salary, wrung from the hand of a mean but sympathetic Government; yet, notwithstanding all these, we honour and revere the man who, when Ireland asks for bread, throws at her what he can—a stone.

Surely, all our sorrows and trials are worth enduring when they provoke an expression of sympathy, a word of counsel, a nod of encouragement, from such a man as Birrell. They are prepared to consider any scheme—blessed words, generous Treasury!

Listen, Leaguers, what more do you want?

What more will ye get? Let us sing and be glad! The Treasury is with us! Birrell is on our side! The British Government is our helper. Seaghan Buidhe[2] is not the hard-hearted fellow we took him to be. He has, after all, a kindly—yea, even a noble side to his nature. We ought, we must remember that the calls upon his generosity are many and great. He has an

[2]John Bull.

army to maintain, a navy to strengthen, a police to pay, and what he can spare he will assuredly give us. Let us not be too exacting. After all, what is Irish Education to a fresh battalion, a new gunboat, or the comfort of the police force? To gain a huge lump of the world as Empire would evoke the admiration of the gods; what doth Seaghan Buidhe profit if Ireland should save her national soul? Let us not expect too much; we act foolishly if we do. Let us remember the wise saying—

Man wants but little here below.

We want very little, and it is well that it is so; for very little we'll get, but we are thankful for even a little.

We are beginning to see that we have regarded the power that rules us unjustly. We will do so no more. While causing all our misery, it only sought our happiness; while destroying our industries, it only wished to strengthen our humility; while banning our education and history, it only endeavoured to educate us. Thank heaven we have had sufficient gratitude to send over a hundred of our leaders to venerate the god of British Rule in the Temple of Westminster. Let us build an idol of that power here in our own land, and deck it with garlands of praise and honour, and prostrate our nationality before it. Will it not be a beautiful thing, this idol of the British Rule, with its heart of gold, a tongue of silver, hands of steel, cheek of brass, head of wood, and its feet of clay? Let us then sacrifice all we have before it—our Language, History, Music, Tradition, Literature, our children's Heritage, our National Spirit, our Glory, our Liberty, all—before the grinning idol of British Rule, and let the High Priest be—Birrell!

AN GALL FADA,[3] *The Peasant and Irish Ireland*, May 25, 1907

[3]O'Casey's first pseudonym, "the long foreigner," or perhaps "the tall Protestant"; O'Casey was, of course, born a Protestant in a predominantly Catholic country.

Room for the Teachers

What authority surfeits on would relieve us: if they would yield us
but the superfluity, while it were wholesome, we might guess they
relieved us humanely; but they think we are too dear: the leanness
that afflicts us, the object of our misery, is as an inventory to par-
ticularise their abundance; our sufferance is a gain to them.

Coriolanus (I, 1)

It is gratifying to think that the sap of discontent is stirring
in the dry bones of the teaching profession. It is a distinct step
forward to realise our misery. A few more progressive steps and
the teachers will be marching in alignment with the rest of the
workers. But they must cast from their shoulders the ghostly
and threadbare mantle of respectability. This fetters their movements and blinds their eyes; but it will not keep them warm,
nor will it, like a magician's cloak, produce in mystery the where-
withal to feed them; nor will it hide from their comrades in
the Labour movement the poverty and silliness of antiquated
pretensions to a status in the good opinion of society which ignores
them—though it sometimes mouths an expression of pretended
sympathy—but let the teachers be assured that the society to
which some of them think they belong, will never lift a hand to
help them. Their one care and only hope is an intense and active
union with the organised workers.

The number of teachers that voted for affiliation with
the Labour movement is a hopeful sign, though it is irritating to
remember how many voted against it, but considering all the
evils they have endured, and how patiently and how long they
have endured them, it is a wonder that they have not degenerated
into slaves of the fourth dimension.

The teachers need have no fear that by identifying themselves with the Labour movement they will lose that curious
and much prized "status," about which so many of them are

fond of talking. They will always command the respect and admiration of the working classes by demanding that position in the nation's life which is their due, and which they can never hold without an intensified improvement in their economic position, and the reverence and admiration of the workers are more to be desired than a reluctant permission from society to enter into a middle-class or a first-rate drawing-room.

The desire for a higher life is brooding now in the breast of the humblest worker, and he is fighting that it may be satisfied. Their progress means a corresponding depression in the social position of the teachers, should they remain quiescent, and, if they refuse to walk in the upward way, they will soon discover that there is not one so poor as to do them reverence.

It would be well for the teachers to learn that they are made of the one stuff as the workers; that there is no degree of clay that moulds humanity; let them remember that as Krishna taught, "that man observes distinctions when he is stupefied with ignorance," and they will find in the Labour movement their one true refuge and their one true strength.

As W. O'Brien and P. T. Daly point out in the Press, the workers, for their own sakes, must stand by the teachers. They are vigilant now and they will not continue to suffer the minds of their children to be cast in the moulds of Welply and his coterie of educational inquisitors. The very system that Labour is out to destroy is being perpetuated in the National schools. Our children are not educated; they are taught to be useful so that they may bring profits to their future masters. They are trained as an exhibitor would train his dogs; not indeed to develop the animals' mentality, but simply to make money out of them. And the teachers are employed at the lowest possible wage to give them an education that will fit them for "their station in life," which is, of course, to make them energetic hewers of wood and drawers of water.

But now—quoting from P. T. Daly's letter—"when the oligarchic National Board speaks to the teachers, it speaks to the workers," and these gentlemen will soon realise that some of us are able to analyse phrases in the English language, in a way so original that it may surprise them. The wage question is, at present, the one that calls for immediate solution, and the fixing of the teachers' salaries should not be left to Mr. Duke nor to Mr. Starkie, but should be settled by the teachers themselves, who are most nearly concerned, and by the Labour delegates, as representing those whose children are taught by them.

Teachers, like all human beings, must eat and drink and clothe themselves, and at present these must be difficulties that their present miserable wage can scarcely overcome. One would think that the reward of the teacher would be such as to entice to the profession the best minds in the country. And the workers demand that their children must be served by the best minds in the country, and this can only be done by creating conditions that will assuredly bring about such a consummation.

What opportunities present themselves to the teachers for self-improvement? Surely, the homes of the Irish teachers ought to be centres of literature, art, science and music; and are they? It is hardly conceivable. How in the name of goodness can they indulge their higher tastes when their salary barely allows them to live? Why some of them would not be able to pay for a course in the cheapest school of art or science. Day by day the workers become intellectually keener, and as they become more and more economically free, their education will increase, and they must, consequently, demand a higher and purer education for their children. So that the teachers' profession will become a more responsible one, and the future, therefore, demands the definite improvement of the present.

Let the teachers shed their hesitation to use the weapons of Labour. They will have organised Labour behind them and surely the National movement will not withhold its help. Should all else fail, let them strike for better conditions.

There are many things that the teachers will have to claim. They will have to fight for a fuller freedom; for the improvement in the lives of the children they teach—for this would mean better and quicker results for themselves—school improvement; abolition of harassing and degrading methods that delay advancement and the clipping of the inspectorial claws and wings. The teacher must be something above a slave that instructs the children of the workers.

But all these will probably follow the happy union with Labour. It was a great feat to demolish the half-god of respectability that frightened you from the temple of Labour.

> Happily know,
> When half-gods go,
> The gods arrive.[4]

Irish Opinion, June 12, 1918

Life and Literature

When one regularly reads the weekly articles under above heading appearing in the *Irish Statesman,* one is struck with the singular circumstances that the double-thought title seems to suggest to the various writers the necessity of dealing only with the subject of Literature, leaving Life to work her ten hours a day, to eat her three meals—when she can get them—a day, and to spend her beggarly leisure time at the Hippodrome. They seem to be interested only in what Literature may think of Life, and absolutely careless (or ignorant) of what Life may think of Literature. It is true, of course, to say that we cannot think too

[4] A slight misquotation of the last lines of Emerson's poem, "Give All to Love."

much of Literature, but then it is equally true that we can (and do) think far too little of Life.

I want to write—or try to write—a little, not about the relation of literature towards life, but about the attitude of life towards literature; and I am going to limit the conception of life to that section of the community that is called "the working class"; and again, to limit the term "working class" to that huge mass of Irish humanity that is gathered into the various folds of the Trade Unions that embrace the Irish Labour Movement.

It is undoubtedly true to say that the working classes are, generally speaking, the most important, and the most ignorant section of the Irish nation. And as they form the largest portion of the people, then we are forced to admit, notwithstanding our intelligence—and we are intelligent—in spite of our sense of humour, and we have a sense of humour—now and again—that the Irish people are an ignorant people, and they will remain so till the working class determinedly walks towards a higher plane of Knowledge.

The higher plane of Knowledge is certainly not to be found in the wilderness of Trade Unionism. Trade Unionism is important, not because of its knowledge, but because of its power. The present-day Trade Unionist is as ignorant and as mechanical as the soldier; and, in many ways, just as dangerous. Trade Unionism may give the worker a larger dinner plate—which, heaven knows, he badly needs—but it will never give him a broader mind which he needs more badly still. Indeed, the thing in which the Trade Unions take the most interest is the very thing of which they are most ignorant—the Labour problem. A few of them think that divinity sprawls over the pages of Karl Marx's *Das Kapital*, and that the infallible indication of this divinity is that the work is beyond their comprehension—possibly a very natural view to take. But to by far the greatest number, Karl Marx is as if he had never been born. They are like the

Republicans, who, swearing by what Wolfe Tone said, and what Wolfe Tone did, have never read his *Autobiography*. A man may be a Trade Unionist for all the years of his working life, and, dying, find that not one cubit has been added to his mental stature. He "comes out by the same door as in he went."

Then what must the workers do if, in the mass, they are not to become an ugly, huge, horrifying fossil? It is useless to plead that other parties are striving as ardently to become crystallised in a single idea, or a single hope, or, worse still, in a single-hearted hate. Cumann na nGaedhael[5] building up the State in its hatred of the Republicans; and the Republicans, in the vain-glory of their self-denial, shattering the nation to pieces. If Manasseh wants to be an ass, well, give the animal liberty to bray; and if Ephraim wishes to join himself to an idol, well, let him alone.

To-day, in its ignorance and vulgarity, Labour is a huge, squirming Fafnir, with its coils in field, factory and workshop, not guarding its wealth, but cherishing its ignorance; and it is none the less repulsive because it has succeeded in thrusting itself into the Senate.

The gulf between the workers and the men and women of genius in Art and Literature seems to be as impassable as that gulf which is said to be between the blessed and the lost, and from what the daily papers say, and what the politicians preach, and what the employers do—or don't do—it seems that all expect the workers to have no higher expression than Calibanistic complaints against hunger and cold and hardship.

The workers must come out of their one-room tenements and out of their dimly-minded Trade Unions—occasionally at least—to pull the plough a little nearer to the stars. They must learn that self-realisation is more important than class-conscious-

---

[5]The Society of the Irish People, the political party of W. T. Cosgrave, which supported the Treaty in 1922, and which was the ancestor of the present Fine Gael party.

ness; and they must learn that there is no possibility in the whining sentimentality of *The Voice of Labour* or the strident sentimentality of *The Irish Worker*.

How then are we to come to a full self-realisation, so that we can no longer be deceived, and our passion be for reality?

"Let a man examine himself," says St. Paul (I think), and this we must do, though difficult, for we are so busy examining others, that we have very little time, and no inclination, to examine ourselves. To realise what they are, and what they may become, the workers must look into the mirrors of the poem, the novel and the play. In these they can see themselves, search their hearts and examine their consciences, for these are they that testify of themselves. Here, and here only, can they develop the power to see themselves as others see them; to gaze at, and meditate upon their own splendour and their own poverty; their own beauty, and their own deformity. And, yet they couldn't understand a poem, even, if by some miracle, they could be persuaded to listen to one; they refuse to read any book worthy of the name of novel, and they hear a play with the same pleasure as they hear the Gospel.

Why?

In the first article of this nature the writer, referring to the decision of the editor to employ a team rather than a single contributor, agreeing with the editor, said: "Better articles will probably be the result. Writers in Ireland are, usually ten-to-fivers, and are very often too weary to write."

The great mass of the Dublin workers who are not ten-to-fivers (more likely some of them are five-to-tenners) will appreciate the saying, "too weary to write," for they themselves are, invariably, too weary to read.

Who would be impertinent enough to throw a stone of condemnation at a Dublin docker, who has pushed a heavy truck carrying frequently half a ton for many hours across a Purgatorially paved quay, because, after having taken his tea, he does not sit down to interest himself (and, probably shock his wife) in *Per Amica Silentia Lunae:* or confound a visiting docker with the stoical wisdom of Epictetus. Or who would venture to point the finger of scorn at a carter who has been all day humping sacks of cement, each weighing sixteen stone, when easing his aching muscles by the fire, does not say when his wife calls out: "There's *The Herald,* Jack!" "*The Herald!* Hand me down *The Garden of Epicurus*—Anatole France."

And why should the docker reading Anatole France, or the carter reading Yeats, be a laughter-provoking conception? Have they then a claim in the Unemployment Exchange, but none in the upward progress of man? His right is as unalienable as the right of others to enjoy the sweet perfumes in the Garden of Literature, or to feel Divinity in the contemplation of the coloured visions portrayed by the Masters in the Hall of Painting. No one can imagine the shade of Rembrandt looking dubiously at a coal-heaver lost in admiration of one of the Master's works, walking over to an attendant, shaking him and saying: "What do you mean by allowing this roughly-clad wretch to dare to try to see the visions I saw!" Or of Yeats—if he were present—snatching *The Wind Among the Reeds* from the hands of a builder's labourer, saying: "Keep the hod in your hand, my good man, these glorious things are not for the like of you."

Rather do these lay their treasures of gold and frankincense and myrrh at the feet of all men, chanting in the radiance of colour, or the melody of song: "Ho, everyone that thirsteth, come ye to the waters, and he that hath no money, come ye, buy and eat; yea, come, buy wine and milk, without money and without price!"

And this is the silent need of the workers: loss of ignorance and acquirement of culture. However the worker may shout for an increase in his wage, or protest against a reduction, be he at work, or waiting wearily in the Unemployment Exchange, his greatest need and most urgent claim is a share in the culture of the society of men.

Governments may come, and governments may go; the carpenter and the labourer may be the carpenter and the labourer still, but there is the need that the one should no longer be an ignorant labourer, or the other an ignorant carpenter, if the people of Ireland are ever going to be something other than a race of fools during an election, and a race of madmen during a civil war.

And to bring this to pass our colleges must become something more than shops for the sale of caps and gowns and chancellor's robes; our schools must be something more than pounds for children that might stray into mischief, and our Trade Unions must shelter literature a little higher than a ledger for recording subscriptions, a minute book and a bundle of envelopes and note paper.

The Irish Statesman, December 22, 1923

Nationalism

I N his youth O'Casey was an ardent Republican who, it is related, would wear only clothes that had been manufactured in Ireland, including even his shoestrings. He belonged for a time to the Irish Republican Brotherhood, a secret organisation dedicated to Ireland's complete independence from England. It was the I.R.B., according to Diarmuid Lynch in his *The I.R.B. and the 1916 Rising,* that provided the principal planning and impetus for the Rising of Easter Week. David Krause, in *Sean O'Casey, the Man and His Work,*[1] reports that O'Casey quit the I.R.B. in disgust with its leaders although not with its principles.

Even as late as 1913, in his argument with "Euchan" in *The Irish Worker* (see below), O'Casey seemed still committed to revolutionary Republicanism. Soon afterwards, however, his concept of Irish political freedom became strongly influenced by the aims of organised Labour. After the labour struggles in the winter of 1913 he was a confirmed internationalist; the struggle for Irish independence was, for him, overshadowed by the world struggle between Capital and Labour. The Rising of 1916 only completed his disillusionment with revolutionary Republicanism, a disillusionment vividly dramatized in his masterpiece, *The Plough and the Stars.*

Guth ar an Ngadre[2]

"Ni lia duine nasamail"[3] is a true proverb emphasised in last month's *Freedom* by the clash of opinion expressed by "Crimal," "Raparee," "Northman," and "Seumas og." Allow me to blow a blast on a little trumpet of my own that I may add melody to the discord of these "beaters of drum and twanglers of the wire." The Separatist movement is, from the lowest root to

[1]David Krause, *Sean 'O'Casey, the Man and His Work* (New York: The Macmillan Co., 1960).

[2]"Ngadre" is apparently a misprint for "ngaoith," in which case the title would be translated as "A Voice on the Wind."

[3]"There are as many opinions as men." The Gaelic phrase should be written, "Ni lia duine ná samhail."

16

the uppermost bough, a Democratic movement, living, moving, and having its being in the fibres of the Irish people. Our work will not have been accomplished when we stand over the grave of the "last of the English." Ireland's star of destiny will not be at its full brilliancy when England's grip is loosened; it will indeed be radiant, but the work of re-creation will daily make it glitter with an ever increasing glow. Our work is not alone to drive far from us our connection with England, but to enter into our inheritance; not to repeal the Union, but to overthrow the conquest; not alone to end our subjection to England, but to labour that we may have life and have it more abundantly. Is it not passing strange that anyone should believe that when Ireland stands free, then Ireland's work is done? Ireland's freedom will be a task glorious to any generation of Gaels—God send it may be ours—but the others shall enter into our labours and reap with joy where we have sown with blood and tears. But woe unto us if we hand over our ideals to be squared and shaped and glossed by those who would write in our skies that socialism is Ireland's hope, and hang around our necks the green ribbons of "Cumannacht na hEireann."[4] Our social progress, present and future, must be garnered from the inspiration, the purity, the fulness of Ireland's past, not from the swelling hearts of England's suckled socialists. There is nothing new under Ireland's sun in Mitchel's or Lalor's doctrines. These were anticipated in the social life of Gaelic Ireland, where kingship affixed no gaudy seal on the grinding of the poor, but where the nation shared his greatness and his splendour; where great men were the concentrated flame of the Nation's souls. "Except ye come as little children," says the Teacher of all men; and behold, as an Piaraiseach has told us in his splendid paper on "Education," when a King's Envoy came demanding audience, there was but one answer for him:—"The King is with his foster children."

[4]The Socialist party of Ireland.

There was in Irish Leadership a more blessed bliss than the decking of the body with purple and fine linen. Life was good for all their people as it was good for themselves. England and her socialists have no new message for the Gael. "Will you not be seated," said the Courtiers to Shane the Froud, when he appeared in the court of Elizabeth. "Not while my gallowglasses stand," said the kingly Sean. "But they are only your servants," was the astonished reply. "They are my kinsmen," was the reply of the "ignorant, half-civilised, Irish chieftain." And instead of Sean we are to choose as our examples men of the race who garnished the Gates of Dublin Castle with the kingly head of our chieftain.

But surely, there should be union between the Separatists and the railway labourer, the factory hand, and transport worker. Surely Democracy follows hard on the heels of Republicanism. "Raparee" advises wrongly when he urges that National ideals should weave a bandage around the toilers' eyes. The men who are linked to Wolfe Tone's soul are mainly toilers, and their condition must be better in a Republican Ireland. We do not demand all the good things of this life, but we do want bread that we may live. The guarantee of a better life is no sop; it is our due. To talk in this way shows that "Raparee" never felt the aching back, the tired arm, the humiliated spirit, the wet foot and the pang of hunger. We are not Ireland's slaves, nor her servants, nor her employees, "Raparee," but Ireland's children; therefore, we claim the children's inheritance in a free Ireland—the best our Mother has to give. "Raparee" says we have, in the Land war, driven out of Ireland the last remnant of her aristocracy. Well, the back of our hand to them, they were never any good, though they did ornament our country with noble monuments such as Nelson Pillar, in O'Connell St.; Wellington Pillar in the Park and the lovely statue in front of Leinster House. Ireland's true aristocracy will take these down, and substitute memorials to Lalor, to Tone, and a living people will, please the God of the

Gael, write with a sword, an epitaph to Emmet on the heart of their foe. We will have Brotherhood and Equality in a Free Ireland; not merely cringing equality based on modern English socialistic ideals, but a bright and living Gaelic equality of opportunity for development of innate strength, talent, and virtue. But we should preach this from the housetops. Why should we fear to proclaim a Nation where unnecessary sorrow shall be no more, and whose unnecessary tears shall be wiped away from every eye?

"Raparee's" article on "The Great Illusion" was most amusing.

Irish Freedom, March, 1913

Faithful Forever

Dost hear the tale the traitors tell,
            Ireland, dear Ireland?
In whisper low or joyous yell,
            Of thee, of thee, dear Ireland?
That thou dost eat the Saxon bread;
That all the hopes thy soul hath wed,
Now prostrate lie with all thy dead,
            Ireland, dear Ireland!

They lie, they lie—the cowards—they lie,
            Ireland, dear Ireland.
Nor blazing guns, nor measures sly,
            Can conquer thee, dear Ireland.
Our blood may tinge our rivers' tide,
Our bodies lie our home beside—
We stand where stood all those who died,
            For Ireland, for Ireland.

Ay, till this earth has ceased to roll,
            Ireland, dear Ireland.

Till death has snatched off every soul
> That pants for thee, dear Ireland.
We'll kindle freedom's magic blaze,
And stand defiant 'neath its rays,
Till, armed and strong, the Gaodheal[5] repays
> His bloody debts, dear Ireland.

Mark that man's face—worn and pale,
> Ireland, dear Ireland.
'Twas fashioned so in England's gaol—
> He fought for thee, dear Ireland.
Her bloody mark is on his brow,
But, as of old, he hates her now,
Her fall is still his prayer and vow,
> His love is thine, dear Ireland.

Beneath thy flag fresh hopes we feel,
> Ireland, dear Ireland.
We'll gild its folds with glint of steel,
> And rifles' flame, dear Ireland.
In garish day, 'neath night's damp dew,
Its green and white and orange hue
Shall signal death to England's crew,
> And hope to thee, dear Ireland.

God of the Gael! our banner bless,
> And Ireland, dear Ireland.
And in the battle's tedious stress
> Oh! nerve our arm for Ireland!
Now Fenian proud, lift high your head,
'Twas vows, but now 'tis blows instead,
For vengeance, for our Martyred Dead,
> For Freedom and for Ireland!

The Irish Worker, April 26, 1913

[5]Gael.

"Irish Freedom" and the "Irish Nation"

Day after day, day after day,
We stuck, nor breath nor motion;
As idle as a painted ship
Upon a painted ocean.

COLERIDGE

How long are we to wait the coming of all men to the cause of Kathleen ni Houlihan?[6] Are we to tarry till every simpering aristocrat abandons the gemmed circle of the garter for the green scarf? Will the Union Jack flutter over Dublin Castle, unhurtful to Republican eyes, so long as even one of Ireland's knightly sons elects to find joy in the presence of an English Viceregal Agent, even though a combination of democratic forces might bring that felon flag down with a run, never to rise again in Ireland? If a union of Labour and Republican forces would result in the achievement of an independent Ireland, or even bring that happy consummation appreciably nearer, would we hesitate and say, "Not yet, not yet; wait for the aristocrats"?

And who are the aristocrats in Ireland, in the name of God, and what are they doing for Ireland? What would they do or what would they risk to make her free? 'Tis well to quote—

Start not, Irish-born man,
If you're to Ireland true.

Are those true to Ireland? Is the planting of a few acres of Ireland with tobacco plants, out of which a profit is made, or the gift of a five-pound note to the Sinn Fein movement[7] by a Meath rancher,

[6]Ireland. For one embodiment of Kathleen, see Yeats's play of the same name. See in this book the story, "The Seamless Coat of Kathleen," and the play, "Kathleen Listens In."

[7]"Sinn Fein" literally means "ourselves." Arthur Griffith, writing in *The United Irishman*, aroused new interest in separation from England. In 1905 Griffith first announced the Sinn Fein policy to the National Council of the Cumann na nGaedheal: "National self-development through the recognition of the duties and rights of citizenship on the part of the individual, and by the aid and support of all movements originating from within Ireland, instinct with national tradition, and not looking outside Ireland for the accomplishment of their aims." In 1907 the Cumann na nGaedheal and the Dungannon clubs merged into the Sinn Fein Party.

or advice given by Castletown, K.P., to the officers of an English regiment as to the best way to equip their force with a pipers' band, faithfulness to Ireland? Are we going to give to the philosophy of Davis a charity and a breadth with which he never inspired it?

True to Ireland! Well, let them be true to Ireland, then; till they are so, let us regard them as those who are against us. Let them give us a sign; let Castletown tear from his breast the pale blue ribbon of his St. Patrick's Castle Knighthood and declare himself "The Mac Giolla Phaudrig";[8] let the Meath rancher give to the descendants of the Meath clansmen the land that is theirs and signify his willingness to go to gaol for Ireland even should his furniture be seized by the Government for his temerity; let Everard renounce the armed forces of England and tell us he will honour the Republican flag and strive for Ireland's Freedom, and then we may no longer be faithless, but believe in the attachment of Ireland's so-called aristocracy to their country.

Irish Freedom appeals to the "Historic Irish Nation." We had our place in the nation then; we are forcing our way to a place in the nation now; we are determined to have and occupy our place in the Irish nation of the future.

Let there be no mistake about it, "we must have Ireland; not for certain peers or nominees of peers in College Green, but Ireland for the Irish." All places of honour and trust and responsibility open to all men of purity, talents, and energy, irrespective of rank or property, and the abolition of poverty, the effective mother of slaves.

"Freedom" says "we must regard every question from the standpoint of the best interests of the nation as a whole." It can't be done in the sense that you must wait till all the National elements are united for Ireland. Unite all you can and use this union to free the nation. Unite the people and the Cause is won. The aristocracy don't count; these are attached to their property, their

[8]The Fitzpatrick.

money, and their honours to-day, as was the celebrated Bishop
of whom Wolfe Tone says, that when he read a certain pamphlet of Tone's, he explained: "If the principles contained in that
abominable work were to spread, do you know you would have
to pay for your coals at the rate of £5 per ton!"

The so-called aristocrats of Ireland have been weighed in
the balances and found wanting, even as they were found wanting in the days of Tone who declared that "The aristocracy
shrank back in disgrace and obscurity, leaving the field open to
democracy; and that body neither wanted talents nor spirit to
profit of the advantages of their present situation."

To-day in the ranks of the democracy we have men of
talents and men of spirit capable of attempting all things, capable
of achieving all things. The aristocracy contains men of spirit
and men of talent, but are apparently incapable of attempting
anything for Ireland.

These we can do without, but the people—not the gentry
and the people—but the people are the effective force of the
nation. The time is at hand for the union of all democratic
forces in Ireland for a general advance. Wolfe Tone turned away
from the Ascendancy gang, and laboured to unite Dissenter and
Catholic to fight for a free Ireland.

It is up to us now to turn away from the self-satisfied gentry
and the soulless controllers of commerce, and to unite the Separatist ranks with the forces of Labour for a free Ireland and
the social advancement of the people.

The Irish Worker, May 10, 1913

Tone's Grave

Once I lay on that sod—it lies over Wolfe Tone—
And thought how he perished in prison alone,
His friends unavenged and his country unfreed,
"O! better," I said, "is the patriots' meed."

DAVIS

Ay! bitterness is there in the reflection upon Ireland's subjection, bitterness in the memory of the lonely grave in Bodenstown; bitterness in the thought of Tone's pallid face and painful wounds and broken heart in the bare cell of Newgate Gaol waiting the approach of Death with an unbroken spirit.

Bitterness in the thought that many Irishmen are offering a final welcome to Home Rule as the joyful crowning of Caitlin ni Houlihan. Shade of the unconquerable Tone did we all elect to utter vows of satisfaction at England's feet because of this, then better that the storm that sweeps down on the plains of Kildare should carry away on its bosom the last trace of thy lonely grave.

For all this bitterness of heart no Nationalist standing beside this lonely grave can repress the feeling that there is near a hope that is stronger than the British Empire; that there is near an inspiration more potent for Ireland's good than sweet words from the mouth of Birrell, political poltroon and liar. If they would do something to stifle stirring memories in the hearts of many a Gael let them run a plow over the grave of Wolfe Tone. England, with all her power, all her ships, all her armies, all her gold-bought traitors, dare not lay a rude hand on the lonely grave of this great Irish Republican. Next Sunday . . . the Annual Pilgrimage to Bodenstown will be held. . . . Dublin contingents will be headed by the O'Toole Pipers and St. James's Band. . . . The Oration at the grave will be delivered by P. H. Pearse, of St. Endas College. . . . Every man who stands as a rebel against

foreign rule is asked to attend. The workers have not sold themselves to England yet.

Sweet, sweet, 'tis to find that such faith can remain,
To the Cause and the Man, so long vanquished and slain!

The Irish Worker, June 21, 1913

The Soul of Davis

> His life was gentle, and the elements
> So mix'd in him that Nature might stand up
> And say to all the world "This was a man!"
> *Julius Caesar* (V, v)

And so he was. A soul that knew no boundaries of class or
colour or creed. Modern exponents of Nationalist thought seem
to have hovered outside the soul of Thomas Davis. They have
successfully veiled his world-wide sympathies from the gaze of
the vulgar poor. What was or would be their human woe and
human pain to such an idealistic soul as Thomas Davis? His love
was no higher than the highest Irish hill and no deeper than
the deepest Irish river—this is what we have been told. But the
love of Davis was no less human than it was Irish, and it sprung
no less from the passion to vindicate the Rights of Ireland, as it
sprung from the passion to vindicate the Rights of Man.

His was a heart that beat for the Irish Peasant made half-
savage by persecution, and the Red-Indian half-savage by inclination. The waves that lashed the shores of Ireland could not
beat back the thoughts that welled from the international soul
of Davis. Too long have we submitted to the touching-up of the
personal portraiture of great Irishmen by present-day leaders who
appear to be interested in the suitable and judicious production
of light and shade in the principles and ideals of men whom they
profess to follow.

To quote an extract that appeared some time ago in

"Irish Freedom," a monthly that, humorously no doubt, declares that it stands for "National ideals as understood by Tone and Mitchel":—"For one reason or another, Irish history has been almost as distorted by Irish writers as by English, with the result that anyone who really wants to know the truth has got to sift thro' the original material himself."

So, too, have many great Irishmen been set upon the revolving basis of a false Nationalism so that the same characteristics face you every way.

But now we dare you to examine the many gleams from the soul of Davis; too many be Orange and Green, but the others are dangerously like the colours symbolising the French Revolution, and indicating the Brotherhood of Man.

The woes and struggles of other countries appealed to Davis as strongly as those of his own; to him there was inspiration in the name of Aodh Ruadh,[9] and there was equal inspiration in the name of Abdel Kader.

The soul of Davis is bred in the "Ballad of Freedom," and the breath of his passion can be measured by the last lines on human freedom:—

> That glorious noon,
>   God send it soon
> Hurrah for Human Freedom!

And that no present-day narrow-souled Nationalist would plumb the depths of his nature is passionately shown in his—

> Oh! for a steed, a rushing steed,
>   And any good course at all;
> . . . For Freedom's Right in flushing fight
>   To conquer if then to fall.

Davis's soul, while it expanded to the light of Ireland's Nationality, also peered into the darkness of human misery and pain.

[9]Red Hugh O'Donnell, an Irish chief of the fifteenth century.

His prophetic vision foresaw the horrors of capitalism, and received from his ardent human soul a prophetic condemnation:—

"We would prefer one housewife skilled in the distaff and the dairy, to a factory full of creatures who live amid the eternal roll and clash and glimmer of spindles and rollers, watching with aching eyes the thousand twirls, and capable of but one thought —tying the broken threads."

"The hazards of the factory system, however, should be encountered, were it sure to fill our starving millions—but this is dubious."

The socialistic nature of Davis denounced the ruin of life that his prophetical vision conjured before his face. He saw in the Future the mother giving life from her bosom to the child, not for Ireland, but for the machine.

To-day we have not the vision, but the actualities leering into our face; the bending back; the drooping shoulders; the peering eyes in sunken sockets; the weak-kneed limb; the uncertain heart and the withering lung; and yet the leaders of National endeavour, who claim affinity with Davis, disregarding these horrors, seem to support the development of the power that is torturing every artery, muscle and limb of Ireland's children.

There is no doubt that Thomas Davis was a Republican in principles and sympathies. His frequent and loving references in his essays to "The People" assert that he realised that without them we can do nothing.

Dealing with the boast of the gentry in his day, that "the wealth of Ireland was opposed to Repeal," he says—"It is an ignorant and a false boast."

> The people of a country are its wealth,
> They till its soil, raise its produce, ply its trade;
> They serve, sustain, support and save it.

Correspondingly contemptuous was the opinion Davis had of Ireland's "Aristocracy." "They were," he says, "its disgrace. . . . They would be the first to sell and the last to redeem it."

Have these shimmering gentlemen changed since the days of Davis? They still think it is their duty to wrong, degrade and beggar the unfortunate people.

Davis spoke clearly; Let the aristocracy come if they wish; but we must have the people.

What to me appears the attitude of present-day extreme National leaders is this:—

Let the people come to us if they wish; but we must have the aristocracy.

To all Nationalists, who are well fed and clothed warmly in Irish tweeds and serges, who, blessed with the satisfaction of regularly well-filled stomachs, can dream in cloudy spiritual Nationalism, I say: Remember us of the working-class who are your strength and right-hand in the day of battle. Help us to realise our destiny; help us to save ourselves from the horrors which Davis himself depicts, and which most of us have experienced, and which, sometimes, form the life of the labourer—

"His food—potatoes and water; his bedding—straw and a coverlet; his enemies—the tax gatherer, the landlord and the law; his consolation—the priest, and his wife; his hope on earth—agitation; his hope hereafter—The Lord God!"

To-day to the workers, Nationalism is a gospel without hope; it does not signify life to them.

National leaders of to-day, if ye cannot sanctify your Nationalism with the breath of humanity, cease shouting at us, and in the name of God, leave us alone.

The Irish Worker, March 7, 1914

A Day in Bodenstown

God prosper the Cause, oh, it cannot but thrive
While the pulse of one patriot heart is alive.

On Sunday last was held the Annual Pilgrimage to the grave of Wolfe Tone. To many it was an inspiration; but it was an hour of pathetic contemplation to a few. The time has come for a change; it is high time to do more than to indulge in a yearly pilgrimage to the grave in Bodenstown Churchyard. To-day Republicanism in Ireland is mouldering even as the wounded remains of the first of Irish Republicans. Up to now it has been from Dublin to Bodenstown; let us now go from Bodenstown to the four quarters of Ireland with Wolfe Tone's message. Even in the assembly that looked reverently at the unpretentious tomb, how many were there that entered into the man's buried life or understood his principles? I would venture to say that to many, to very many in that crowd Wolfe Tone had died in vain. Wolfe Tone is dead, and all the ideas and dreams of Ireland are to-day suffered to repose and decay within the massive head of John Redmond.

Even some of those whom we were called upon to trust as Republican leaders have announced by their votes on the Provisional Committee of the National Volunteers that it is expedient to believe that John Redmond is the fountain-head of Ireland's Hope. John Redmond and his policy is the slough of Ireland's political damnation.

Would to God Wolfe Tone were here to-day! In his day he abandoned Grattan, his scintillating Volunteers, and his property-protecting Parliament, and linked his fortunes with the oppressed people of Ireland.

Grattan got his thirty-thousand pounds and Wolfe Tone suffered martyrdom in an English prison. To-day we have a miniature Grattan in John Redmond. Who is going to take the place of a Wolfe Tone in the vanguard of an oppressed people that we may fight again the battle for an Irish Republic? That is a question the Irish people will have to answer, and answer quickly.

The Chairman of the meeting in the course of his remarks, referred with hope to the fact that Irishmen were drilling and arming everywhere. What are they arming for and for what do they drill? We wish we could share his hope. These drilled men may be used by an unscrupulous Government, even though a green flag over its Senate House proclaims it a National Government, to postpone the day the speaker conjured up in his mind's eye. They may be used to break up democratic progress, even as some of the Volunteers of '82 hunted down the followers of Wolfe Tone in glorious '98.

Mr. Ryan, who delivered the oration, was evidently afraid to let himself go, as he said it was a place to refrain from offending the susceptibilities of any class or shade of political opinion. We believe Republicanism should be more aggressive. False gods in Ireland must be thrown down, and the groves and high places of political trickery must be pulled to pieces. The earlier the Republican Party of Ireland realise they are out against all opposition; that all parties must be made Republican thro' a vigorous propaganda, the better for themselves and the better for Ireland.

This talk of a union of all classes is impossible, and foolish because it is impossible. Talk of peace is nonsense, and deep down in their hearts they know that this talk of peace is nonsense. There should be less talk of peace and more about the principles of Republicanism, about which most of us know so little.

We were advised to regard the points of agreement between different sections of Irishmen rather than the points of difference between them. We venture to suggest that the Republicans should act upon their own counsel and take into consideration the points of agreement between them and the workers' organisations.

If they took time to think this over they would discover that all workers are, thro' force of necessity, rebels, and that from their ranks thousands of vigorous Republicans can be recruited. That was the policy of Wolfe Tone in '98. He held no foolish hopes of a possible union of all classes. He hated the aristocracy and he thoroughly despised the propertied class and the merchants. He saw that these served their own interests and looked upon not Ireland but on the stake they had in the country and the business they carried on in Ireland. He passed by the members of the Church—of the Ascendancy Church—and linked up to the oppressed Catholics and the oppressed Presbyterians. This union created the Society of the United Irishmen. The only possible union to-day for the men who still believe in Republicanism to look for is one between themselves and the workers, whose principles are practically identical. Looking for the support of the propertied class is even as a man fishing with a rod; searching amongst the workers, they would be even as a man employing a net in a fruitful sea. Let us all, who believe in Wolfe Tone's principles, take courage of heart, and preach not peace, where there can be no peace, but at all costs, the principles of him who, being dead, yet speaketh to all the people of Ireland, whose oppression calls loudly for economic and political enfranchisement.

The Irish Worker, June 27, 1914

D

The Irish Language

THE Irish language has been a major issue in twentieth-century Ireland, for the language revival was inextricably tangled with both the fight for political freedom and the cultural renaissance.

"By 1900," points out Edward Curtis in his *History of Ireland,* "the Irish language, though something like half a million people still spoke it along the western and southern coasts and great numbers of the older people spoke nothing else, was rapidly dying."

To arrest the death of the language Douglas Hyde in 1893 founded the Gaelic League, and shortly after appeared the weekly Irish newspaper *Fainne an Lae* (Dawn of Day), which O'Casey sometimes refers to.

O'Casey became an enthusiastic Gaelic Leaguer, but his critical intelligence soon perceived that the League was a sickly and ineffectual organisation. In his second published articles, which appeared in *The Peasant and Irish Ireland* for July, 1907, he criticised the League and presented a full and plausible plan of reorganisation to pump new life into it. In 1918 he published two articles in *Irish Opinion;* both were critical of the League, and both again offered constructive suggestions.

In 1922 the language movement received apparently a considerable boost, when the Free State government made the teaching of Irish compulsory in the schools. But by 1924 O'Casey saw that compulsory Irish was little more effective than the Gaelic League had been, and he published a story, "Irish in the Schools" (see page 261), in *The Irish Statesman,* a story that was coldly critical of the entire attempt to legislate the language into being. To the mature O'Casey an Irish Ireland was highly desirable, but it was criminal to squander money and effort in teaching Irish ineffectually, when thousands of people yet languished in poverty in the Dublin slums.

Such a short story, however sound its criticism, could but ruffle tempers; and O'Casey had to defend and amplify his view in two letters (see pages 116 and 122) which the *Statesman* printed early in 1925.

His comments and criticisms seem just. Now, thirty-five years after O'Casey's letters and after more than half a century of concerted effort by devoted people, English is yet the language of Ireland's life and literature. Irish has made little more impression on modern Ireland than being written on its postage stamps and printed above the English on its street signs.

If O'Casey were to walk through Dublin, along the street on which he was born, and to survey the unchanged tenements, it would still not seem very important to him whether he called the thoroughfare Sraid Dorsait or Dorset Street.

FROM *The Gaelic League in Dublin:*
How to Make it a Great Power

Notwithstanding our numerous branches, our many committees, our Coisde Ceanntair,[1] our swarms of critics, and our never-ending talk, the Dublin Gaelic League is weak, and its hold upon the Dublin people has loosened ever so little. Now the hold must become a grip, and that same grip must tighten, and pull forward the people on the road to Nationality week by week, day by day. The work of the League here is to make Dublin Irish. Is it making Dublin Irish? If present conditions continue, will it ever do so? Never. At the present rate of progress *backwards,* we will be a long time before we realise our ideals. No matter what we say on one day in the year, Dublin is not Irished, it is not even being Irished. On Language Day alone does Dublin put on her best Irish attire, paints her face, and sallies out with a light careless heart to strew flowers in the way of the marching Gael, but on every following day of the year, Dublin's offences are as deep and as crimson as ever. The Dublin League is not the force it ought to be, nor does it even apply properly the power it undoubtedly possesses. Through bad, or rather lack of organisation, there is a tremendous and painful waste of energy.

A change, a re-constitution, a general improvement is needed, needed badly; such is essential if the League is to win to her standard the fair city of Dublin.

All agree that something should be done. The meeting in the

[1]District Council.

house of the Lord Mayor endorsed this. It declared trumpet-
tongued that the Dublin League was not perfect, was not even
tolerably good. It was a strange sight, this meeting in the Mansion
House. Miserable and august! Tense and exciting at first; then,
as nothing was born of the talk, interest flagged, and a tired feeling crept softly over the assembled Gaels, and all chance of reform, suggestion, fruit was over. From 8 o'clock till 11 o'clock
there they were—speaker succeeded speaker; bell after bell rung;
still hopeful, we waited to see if anything would come. No. Compelled were we to march into the stilly night with no new hopes in
our hearts, no fresh ideas in our minds, only sounds ringing in our
ears that were—Words, words, words! Alas! Liam's plan was too
revolutionary, impossible at present. Leaguers paled before the
suggestion of running from one extreme to another. But, even
those who opposed him most strongly admitted that some reform
was urgently required. A *via media* must be chosen, and less
drastic measures considered for the strengthening and development of the League amongst us. The Dublin League is disorganised and weak. Reorganisation then is first needed, for it must be
strong before it can be developed. Growth will succeed strength.

Very shyly do I venture to lay before Dublin Leaguers this
simple plan for the betterment in many ways of the Organisation,
and earnestly appeal for the consideration of my fellow-workers
in respect of this little measure. . . .

[There then follows a detailed and lengthy plan of reorganisation, which I have omitted for it is probably of minor interest
to the modern reader.]

. . . Let the Dublin Leaguers impartially judge this scheme of
one whose strongest prayer and hope is for Ireland's regeneration.

AN GALL FADA, *The Peasant and Irish Ireland*, July 6, 1907

Down with the Gaedhilge![2]

Down, down to hell; and say I sent thee thither: . . .
   3 King Henry the Sixth (V, vi)

Should the Irish language die, we may blame, not the
British Government, but the Irish people. For years the Gaelic
League endeavoured to fling aside the mould that held it in its
grave, and a few handsful were removed, but the Irish people are
again shovelling the clay of indifference upon grasping life. We
may prate as we like about our language, listen reverently to some
gifted speaker, who boldly reminds us of its existence, piously
mark down one Irish song at least upon our concert programmes,
religiously say "slan leat"[3] to our parting friends, but if we say
that we love the language, and that we believe that the Gaedhilge
is the basic power of Irish expression, we are liars, and the truth
is not in us. The plain, unvarnished truth is that the Irish people,
United Irish Leaguers, Sinn Feiners, and Trades Unionists say,
day after day, moment by moment, in their indifference and
neglect: "To hell with the Gaedhilge. . . !"

Consider the Gaelic Athletic Association. Some years ago a
resolution was passed at the Annual All-Ireland Convention declaring that the Convention of 1917 should be an Irish-speaking
Convention—how easy it is to resolve for the future—and the
speaking of Irish was made obligatory upon all the delegates. But
1917 has come and gone, and the day of an Irish-speaking G.A.A.
Convention is as far distant as ever!

Some time ago in the *Claidheamh Soluis*[4] the decrescent
enthusiasm for the Irish language was commented upon. It was
pointed out that 15 years ago at Aeridheachta and Cuirme Ceoil[5]
an English song was a rarity; now at any of these events an Irish
song is seldom heard. At the same time in the streets Irish was

[2]Gaelic.
[3]Goodbye.
[4]*Shining Sword*, the weekly journal of the Gaelic League.
[5]Outdoor concert and concert.

spoken even aggressively, but now is it ever heard? The people have grown tired of it, and, for good or evil, political zeal has dissipated the attachment once so vigorously bestowed upon the Irish language.

In last week's issue of *Fainne an Lae*,[6] we found an Educational Committee of the Gaelic League recommending that an effort should be made to have Irish taught in the schools to lower standards as an ordinary subject for one hour per day, and to higher standards as an ordinary subject for one half-hour per day, and an additional half-hour as an outside subject, after or before school hours, the teachers to receive added remuneration for this work. It is also suggested that each class should not consist of more than twenty-five pupils, and that the teachers might be able to teach five classes in the one day. Does the Committee think the teachers can do this? They are shamefully overworked and shamelessly underpaid at present, and it would be silly to impose upon them an additional worry and labour till time and struggle place them in the position of security against any difficulty in living a life free from economic cares, so that they may be able to teach the workers' children from the heart as well as from the head. If we are to restore the Irish language to Ireland, then the teaching of it must be a happiness to the teachers, and the learning of it must be a joy for our children. At present, wherever it may be taught, the children hate it, for it is not taught, but administered as a noxious medicine. If we hope to restore the Irish language through the schools, then the whole system of Irish Popular Education will have to be revolutionised. The teachers must be lifted to a plane of elevated citizenship, free from economical worry of every description, so that they may teach, and our children must be comfortably clad, and fully fed, that they may be able to learn. These are the first things. Then it is for Labour and Learning and Nationality to decide what shall

[6]*Dawn of Day.*

be taught in the schools, and the methods and means to be adopted.

Irish Opinion, March 9, 1918

The Gaelic Movement To-day

The programme of the Gaelic League is miserably insufficient. The outcome of limited outlook of the present committee, it ignores entirely the working class movement.

This is a question that vitally concerns the workers, as "C. U." wisely says in his article on "The Language in the Primary Schools." As he points out, "those in affluent circumstances can choose the schools to which they can send their children, and they have strength and means to add at home to the education that their children receive." This the workers cannot do, for after their work they are too tired to interest themselves in their children's improvement, or, perhaps, lack of early opportunity has left them knowing less than a pupil that is in the fourth or fifth standard. It is important that the workers' children should receive the best possible training during school hours. And if the workers wish our children to be Irish, then the instruction they should get should be Irish, not for half an hour in the day, but from the calling of the roll till the last chime of the clock. This would be possible if we had leaders in the Gaelic League with sufficient faith to remove, not mountains, but little obstacles not larger than molehills. The vision of these leaders is small and narrow, and eminently respectable, and they cannot conceive that a thousand workers speaking Irish would savour more fully of an Irish life than one eminently respectable person lisping a few words of Irish in a Gaelic League class. Take "An Fainne"[7] for example, an organisation for Irish speakers who undertake

[7]"The Ring" or "The Circle."

to speak nothing but Irish to those who are also acquainted with the language.

Before admission is allowed to "An Fainne" a candidate must be recommended by two members and an annual subscription must be paid before you will be allowed to speak Irish habitually to other Irish speakers!

One would think that the Gaelic League would honour Ireland's sons and daughters that had the perseverance and courage and love to learn Ireland's language by a badge that would proclaim to all that those who wore it were true to the first essential of Irish nationality without a fee or a call to vouch for your untarnished respectability!

Shoneenism is creeping back to Ireland's bosom again. "The Tango" and "The Turkey Trot" embellish the joys of social events organised by the "National Aid," and foreign dances elbow out our Irish dances in many scoruidheachta[8] held by societies whose ostensible purpose it is to develop and perpetuate our Gaelic characteristics. We hear everywhere around us the phrases, "Up Valera!" "Are we downhearted," "he's a slacker," "he did his bit," and many other indications reveal to us that the Cock of Anglicisation is again crowing lustily.

Some weeks ago Mr. Griffith suggested that the best monument to Tomas Aghas[9] would be 800,000 additional Irish speakers. So it would; but how is it to be built? Is the Gaelic League equal to the task? Davis, in his own day, recommended that efforts should be made to save it "by inducing the upper classes to teach to their children, as the introduction of the language through the National schools was a dream only to be thought of a hundred years hence." We workers know now more than Davis did then. The language can only be saved by the help of the "lower classes," and the Gaelic League must rec-

[8]Country road dance.
[9]Thomas Ashe. See "A Lament," page 153ff.

ognise this, must help the workers to secure conditions that will allow them to practise their duty to their country.

They must not act so insensately as they acted some years ago when they "made all hell stir" because Jim Larkin spoke at one of their meetings, who showed by his burning and earnest words that the language question could only be solved by the working class. We are to have an All-Ireland Conference with reference to the Food Problem. Why not an All-Ireland Conference to deal with the education of Ireland's children?

Why not elect an All-Ireland Executive, representative of the Gaelic League, Labour, the Teachers, with men of science, art and literature to resolve upon all educational problems, and frankly to make the continuance of the "National Board" impossible? If we are earnest over the Irish language let us show it; if not, then let us abandon the idealistic attempt that we may economise our energy "for the greatest of all waste," says Ruskin, "is the waste of energy." We abhor partition, and shout sarcastically about two-thirds of a nation; but there is worse than partition, and that is the loss of the language; for, as Davis says, "a country without a language of its own is only half a nation."

We may anticipate comment by saying the obvious reply to Sean's strictures on the Gaelic League is that the Labour movement has shown little enthusiasm in relation to Gaelic. How many trade union branches have organised Irish classes—or indeed any other kind of class? The Gaelic League is the creature of its members. Its faults are those of the men and women who compose it. We do not want Labour to stand outside and jeer, but to get into the League and take a hand in the work. Then it will have its chance to remould the Gaelic organisation.—Ed. [Andrew E. Malone.]

Irish Opinion, March 23, 1918

Labour

O'CASEY was not an official of the Irish Transport and General Workers' Union, but he inevitably became a union member. He also wrote frequently for Larkin's labour paper, *The Irish Worker,* and he was the first Secretary of the Irish Citizen Army which was composed of working men and had its offices at Liberty Hall, the home of the union.

Before Jim Larkin came to Dublin and organised the Irish Transport and General Workers' Union, the plight of the Dublin labourer was desperate indeed. Consider this description of Dublin in 1909, which I have extracted from *Fifty Years of Liberty Hall,*[1] a book commemorating the first half century of the Transport Union:

> When the Irish Transport and General Workers' Union was founded half a century ago, Dublin had a population of 305,000. It was a commercial, distributing and shipping centre rather than a manufacturing city. Except in brewing and biscuit-making its productive power was comparatively low and most of its factories were small and gave little manual employment. . . .
>
> Extremely low wages and wretchedly bad housing, preventing workers from reaching decent living standards or securing adequate nourishment and clothing, were reflected in a death-rate in Dublin city of 23 per 1,000 of population compared with a mean death-rate of 15.8 in the largest towns in England, the highest of these being 19.8 in Oldham.
>
> Mortality among infants under five years of age was 2.5 per 1,000 in the professional, independent and middle categories and 14.2 among the hawkers, porters and labourers. . . .
>
> By 1911 Dublin's death-rate had risen to 27.6 per 1,000 when Calcutta's, infested with plague and cholera, was 27 and in Europe the next highest to Dublin's was 26.3 in Moscow groaning under Czarist tyranny. . . .
>
> The living and housing conditions of these wage-earners, particularly in the decaying and over-crowded tenement buildings in

[1]Cathal O'Shannon, ed., *Fifty Years of Liberty Hall: The Golden Jubilee of the Irish Transport and General Workers' Union, 1909-1959* (Dublin: The Three Candles, Ltd., 1959).

40

which the majority of general labourers were compelled to rear their families, were miserable almost beyond endurance, but attracted no public attention until trade union agitation and the collapse of a number of these buildings with a death-roll of their rent-paying slum dwellers exposed the horrible scandal. Over a third, 33.9 per cent, of the total number of families in Dublin had only a single room each to live in. . . .

General labourers, the bulk of the wage-earners, were rarely paid more than 20/- a week in regular, full-time employment, and the common rate ran from 15/- to 18/-. Because of the scarcity of employment for women thousands of families had to exist on no more than 15/- a week and cases were recorded of total family earnings as low as 10/- and less.

Actual cases noted in the sparse official reports of the time show:

a van driver, with mother-in-law and three children, in constant employment at 15/- a week, paying 2/6d. rent, and having tea, bread and butter for breakfast, with cheap American bacon and cabbage, or occasionally herrings, for dinner, and tea and bread, for evening meal or supper; . . .

another labourer with wife and five children, in very irregular work at 14/- a week, paying 1/6d. rent and having bread, butter and milk for all three meals, except that on Sundays there was bacon for dinner. . . .

The minimum hours worked in a day were ten to twelve. Carters worked twelve to fifteen hours a day for 18/- to 20/- a week, and the highest paid dock labourers were paid up to 24/- for a 70 hour week.

Larkin was of enormous benefit to the Dublin workers, and his influence among the workers was enormous. The pages of *The Irish Worker* amply attest the passionate devotion that he attracted. (O'Casey describes Larkin in the "Prometheus Hibernica" chapter of *Drums Under the Windows,* and presents a stylized portrait of him as "Red Jim" in the play, *The Star Turns Red.*)

Yet the struggle to establish an effective union was not easy, and Larkin and Larkinism were as violently denounced by the clergy as they were by business and property. To combat organised labour the Dublin Employers' Federation was formed. A chief mover in this organisation was William Martin Murphy, who owned the Dublin United Tramways Company and the Irish Independent newspapers. On August 15, 1913, Murphy told the workers in the dispatch department of his newspapers that he would dismiss any member of the Transport Union.

There had already been, reports R. M. Fox in his excellent *History of the Irish Citizen Army*,[2] about thirty strikes in Dublin in the previous six months. Murphy's ultimatum released all of the culminated anger of the workers and allowed it to burst forth in the last days of August. First the tramway workers put on the Red Hand badge of the union and left their tramcars sitting in the middle of the streets, despite the heavy passenger traffic for the famous Dublin Horse Show.

The next few days included many riots and built up to the explosion of August 31, "Bloody Sunday," when Larkin was to address a meeting in O'Connell Street. The meeting had been proscribed, but Larkin, disguised as a bearded invalid, appeared on a balcony of the Imperial Hotel —which was, ironically, owned by Murphy—swept off his beard, and began to speak. As soon as Larkin began, the police charged into the great crowd, swinging their batons. According to Fox, there were at least five hundred casualties.

On August 30 and 31, the police broke into tenements, destroyed property, assaulted the innocent—including women and children—in short, committed every barbaric atrocity, including murder. The battle lines were now drawn, and "battle lines" is scarcely a metaphor. As O'Casey writes below, "The whole forces of the Transport Union are wheeling into the battlefield."

Under Murphy's prodding, the Employers' Federation agreed not to employ any union member and to demand that each employee sign this pledge:

> I hereby undertake to carry out all instructions given to me by or on behalf of my employers and, further, I agree to immediately resign my membership of the Irish Transport and General Workers' Union (if a member), and I further undertake that I will not join or in any way support this Union.

Hostilities did not break out again into violence of the magnitude of "Bloody Sunday," for the struggle became now a war of attrition. The employers attempted to starve the workers away from the union, and ultimately so many people were involved that Dublin took on the character of a city under siege. Against the 403 employers, says Fox, were

[2]R. M. Fox, *History of the Irish Citizen Army* (Dublin: James Duffy & Co., Ltd., 1943).

ultimately arrayed 100,000 men, women, and children, roughly a third of the city's population.

The union organised a relief committee to collect contributions for the strikers' fund, and O'Casey was one of the secretaries. Food ships from England afforded partial relief, and notwithstanding vehement denunciations from members of the clergy, some of the strikers' children were evacuated to England. Yet, despite spirited condemnation of the employers by Ireland's leading intellectuals—Yeats, Maud Gonne, A.E., James Stephens, P. H. Pearse, Padraic Colum and many others—despite horrified reaction in England and even sympathetic strikes in several English cities, despite contributions from organised and individual workers all over the world, the struggle wore on into 1914.

Writes William O'Brien in *Fifty Years of Liberty Hall:*

Throughout the whole struggle the combination of Dublin employers had the valuable support of the British Government forces in Ireland, armed and unarmed, law, police, military, and prison. From time to time one or another section of these forces was brought into action against the workers. The police not only protected black-legs but as well forcibly broke up meetings, raided the working-class quarters and batoned two workers to death—James Nolan and John Byrne—and imprisoned leaders of the Irish Transport and of other Unions and hundreds of workers.

To O'Casey, who was in the middle of it all, these facts must have made one point indelibly clear: the real battle in Ireland was not, as he had suggested a few months before, for Irish freedom but against Irish poverty; the real struggle was not between the English Imperialist and the Irish Republican, but between international capitalism and the workers of the world.

This was a time of great hope and activity for O'Casey. Besides his work on the relief committee, he was the secretary of the newly formed Irish Citizen Army, and he continued, when he could, to write fiery notices for *The Irish Worker*. But, though it was an active and exciting time, it was also a terrible time for him and for Dublin. As Fox says:

The tenements were in the firm grip of starvation. Their women and children were drained of vitality. Their wretched tenement homes were stripped of everything that the pawnshops would take. . . . In the latter months of 1913 and early in 1914, it was an army of hunger, a militant host of the poor.

Early in 1914 the workers and their resources were utterly exhausted, and one by one they drifted back to work. The strike was over. Neither side had really won. The workers had been forced back to their jobs by hunger, but the Transport Union had not been broken.

The Great Lockout had, however, despite its toll in misery and human life, accomplished something. It established organised labour as a force to be reckoned with in Ireland; and, according to some writers, by the formation of the Citizen Army it laid the groundwork for the Rising of Easter Week, 1916.

I think that for O'Casey the Great Lockout was the crucial public event of his first forty years. I think that it solidified in him the yet unaltered conviction that a man of good will must strive for the international abolition of poverty and the ownership of the means of production by the worker.

Declenda Est Larkinism![3]

> When shall we three meet again
> In thunder, lightning, or in rain?
>
> *Macbeth* (I, i)

A monster meeting was held in Amiens Street last Sunday by the National Workers' Union. The concourse of people that attended was awe inspiring. The Borough Surveyor was present

[3]The title is an O'Caseyan version of "Delenda est Carthago," or "Carthage must be destroyed," a phrase with which, says Plutarch, Cato the Elder ended his speeches.

The subject is an ineffectual rival to the Transport Union, and the manner is perhaps the earliest example of O'Casey's blending of phantasy and satire.

Mr. Cathal O'Shannon writes me that "William Richardson . . . was in his way something of a civic reformer addicted to writing letters to the newspapers. . . . He was fairly well-known in Dublin for some years and at one time was connected with an attempt to form an anti-Larkin union but with no real success. I am reminded that in the great Dublin conflict of 1913-1914 he ran for some time an anti-Larkin weekly called *The Liberator*."

Of T. Greene Mr. O'Shannon writes, "I'm told that T. Greene was the first secretary of the first branch . . . of the Irish Transport and General Workers' Union for a time after its foundation in 1909. I have no personal knowledge of him but I don't think he was in office for any considerable length of time or that any member except the few hundred of the first months would have known any secretary of that branch except John O'Neill who was its secretary for a great many years. How and why Greene and Larkin parted I don't know but from Greene's association with Richardson in O'Casey's reference it is obvious that the parting wasn't friendly."

in expectation of seeing the adjacent buildings fall through the
pressure of the crowd. Mr. Richardson, who came to the meeting in a patent airship inflated with beer, was the recipient of
a terrific cheer, which caused even some of the minor stars to
fall from the sky, and Nelson's Pillar shook tremulously. The
vast assembly sang with a quivering roar the modern madrigal
of Labour, "God Save Plain Bill"; and when the tears trickled
down the cheeks of Mr. Richardson with emotion, the scene was
most impressive.

The meeting was opened by T. Greene, who spoke in a
voice husky with emotion, or something else, read a letter of
apology from the Lord Mayor. His Lordship mentioned in his
letter that he had obtained a photograph of himself dressed in
the crimson silk-lined robe of an LL.D. of Trinity, and that he
looked lovely, and that he would be pleased to present a copy
to his friend Bill, which he suggested should be placed in a
conspicuous position in the rooms of the National Workers'
Union in Mabbot Street. His announcement occasioned a furious
outburst of applause. Mr. Greene then read a letter from Earl
Aberdeen wishing them God speed in their efforts to make all
Irish workers respectable and intelligent. His Excellency then
impressed upon Mr. Richardson the advisability of convincing
his hosts of followers that, with judicious handling, 8s. 6d. a
week could be made to do wonders. He begged leave to quote
from one of Ireland's poets the beautiful inspiration that

> Man wants but little here below,
> Nor wants that little long.

He also suggested that Mr. Richardson, who now, happily, had
ceased to pray with his face towards Bodenstown, should immediately hoist the Union Jack over his Union premises. That
flag waved over Mountjoy Prison, and why should it not adorn
the glorious façade of the National Workers' Union? Mr.
Greene, in the course of his remarks said that he in the fulness

of simplicity and honesty, had originally loved Larkin. That was past now. But even at the eleventh hour, if Larkin repented, and came to him in sackcloth and ashes, begging forgiveness, he would pardon all! (Great sensation.) He would fall on Larkin's neck and kiss him! A voice here shouted that Larkin didn't like the smell of drink, whereupon Mr. Greene declared that that was not his business. If Larkin wanted a kiss he would have to put up with it (loud applause).

At this juncture a poor collection of ten or twelve men, headed by a single piper, came marching up Amiens Street, in the midst of which Jim Larkin marched with downcast head and a demeanour of utter dejection, followed by a contingent of 970 stalwart policemen. They wheeled up Talbot Street, and were greeted with loud, long, and derisive cheers by the enormous gathering of Richardson's followers, who again broke into the enthusiastic chant of "God Save Plain Bill."

Mr. Richardson then attempted to address the meeting, but his supporters were so wildly happy that it was a long time before he could be heard.

At last he was heard to say that he did not fear to "pit" himself against Larkin, even if Glasnevin was the ultimate consequence. He was not out against strikes. It was demoralising to give men 12s. 6d. or more a week for doing nothing. 'Twas better to make them work for 8s. 6d. per week, provided they had a family of at least five, than that they should get a wage while idling, which promoted mischief and dislocated the commerce of our beloved country. The voice of some ignoramus here interjected, "Who robbed the Treaty Stone?"

Mr. Richardson said that was a lie. He had knocked a chip off it as a curio, which was to be seen any day under a glass shade in their Union rooms. He was delighted to be able to say that Liberty Hall was tottering to its fall; its days were numbered. He appealed to his thousands of followers to show mercy in the hour of victory. His devoted fellow-labourer, the Labour Prophet, Jeremiah Greene, had told them that Liberty Hall would before long be destroyed; that one stone would not be left upon another; that it would be burned with fire, and that the place where it stood would become a place of desolation. In the hour of its ponderous fall he appealed to them to spare Larkin's life. It was more than he deserved, but let justice be tempered with mercy. He was proud to announce that they were now so financially strong that the Committee had almost dared to decide that they would get their Union rooms white-washed. (Tremendous applause.) He begged to tell them, in conclusion, that the arms of the Union would be on a green field, indicative of their nationality; in chief the Treaty Stone, in honour of their leader—(applause)—below an Aberdeen herring and a crab, symbolising Progress Backwards. Their motto would be "Ni Bhuailem—I don't strike!"

At the end of the meeting the enthusiasm was unspeakable. Mr. Richardson was carried home on the shoulders of his followers, while tens of thousands marched behind singing again "God Save Plain Bill."

The Irish Worker, April 19, 1913

The Gathering

Ye who despoil the sons of toil, saw ye this sight to-day,
Great stalwart trade, in long brigade, beyond a king's array;
And know, ye soft and silken lords, won we the thing ye say,
Your broad domains, your coffered gains, your lives, were ours to-day.

The whole forces of the Transport Union are wheeling into the battlefield. Dressing their ranks, cheering with enthusiasm, deploying to their several places, looking up at the banner that shall never weaken in the grasp of those who carry it, the symbol of their hope—the banner of the Red Hand. Look over

E

in the distance at the army of opposing Generals in their gaudy uniforms, which greed and plunder with deft hands, have decorated. Look at Marshal Murphy with his drum-head court-martial at his back, with his manifesto on the drum-head, draped with the Union Jack—swear away the Transport Workers' Union! If not, then starve!

Have a care, Marshal Murphy. Starvation is not a pleasant anticipation, it is always a difficult thing to starve thousands unwilling to suffer where food is plentiful.

Hunger makes men weak; it often makes men desperate, and the ferocity of hungry men and hungry women is a dreadful thing.

Other countries have experienced it. Let Murphy take care that Ireland does not furnish another dreadful example of men mad whom the capitalists would destroy.

"That ancient swelling and desire for liberty" is again stirring in our souls. The workers have lifted up their eyes unto the hills. They have no friends but themselves: but in their own strength they can conquer. Their only hope is their Union.

"Sacrifice the Union," say the employers, "and all is gained."

Sacrifice the Union once—all is lost.

What life would remain in a human body if the heat were plucked out and cast away?

We know that the Transport Union is the heart of all our strength and all our hope.

We are not deceived. The workers can do as much without their Union as Caesar's body when Caesar's head is off!

We know our friends now. How fond they are of the workers when strength and recklessness is needed to secure some end!

"We must have Irish in the National University," and the

workers all over Ireland are heraldic to public meetings by the "most democratic organisation in the country."

What expression has this "most democratic society" made of the efforts of a few tuft-hunting employers to suppress every spark of individual liberty in the heart of the workers?

What has the democratic G.A.A.[4] to say of the foul means that are being used to starve life and freedom in the capital of our country?

What has the patriotic U.I.L.,[5] who spend night and day sleeplessly, with one eye on Larkin and the other on the Liberal Government, to say to the employers' cursed declarations that Home Rule or no Home Rule the workers can have no vestige of individual liberty? How many of them jump on and jump off jauntily, as if to the manner born, the various trams still meandering through the city? How many of them have contributed to the Strike Fund to preserve the labourer's manhood striving to assert itself into a fuller development? Damn few.

Many Irish Irelanders speaking to me have expressed the hope that the workers would win. God be praised for their kind wishes, anyway. But it is easy to praise us with their lips while their hearts are far from us. The Nationalists are afraid of us; we are strong and numerous, and might hurry them on quicker than they are prepared to go. They want to save the whole nation, which they seem to think are the employers and the aristocracy. Well, workers, we are the whole nation. What care we for those who, as Wolfe Tone said, "would sacrifice everything for their own security." They are only a few; we are all. And what are five hundred or a thousand Irishmen, more or less, to the economic and political independence of the Irish people?

"Men, be men!" Who shall stop the onward march of the

[4]The Gaelic Athletic Association.

[5]United Irish League, the political machinery of the Irish Parliamentary Party the Home Rulers headed by John Redmond, with branches throughout the country.

people? Those who oppose us we will sweep aside; those who ignore us we will ignore. The Transport Union—or—

> Then gather, gather, gather!
> While there's leaves in the forest
> And foam on the river,
> Despite them, M'Gregor shall flourish for ever!

The Irish Worker, September 27, 1913

Striking for Liberty

Say are ye Friends to Freedom?

Evidences are everywhere manifesting themselves of the Gael's determination to stand by the workers in their magnificent fight to vindicate the liberties of man. The G.A.A. has nobly taken its stand with the workers. Go neartighidh Dia e.[6]

There are many Irish Irelanders, I feel sure, who are anxious to help in this historic battle, and I would like to suggest that they may help to strengthen the funds of the workers by contributing to the Strike Fund or by collecting among their friends. All information about collecting will be gladly given at Liberty Hall, and I shall be glad to receive or call for any subscriptions that Irish Irelanders may be willing to give towards preserving the elemental Rights of Man.

It is our right to decide for ourselves the best means of protecting ourselves. Freedom of speech and freedom of action—who will deprive us of them? Shall we be slaves for ever?

The Irish Worker, October 18, 1913

[6]God give it strength.

Ecce Nunc

What a happy country Ireland would be if Jim Larkin took everybody's advice.

The pulpit, the Press and the platform have all echoed, with burning words of counsel, warnings and deprecations to the Labour leader. The clergyman confronts him with the rebuke that his policy and his preaching threatens the tranquillity of the Church; the economist stands at his right hand telling him that his policy will quickly ruin the class he labours to serve; the nationalist stands at his left hand sighing into his ear that no doubt this policy will shiver into fragments—the quivering remains of Ireland's nationality. Terrible man, Larkin! Destroyer of Church and State and Nationality!

We are told by the greatest of all seers that "in the multitude of counsellors there is safety"; but Jim Larkin seems to have concluded that they simply breed confusion.

The majority of scholars are against Larkin, certainly; but is the majority always wise and always right? If it be that the theologian, the economist and the patriot are right, then Larkin is a colossal fool and has been working miracles; but if Larkin be right, what are we to think of the patriots, theologians and economists?

Perhaps, 'tis true, what Carlyle said:—"The world is composed of wise men and fools—mostly fools."

Is it not passing strange that to-day it is declared that all the love of country, all the wisdom, all the faculty for holding fast that which is good, belongs to the moneyed and employing class. We have nothing but empty stomachs and empty heads—they have taken care to see to that.

How the class whose stomachs are always lined with best of things have often chanted a protest against the foolishness of the Irishmen striking at the dictation of an English Executive; now they declare the Irish Transport Union must be re-organised, and governed by officials approved of by British Joint Labour Board. Love Ireland! Of course they do, the hypocrites! And how anxious the Press and employers are to save the few remaining Irish industries! And the other day Dockrell's summoned the City of Dublin Co. for non-delivery of a number of kegs of paint they had obtained from England! And all the Dailies are printed in foreign ink on foreign paper. Are there any employers generously interested in any industry outside of the one they stand to profit by?

Don't we know them, workers! the pack of hypocrites! Then the hysterical cries of the Nationalists have been reverberating in our ears that this industrial war would smash the determination created by agony and toil, to buy nothing but Irish industries; and the familiarity of the Irish agitator with the English workers would sap the first principles of Irish Nationality.

These patriots have much to answer for. The preservation of Ireland's identity is a poor thing beside their own personal interests.

We all remember Kettle referring the question of the unloading of the "Hecla," not, mind you, to the Irish leader of the Irish Union, but to the English leader of an English Union!

These patriots prefer the accommodating Irish labour leader to the equally accommodating English leader—that is the extent of their patriotism. Let a MAN arise in Ireland, and any means that present themselves to curb and confine him are embraced by the official patriots and the country-loving commercial class!

There was a great dash for "Faith and Fatherland" when the labour leaders dealt with the question of proper provision for the strikers' children, The clergy, most of whom patriotically spend their holidays, and consequently, their money, on the Continent, in England or in Wales, hastily came to the conclusion that every deported child would become English and Protestant! It was recorded in the papers that Father Doherty asked one little fellow, shivering on the boat, would "he like to become an Englishman and a Protestant?" He might as well have asked him would he like to become a Dutchman and a Protestant.

But there are many children in England and they are neither English nor Protestant, no more than Father Doherty is, tho' a native of the Blasket Islands would hardly be able to identify, perhaps, Father Doherty from an ordinary English priest.

Parnell, too, I think, was an Irishman, and it was the clergy whipped energy into the pack of hounds that hunted him to death.

And some of us have not forgotten yet the clergy's attitude towards Essential Irish in the National University.

The clergy's passion for the preservation of Irish nationality is certainly exemplified in the thorough manner Irish is taught in their schools; in the songs and recitations they allow the children to be taught, and in the same manner in which they guide the members of the A.O.H.[7]—the divinely selected guardians of faith and fatherland—in the ways of Nationality, by sanctioning the taste of that body for such Irish activities as card-playing, foreign dances, music-hall songs and Christy Minstrel Troupes!

It was certainly instructive to hear these members of the Order for the Incubation of Scabs, singing the other night that "they would preach the Faith, as love knows how."

"With kindly words and virtuous life"; and evidently if the "kindly words and virtuous life" failed, they were prepared to use sticks. There are searchings of the heart over the countless

[7]Ancient Order of Hibernians. Cathal O'Shannon writes me that the A.O.H. "was an exclusively Catholic organisation and bitterly opposed to Sinn Fein, Socialism, Liberty Hall and the Irish Transport & General Workers' Union. By these it was regarded as a kind of Catholic counterpart to the Orangemen of the North and a very bad influence in politics, owing to its exclusive sectarianism and its use by [Joseph] Devlin [its national president] as a body of political shock troops."

deportations from the home to the hospital, to the sanatorium, and subsequently, now often—to the grave! Everything is right and commendable, or, at least, forgivable, save Labour's effort to save life or to preserve the workers from shame and disease incurable. Ours is the most just Cause, the Cause of Labour.

The Hibernians scream and scratch to guard their jobs and open new avenues of emolument to themselves; the commercial and aristocratic gang manipulate penury and want to kill the workers so slowly that no one can call it murder.

The politicians are, I suppose, still considering the question they raised during the week of blood and murder, "Is the Gaelic League Political?" and have no time to think of life and progress; so it devolves upon the workers to preach the Gospel of Human Development and call upon the young and hopeful to flock to the banner that waves nearest the skies.

The enveloping forces of the workers are on the march.

> Such a phalanx ne'er
> Measured firm paces to the calming sound
> Of Spartan flute! These on the fated day
> When, stung to Rage by Pity, eloquent men
> Have roused with pealing voice the unnumbered tribes
> That toil and groan and bleed, hungry and blind.

The Irish Worker, November 15, 1913

To the Editor of
THE IRISH WORKER

LIBERTY HALL, BERESFORD PLACE, DUBLIN
26th November, 1913

DEAR SIR,—My Committee take the liberty of claiming the hospitality of your paper to announce the receipt of a subscription of £5 from the Mary Street Cinema Company. Especially do we wish to acknowledge through your columns the encouraging and generous help we have received from the Dorset Street Picture House in the shape of a subscription of £10, and a promise of £5 weekly till further notice. We wish to convey to the management our earnest appreciation of their sympathy with our work, expressed in such a substantial and practical manner. The Dorset Street Picture House has invariably stood by the workers and the poor when in especial difficulties, and we are not surprised at their generous action on this occasion. Our Committee sincerely hope that the kindness of the Dorset Street Picture House will act as an incentive to other firms of a like nature to help the good work we have in hand by subscriptions or by benefit performances, or, preferably by both. Many other contributions we have received will shortly be published.

Sincerely yours,

P. Lennon,

Sean O Cathasaigh,

Hon. Secretaries

I Been Workin' on the Railroad

Great Northern Railway, Ireland
Some of Its Works and Pomps
The Charity of Its Officials

Charity, says St. Paul, is a Virtue, greater even than Faith or Hope. Amen, say the gentle-hearted officials of the G.N.R. "St. Paul," they murmur, "must have been a rare philosopher, for charity begins at home." In few places within the four seas of Eireann is charity to ourselves so esthetically practised as with G.N.R. officials within the boundaries of their system. But there are exceptions. Some have coaxed into their hearts the merry principle that it is "more blessed to give than to receive." One of these jaunty-hearted philanthropists is Foreman Reid, of the Engineering Department. He was ever anxious for the comfort of his men. Unpleasant to his eyes were broken boots, or coats windowed by the hand of time. So the kind-hearted foreman started a club, which, I suppose, is still flourishing, to clothe the naked workman, and to place means at his disposal to secure articles indispensable to his health and enjoyment. All the workmen were invited to join except a few turbulent spirits, who, like Demophon, the emblem of bigots, would shiver when the sun shone upon them. A magnificent suit would be dangled before your eyes, if you were a member of the club, and, of course, workmen have no choice. You generally accepted it with gratitude and joy, regardless of colour, shape, or price. The price was necessarily very high, perhaps three times more than the price you would pay for a better article in the shops, but consider the

convenience and pride of being allowed to purchase your wants
from your own dear foreman! The happy commerce produced
a happy and edifying union between the master and the slave.
Even the tradesmen—carpenters, masons, plumbers, and all—
hesitated not to clothe themselves with club suits, and deck their
persons with club jewellery. This connection ensured them favours
of overtime, etc., which those who did not hail as members of the
club would not be allowed to enjoy. Some were found to murmur
that it was not fair, and a few imprudently insinuated that Foreman Reid made a good thing out of the workmen who rose early
and retired late that they might have more to present to their
foreman when the hard week's work was done. Even a few
daringly said that to join the club was slavish, and to make men
take cheap and shoddy goods at enhanced prices was neither
honest nor Christian. But it was hard to withstand official bland-
ishments.

> Dear R———, the slee'st paukie chief!
> That e'er attempted stealth or rief,
> Ye surely have some warlock breef,
>   Our human hearts;
> For ne'er a bosom yet was prief
>   Against your arts.

One man indignantly told me that a pair of blankets he
bought for a big price were like tissue paper; some men are very
silly. The staff was introduced once to an Englishman who took
a photographic group, and the men delightedly bought copies
at the foreman's request. Some evilly-disposed person hinted that
the foreman got a full size portrait of himself free, but you can't
believe everything. The foreman got tired of a camera he bought
once, and how it lifts one's heart to remember how we all bought
tickets for the raffle in which it was to be the prize. Of course,
we didn't want the thing; it wasn't any use to one of us, but we

felt eager to oblige our loving foreman, who felt constrained to get a good deal more than he paid for it, for he could hardly live on £3 5s. per week. Of course, it was safer to buy a ticket than to risk a refusal; it kept the "gaffer" in a good humour. A bicycle, too, that he got tired of was put up, and the men, some of them, only living from hand to mouth, forced smilingly to take shilling tickets for a machine which none of them wanted, and which none of them got. Now, perhaps, this article will encourage Reid's men to never again submit to his raffles or his club.

After all workmen can do without charity—at least the charity commended to their attention by their foremen. The man whom Reid succeeded, who now has a better job in Dundalk, I hear was very fond of these raffles, as a convenient and modest way of befriending those less fortunate than himself. I wonder does Dowrick help the worker yet in this way?

I have heard that Hayden, a kind of overseer at the Dublin running shed, a genteel, cultured "boy," has a habit of receiving money from cleaners to back his own selection. Should his choice come home they get their money back; should he fail to "spot the winner" there's nothing more to be said about the matter. The superintendent of the goods, Turkington, too, takes a great interest in the moral welfare of the men, and at present is forming a Temperance Union amongst those under him. The story of the Shaughran[1] here comes into my mind, "Sure Conn's father," says Mr. Kelly, "was a real good man when he was sober." "But you said, Mr. Kelly, he was never sober." "Never, and Conn takes after him."

I hear the men in the workyard now won't be allowed to leave their food in the dining-hall the first thing in the morning. They must carry it with them, leave it on the sill, or hide it some place till Foreman Reid graciously allows the door to be opened

[1]A play by Dion Boucicault, a nineteenth-century Irish-American dramatist much admired by O'Casey.

a little time before breakfast. When these men knock off for meals they are forced to leave the yard, where the dining-hall stands, march through the gate, around the roads, past the goods stores, and back again to the dining-hall, from whence they started, like a crowd of unhappy criminals. This is done simply to make the men appear as mean and as passive as it may be possible to make them.

I saw one man threatened with dismissal one day because he stopped to give a drayman a lift with a bag of flour which had fallen off his cart. Space is not ample enough to enumerate all the mean, cowardly efforts to make the workmen feel that they are dust and to dust shall they return, but this tyranny of the foremen is only equal to their slavish adoration of their own superiors, who are, to them, as crescent-headed Astarte was to the Egyptians.

In subsequent articles we may deal with the officials and their patriotism, their competence, their nationality, their honesty, and their culture. Perhaps this article may induce the men to keep the foremen from robbing them of their manhood.

We are sadly afraid the foremen would have a difficult task. You cannot take what is not there. The few men left on the G.N.R. are surrounded by a herd of backboneless, selfish, bigoted tools.—Ed. [Jim Larkin.]

The Irish Worker, June 8, 1912

Chiefs of the G.N.R.I., I

So let us join both heart and hand, and lovingly agree,
For we're the loyal branches of the old Orange Tree.
Orange Song Book

I was more than interested in the articles contributed recently by Mr. Partridge concerning the works and pomps—

particularly the pomps—of the G.S.W.R.[2] The many facts he marshalled before all our eyes, of the incompetency of some, and the intolerance of all the magnates who sit in the places of judgment on that Railway, showed all that there was, and is, something rotten in the "State of Denmark."

I was struck how comparatively the G.N.R. surpasses its rich railway brother in the happy possession of Managers, Engineers, and Bosses, who in their persons combine a sublime knowledge of the Geometry of Euclid, Arithmetic of Nicomachus, the Mechanics of Archimedes, the Logic of Aristotle, and the Charity of all the Saints. All these gods of paper, and stone and mortar and brass, unlike the poor, undeveloped, groping moles of the G.S.W.R., are of Ireland Irish; indigenous to the soil. There was lately Plews, or, as he was affectionately called, Col. Plews, of an ancient Kerry stock, who derived his love for a position in the English Militia, by instincts inherited from, some said, King Billy, others said from Conn of the Hundred Battles. In his place is now the celebrated native speaker from Inis Diomain in the heart of Yorkshire, Mr. Bagwell—you'd know he was a Gaedheal by his name! And sure it 'ud do your heart good to see the Goods Manager, MacTurkington—or should it be O'?—dancing the Kerry Jig at Father Mathew Hall, or any other Temperance Entertainment. Then there's Milling and Wheldon, two ripe engineers who proudly trace their ancestry to Goban Taor or Goll MacMorna, who we all know wore cloaks with the blended colours of purple and orange and blue. Indeed all the "Heads" of the G.N.R. are first in knowledge, skill, and resource:—

> They are the true sons of Levi,
>   None on earth can with them compare;
> They are the root and the branch of David,
>   The bright and glorious morning star!

Orange Song Book

So intellectually keen were these true men of genius, that when they wanted to do a task in a right way, they had only to essay that task—three or four times! Perhaps a few experiences of my own would be interesting, which happened while I had the joy of working in that abode of harmony and love, and unending bliss—for the Bosses—the G.N.R.I.

Once upon a time the authorities decided to run what was called a "Special Motor Service to Howth." Then they had to build a shed for the "motors." They set about the task, and thereby hangs a tale or two. Elaborate plans were sketched; a cargo of bricks was secured to be used as flooring; every available man was told off to work at the "New Motor Shed." The horizon was black with engineers running with tape measures, rules, levels, and other tools of architecture.

The shed itself was too much for them, so they employed a foreign firm to erect that, a big structure it was of iron standards and corrugated iron walls, with three heavy wooden, iron-clamped gates to form the entrance. At length it was standing! Then there was a hitch! The gates wouldn't work; they couldn't shut the three gates together. If they shut a certain one, the other two would have to remain open; if they shut the other two, the certain one would have to stand extended! But that difficulty was nothing. They promptly overcame it by taking that certain one off and laying it aside altogether! They dug a pit six feet, placed a post therein thirty feet high, and surrounded it with concrete. This was to hold a big electric lamp. At last the "new motors" sidled along, and standing inside were a crowd of joy-filled overseers, each with all the dignity of a child with a Christmas toy. There was Mills, the "chief," or, as he was lovingly called by his men, "oul' Mills," and Hargreaves, his assistant, and Ogle, THE inspector, and Milling, District Engineer, and Whelden, the Assistant Engineer, and other "great men," all enjoying themselves on the slowly-moving "motor," which was soon to repose in its costly receptacle. And they were comical motors; they didn't seem to work well. "First they would, and then they wouldn't; then they could, and then they couldn't." Eventually they abandoned the original car, which contained the motor engine, and fell back upon the little, reliable Howth engines to propel the motor carriages to and fro from Howth. This alone must have cost the shareholders a bit of money. Well, as I said before, they tried to get the motors into the New Shed. But after knocking a cloud of bricks off one of the entrances to the Running Shed, after a multitude of orders and counter-orders, after running on this line and running on that, it was discovered that the rails leading to the new shed had been laid wrongly. And so the motors were led back and bandaged up to keep them from the harm of sun and air (they're not bandaged now!), while a gang of men who KNEW how to do things for a long time were engaged in rearranging what had been first been done on the G.N.R. regular way—wrongly. These men, with their fourteen shillings a week, and the gaffer's eighteen or so, made everything right, and again the motors sidled merrily towards the motor shed. But stop! the light-hearted engineers had planted that huge lamppost right in the way. There was a ripping noise, loud shouts, a frantic backing of the lovely new motors, and they were removed in safety minus one of their footboards. A cross-cut was hastily procured, the enemy attacked, and the huge post, which had been erected with so much labour, that evening lay on its back like a stricken giant.

Then they seemed to have miscalculated the proper length of the rails running the length of the shed, and to allow the motors to receive the protection for which the shed was presumably built, they had to strip the back elevation to permit the stop buffer stanchions to pass, and so find room for them outside. But notwithstanding all their mighty ingenuity, the motors still stood out fifteen feet or so beyond the two great gates, and so after a while the other gates were taken down and left in pitiful repose beside their brother. Then they got a huge quantity of "smoke boards," which are used to convey the steam along by the roof till it is dispersed in the open air. Two rows of these were to run parallel from one end of the shed to the other. While fixing these it was discovered that they would impose an excessive strain upon the roof, and to-day the bulk of these are hidden away in some obscure corner of one of the many railway departments. This was another dip into the shareholders' profit. They added an elaborate system of water hydrants and drainage, and after all the pipes had been laid, the floor put in, in fact, three months or so after the whole job was done, they came to the tradesman and asked him to make a chalk line over exactly where he had laid all the pipes! Of course it wasn't fair to expect these over-paid janissaries to think of everything; the curious thing was they seemed incapable of thinking of anything. They installed an elaborate system of electric lighting; they protected it with an expensive slate roof—slates and all, of course, imported; and yet I never could see, nor could anyone else whom I spoke to see, the need or the utility of this great expenditure. I have often seen the motor carriages scattered about the yard mixed with the ordinary carriages, neglected and uncared for; and, as I said before, the original "motors," all the way from Glasgow, were laughable and a dismal failure.

Let me relate an incident which curiously shows how these imported engineers regarded economy and extravagance. The foreman, Reid, sent me once to Booths, of Stephen Street, for a blow lamp, such as painters use for removing paint from woodwork; there was a lot of painting to be done. I was to get a good, serviceable article. I chose one for 30s. I brought it back.

F

"That's a good one," remarked the foreman, examining it critically, "How much is it?"

"£1 10s.," said I.

"My God," was the startled answer, "bring it back at once. If Mr. Milling (another importation) saw that bill he would be 'mad.' We want one for 3s. or 4s."

I brought it back. I had to take the cheapest one in the shop, which, I think, was 6s. 6d.

I daresay it's necessary to hold on tightly sometimes to make up leeway for blundering incompetency. They know well how to strain at a gnat and to swallow a camel. These Birmingham and Yorkshire and London importations come over here, secure the best of jobs, and set about convincing the Irish that they are those who guide the planets in their course. I have been amused to discover that those on the G.N.R. leave a lot to be desired in skill, education and manners.

However, with the Editor's permission, I will next week give further examples of these titanic men of science.

The Irish Worker, January 25, 1913

Chiefs of the G.N.R.I., II

In Uibh Laoghaire na nGaor seadh chaith sí a saoghal,
Níor fhás sí puinn riamh mar ba dhual di ó gach taobh dá gaol,
Gidh gur mó mála coirce 'gus mine d'ith sí go slán,
Is fíor-bheag dá chomhartha bhí ar chroiceann an chapaillín bháin.[3]

The G.N.R. officials have reasons to rejoice that a large share of Ireland is devoted to the rearing of cattle to feed their

[3]This is the second verse of a song called "An Capaillin Ban" or "The Little White Pony." As originally printed in *The Irish Worker*, it was somewhat garbled by the printer. Mr. Alf Mac Lochlainn, Assistant Keeper of Manuscripts at the National Library of Ireland, has freely versified it for me as:

Her sire and dam were tall and strong,
But she hardly grew at all herself;
They stuffed her with oats in S. W. Cork,
But damn the sign on the pony's pelt.

children. In a land living on the strength of its soil short shrift would be given to imported incompetence. Besides the latter traffic adds assurance to the security of their too well-paid positions. For a long time this traffic was accommodated on the "banks" from which all other commodities and goods were loaded. It was always an exciting time on a market day when the cattle would arrive for transit from Dublin to Belfast. Then would it become a scene reminiscent of a disorderly retreat on the part of a defeated army. Everything was in confusion; running hither and thither; carts, drays, lorries, floats, horses, men, cattle, sheep, and pigs inextricably mixed together! And then the deafening and discordant Babel of tongues! Carters shouting for their waggons and inquiring in forcible tones from the two heartworn and harassed checkers if they were going to be kept there all night; the checkers calling a carter to come on in an irritable manner, or cursing a dray up to the "other end of the bank"; and louder than all, clear and unmistakable, the imprecations, full and free, of the long-suffering cattle drovers. It was chaos gone mad.

It would appear as if no human ingenuity could possibly evolve order from such a medley; and yet, when evening shades fell, the cattle were safely housed in their waggons, the carters contentedly wending their way back to their respective firms, and two poor dead-tired checkers in their "hut" looking forward to the hour when they might be allowed to go home and find strength for the return of strife and turmoil on the morrow. And these poor slaves of checkers, with their paltry pound a week (or maybe less) and a little "overtime" thrown in, daily performed a feat of organisation, of evolving order out of chaos, of surmounting obstacles occasioned by the incompetence of richly-paid officials, which the latter, even in the self-confidence begotten of five hundred, seven hundred, or a thousand pounds a year, would never have been able to accomplish. But the toiler does not yet know his value. At length, owing probably to the frequent growls of the various city merchants, an idea penetrated the colossal skulls of the managers and engineers that the laughable and ponderous congestion of traffic on a tiny piece of ground could be allowed to continue no longer; and that which had for years been a subject for comment and joke on the part of checker, labourer, and carter, at length received the attention of fat-salaried mathematicians, who, in their own estimation, could, if they liked, cause as Mahomet is said to have done, the moon to so contract her sphere that it would enter in at their collar and come out again by the sleeve of their shirt! So they determined to build on the site of the old coal bank a new siding and a new means from which to deal with the cattle traffic.

Heavens! that was the siding and that was the cattle bank! I believe that it took fully five years to accomplish this task; it was scarcely worth the trouble. Who would dare to say it was worth the money it cost? This cattle bank, built and rebuilt, and rebuilt yet again, would to-day fail to comfortably enclose two ordinary herds of cattle.

Milling was the engineer selected by the gods to superintend this gigantic task. It was carried out on the principle of "slow, but sure." At one time there would be twenty men "hacking," delving, and harrowing like niggers; four days hence some fear or other would appal the hearts of the overseers, and you would see one man like a bird alone in the cutting, all the others having been gradually drawn away to other jobs. Asking this lone man the query of "What's up," the invariable answer would be—"Oh, some change in the orders; God knows when they start again." And how many times did this occur, almost at every job? Very often, indeed. However, after innumerable hesitations, the cutting was made, the line laid by the men with the fourteen or fifteen shillings a week. Then they gave to a contractor the job of building the enclosing concrete walls, one of which was built too high.

I have heard that the cement for this job was procured from "The Eblana Cement Works," the head man of which was the then chief engineer's son, George. However, that may be only a coincidence. Also, is it not a fact that on this job the Company placed twenty men to watch how the job was done? A costly mitred timber iron clamped railing was built on the right hand bank. Where is it now? It got in the way, and, of course, it came down quicker than it went up! Elaborately made concrete steps were made at the near end of the siding, on each side; these were never used. They are now grass-grown, and only serve to insure that the end waggon can never be loaded or unloaded without the aid of an engine or a gang of men to push it up into a more suitable place. If an engine be not available each waggon in front of it has to be pushed up first that the end one may be utilised. But the cattle bank! Then men were disposed of on each side of the bank to dig parallel trenches about six feet deep by seven. Tons of stuff which had previously been dumped there to raise the bank, were again flung up, and for a long time the work went merrily on, till on each side was the trench sentinelled by mountains of "filling in." Then one evening Milling appeared with the foreman; the trenches were to be stopped for awhile! This was done. After awhile they recommenced; waggons and waggons of stones were sent in; the bank was "patched" with them; they were tightly wedged together, their tops "feather edged," and the interstices were filled with sand, clay, and broken stones. Then it was flattened out and hardened by the continued operation of a road engine. After this was done, it was discovered that no space had been provided in which to sink the wooden piers on which the gates were to be swung. That was nothing, though! So the bank on the two sides was again attacked, the clay, sand, and broken stones hacked up, and the pitching, which had been laid only a few weeks before, was torn up every place where a pillar had to be placed, and by the time that was done that "cattle bank" presented the appearance that its last state was nearly as bad as its first!

I do not wish to give the details of the sinking and erecting of the pillars to hold the gates which were to admit of the cattle being driven from the bank to the waiting waggons. It was a long-drawn out comedy. This task was confided to a so-called carpenter, general pimp and spy, and particular confidential servant named Higgins. This creature—huge of stomach, huge of limb and huge of head, in which was said to be a microscopical brain, of which I have my doubts—was a genius for doing everything wrong. However, in faith and in politics he was of the "elect," and this does or ought to cover multitudes of sins. We shall bring him on the stage again. The day came when the bank was smooth and level beneath the critical and complacent gaze of the doughty Milling and his henchmen. They wouldn't let a crow alight on the bank till it was "dry and settled." You should have seen that bank a few months after. The pitching forced its way through the sand and clay, and very soon that bank was as bad as a rocky and flinty ravine in the heart of the Rocky Mountains. It was simply disgraceful for months; could never be properly cleaned; skimmed with a brush lightly, as a barber would brush a gent's hair, so as to, as the men were told, prevent the "broken stones from being carried away." A sprinkling of lime once a week completed its toilet, and it was always a mystery to me how our "Inspectors" allowed that bank to remain in such a condition for such a long time.

However, another attempt was made by doing again; what they had done before was useless. Waggons of broken stones were spread on it, and again it was rolled by a road engine smooth and level, and again in a few months it was as bad as ever. Then the new Chief came—Campion—another importation of course—by the way, at first it was whispered tremulously that he was a Catholic; but he wasn't; and that "cattle bank" was again the object of earnest attention. This time it was given to a contractor, and mountains of ballast and clay, and pitching stones and broken stones, out of which Milling tried to make a cattle bank, were taken forever away and heaped on the roadside. It gave employment, however, to a lot of men, and "it's an ill wind that blows nobody good." However, still it was waste of labour, and I think it's Ruskin says: "Of all wastes, the greatest waste you can commit is the waste of labour." It would be interesting, too, to find out, in all these years of effort, exactly how much this tiny, miserable, comical cattle bank cost the shareholders; and even when concreted, as it is now, I have seen in some places the water lodge after rain, due to faulty levelling on the part of those in charge. A lot of trouble would be often saved if these "college educated men" took the simple workmen into their confidence more frequently. Some of us have brains, and many men in this world, and in this country particularly, are in their wrong places.

The Irish Worker, February 8, 1913

Chiefs of the G. N. R. I., III

'Twas Flanagan found out the secret of flight,
    And made such a perfect affair,
That Farman and Bleriot, Latham and White,
    Proclaimed him the king of the air.
And, mind you, I think, he deserved his success,
    For really he worked very hard,
Six days out of seven; his private address
    Was—the hospital accident Ward!
        Song of the Modern Bardic School.

Henry, Hugh, or Herbert Milling was a remarkable man. He was originally an Englishman, and, as is well known, a prophet is never honoured in his own country, he shook its dust from his feet one day, embarked on a ship, came over to the

"Emerald Isle," was received with open arms by the officials of the G.N.R., who fell on his neck and kissed him. He has been here ever since. He bears on his lofty brow the sure mark of election. Anxiety and wistfulness for the company's success have furnished him with a grey head, trembling hand, and haggard cheek. No one who knew him well would venture to doubt that the Company's interests were only to be considered second to his own.

The old Greek or elder Gael would learn much from the polish and exalted benevolence of his manners.

The uninitiated sometimes conceived that his addresses to his men were usually blended with profanity, but this opinion was due to a mistaken conception of his method of administering lavish benedictions on those who hewed wood or drew water for the Company.

The writer himself remembers with becoming gratitude a few occasions when he profited splendidly by this Engineer's engaging conversation. Still, to be called upon to hear what the meanest thing in the Jungle could not endure, where the only law is the power of the strong to terrorise and prey upon the weak, inculcates patience in the character of the worker, and makes him—perhaps—fitter for the world to come.

When I bowed my head first before this gracious Buddha of Science, he was Engineer at the "Dublin End," and now is District Engineer from Dublin to Dundalk.

H. Milling, Esq., was a young "sport." He, like most people, knew how to enjoy himself; but, unlike many, he found many opportunities. I often wondered when I saw him in his natty, nautical costume of reefer jackets, blue pants and peaked hat, was he on a holiday, who gave him that holiday, or was he enjoying himself on the Company's time? Well, of course, Mr. Milling could not walk on the sea, so he built himself a yacht. When was the yacht built? Well, it wasn't a work carried out so

publicly as the building of the Ark by Noah. It was put together
by the Company's men in the "Test Room" at the Permanent
Way Stores, Dublin, and I'm told many amusing scenes occurred
of "clapping to the door" when anybody particular was knocking
around. Everyone, of course, heard the story that the men were
paid by Milling himself, but even so, what bye-law, rule, or regu-
lation of the Company permits its men being utilised in this way
for the pleasure of officials who are woefully overpaid already?
This was the identical engineer who, according to the complaint
of the Society of Painters of Dundalk, published some time ago
in the columns of "Sinn Fein," permitted painters and labourers
in the Company's services to be employed in the decoration of
a merchant's house in that town. It was the revealing of the incident which caused, as was generally understood, the issue of
time sheets, with which we will subsequently deal.

It would be also interesting to be able to gather details as
to the exact number of articles which were made by the Company's workmen for the elaborate house that Milling built for
himself in Malahide, how much were paid for these, and how
much they cost, such as window frames, etc.; how many times
the men from Malahide had to dig the boss's garden for him, or
go for messages, or gather moss or ferns for him in return for the
miserable security of their jobs. How often I grew indignant
when I noticed the fear and timidity that would smite the hearts
of any group of men when this ill-mannered tyrant would present himself. When will the toiler lift up his head and realise
that many of the lords appointed to reign over him are not worthy
to unloose the latchet of his shoes?

And it came to pass that Yachting palled on Mr. Milling,
and he secured a Motor Car—from the Company. This motor
car ran on the permanent way, and was used to carry the engineer from station to station, and a proud sight it was to see
Milling flitting about from place to place like a happy hearted

butterfly. But, in my opinion, the amusement it gave to Milling was greater than its utility to the Company. One day he travelled from Howth Head, via Howth, and returned via Sutton, and then found that there was no cross over road from Sutton tram line to the permanent way. There you are! A district engineer who did not know there was no cross over road from the tram line to Howth permanent way! and as the gradient was, presumably, too steep to return, the comical spectacle was witnessed of a crowd lifting the motor from the tram line to the permanent way. But the end came at last.

Travelling up north, with Ogle and some friends, Milling, like Don Quixote charging a windmill, ran full speed into a level crossing gate, and he and his friends described a circle in the air, that would delight the heart of any Mason, except, of course, Milling and his friends, and these gentlemen came out of hospital sadder and wiser men. Moral: If any engine driver had done such a rash act, or acted even much less rashly, he would have been sacked. Milling was not sacked. Why? I have heard the Motor was taken off him, and is not used now. More waste of money. I remember working at a job where artificial light was required, and I recollect refusing to go and purchase twopence worth of candles for the mason, which he bought himself out of his own pocket. More fool he! For if a Company can purchase motor cars, useless and burdensome, which serve only to half kill their occupants, they can surely afford to buy twopence worth of candles for the carrying out of necessary work.

The Irish Worker, February 15, 1913

Some Slaves of the G. N. R. I.
and Others

In the beauty of the lilies Christ was born across the sea
With a glory in His bosom that transfigures you and me;
As He died to make men holy, let us die to make men free.

—HOWE, *Battle Hymn of the Republic*

The recent leading article in *The Worker* presented a nice little mathematical problem before Mr. M. Murphy, Watson, Callaghan, and their hired helpers, who pictured with Dantean fervour the starving agonies of the strikers trying to live on 12*s*. 6*d*. a week. It is to be sincerely hoped they will give the problem an answer. If a man receiving 12*s*. 6*d*. weekly for one or two weeks starves in seven days, how long will it take a man to starve who receives 12*s*.—or less—a week for the whole of his unnatural life?

Callaghan and Murphy should be good at figures. How magnanimous and pitiful are these becoming; so anxious to rejoice when the workers rejoice and to mourn when they mourn. How solicitous these hypocrites are that the workers should suffer; no lack when their own revenues are in danger of reduction!

What about a man who falls sick or who meets with an accident, and who is, perhaps, for a long time forced to survive and recover on half-pay, which, in the case of sickness, he receives from a fund contributed to by himself? A sick man has to pay the same rent, needs better and more costly food, has need of the same warmth, has to meet the usual and unusual expenses, and will the Murphys and the Watsons in his sickness give him then what they give him in a job that is "clean and comfortable with very little to do?"

I was working in Balbriggan some time ago, and in conversing with one of the porters there I asked him what he had to pay for his lodging? "Eleven shillings a week," he told me.

"How much does the railway give you?" I asked.

"Ten bob a week," was the reply.

"How on earth, then, do you pay 11s. a week for your lodging?"

"You see," said this poor slave, "I work every Sunday and get 2s. for it, and so have a shilling for myself."

I often wonder did he put that shilling in the "bank" that the Company established to "encourage thrift among their employees." How many of the G.N.R. are in receipt of the colossal wage of 10s. a week?

I knew a "gatekeeper" at the "level crossing" at the Golf Links, Sutton. This young fellow had to be at his post every morning before seven o'clock, and they let him go to bed when the "last up" would pass for Dublin somewhere near twelve o'clock. The same on Sunday—no time allowed for Matins or Mass—and all for the "God-save-you-kindly" wage of nine shillings a week! The married men at the gates of Kilbarrack road and Claremont Hotel were granted hovels, which the Railway called "houses," less healthy and picturesque than the caves inhabited by pre-historic man. The "ballast men," the finest and best-built men of Fingal, get in return for the hardest and most exacting work in all weathers, the tidy sum of fourteen shillings a week; but they must keep the station masters on their hands, and the engineers, inspectors, and other bosses, too, by digging their gardens, whitewashing walls, so that the wages they get may not make them proud and overbearing.

Talking to a ganger once, I was much amused at the way his eyes gleaméd with enthusiasm about the "rise" that the "Conciliation Boards" would bring to the "labourin' man." How indignant he was when I ventured to say that the "Boards" would do little without the propelling force of organised labour. They got a rise of sixpence! Fourteen and six for hundreds of men, most of them married, out of which they have to pay for the Insurance Society, controlled by the railway directors, and to the Company's Pension Fund, not less than 8*d*. per week!

I used to know a man who guarded the entrance to Amiens Street Terminus, dressed in gorgeous glory of gold braid and blue cloth, and fourteen shillings a week, paid fortnightly! I knew a man on this same railway who served on the platform and then in the permanent way for fully twenty years, then was sent about his business—that is to starve—because he was not as active when he became old as when he was young. The last I heard of him was his death in the Union. He was neither a Mason nor an Orangeman.

There are hundreds on the G.N.R.I., boys and men, who are receiving starvation wages. Not only though do they give their energies, heat and activities of their bodies for a miserable fortnightly dole, but also sacrifice independence of mind and sturdiness of soul that they may drag out a miserable existence.

I was in the vestry attached to a Protestant parish one day talking to the Rector, when a young man entered and made inquiries as to the cost, etc., of the Church's blessing on his marriage. He demurred when the Rector mentioned the usual fee. The Rector kindly asked him how much his wages were, and was thunderstruck when he was told that it was 12*s*. 6*d*. per week!

"Has SHE anything?" inquired the anxious pastor.

"Not a ha'penny," was the reply.

"How on earth do you expect to live on 12*s*. 6*d*. a week?" was the astonished query.

There was no answer.

How, indeed! But if the unfortunate swain was foolish, what opinion must we have of the commercial gang of scoundrels who thought this poor fellow could perform the sacred duties of citizenship on 12s. 6d. a week? Sure, after paying even for the barest necessities of shelter and clothing and coal, they wouldn't have enough to give themselves one hearty meal of porridge in the week! I have before me a "One Day Menu for Lent," which won a prize of 10s. 6d. in a recent competition promoted by the *Saturday Herald*. This is, as the paper says, "a menu to suit the requirements of ordinary people; the dishes are easy to prepare, and are quite inexpensive." Here it is—Menu:—Breakfast—Porridge, buttered eggs, marmalade, tea and coffee. Lunch—Stuffed haddock, apricot pudding. Dinner—Lentil soup and steaks with tomato, roast lamb, cauliflower, baked potatoes, Charlotte Russe (whatever that is); biscuits and cheese, café noir (if required.)

I hope that all the workers in the employment of Martin Murphy are able to regale themselves even on Feast Days with these delectable dainties, "which are inexpensive and suit the requirements of ordinary folk"! It's high time that we should see that all toilers should be provided with the fare that gave sustenance to the poor that the Divine Founder of Christianity said we would always have with us.

At present we don't even get that much.

The Irish Worker, March 1, 1913

Religion

I HAVE found no essays from this period that deal other than obliquely with religion. Yet the autobiographies indicate that organised religion was once as vital a matter for O'Casey as the Nationalist Movement, the Gaelic League, or the Transport Union. In his book on O'Casey, David Krause has offered evidence that Michael, the playwright's father, was a militant Protestant. O'Casey's mother was a pious woman, and O'Casey himself was active in St. Barnabas Church which was just around the corner from where he and his mother lived in Abercorn Road. The rector, the Reverend E. M. Griffin, was his great friend, and to him O'Casey dedicated *Pictures in the Hallway:* "A fine scholar; a man of many-branched kindness, whose sensitive hand was the first to give the clasp of friendship to the author."

O'Casey's censure of organised religion doubtless began when he observed the obstructionism and bigotry that the Reverend Mr. Griffin encountered in such parishioners as the Dowzard whom O'Casey pilloried in *Red Roses for Me* and in an early vitriolic essay, "Dowzard: the Hector of the Quays." O'Casey's censure and distrust could only have been intensified by observing that most of the clergy were fervently opposed to Nationalism, Irish in the schools, and the labour movement. He was also much incensed by the cases of the unfortunate Dr. Michael O'Hickey and Dr. Walter McDonald of Maynooth College, whose difficulties with the Roman Catholic Church he sympathetically retells in his autobiographies. But perhaps the conclusive proof for him was the narrow religiosity of a school teacher with whom he fell in love. (The school teacher is surely the Sheila Moorneen of *Red Roses for Me,* and probably a bit of her is in Nora Clitheroe of *The Plough and the Stars.*)

At any rate, although there is little early evidence from O'Casey's own hand, the same pattern of growth can be seen in his religious thought that we have seen in the other causes which he espoused. First there was a passionate involvement; later his critical mind saw many flaws, sometimes outrageous ones, in the practice of religion; and ultimately he became an outspoken critic. A critic of the practices of religion need not be irreligious; he may be more intensely religious than the conventional churchgoer. O'Casey is.

77

"The Soul of Man" is the earliest work of O'Casey's that I have found, and this is its first publication. It is interesting to note that an intimation of the pattern discussed in the preceding paragraph appears in the poem when Faith is superseded by Self-Reliance.

The Soul of Man

Poor man, all human, half divine,
    With natures both absorbed in each,
Stands on the top of Life's incline,
    And looks as far as thought can reach;
And wonders if Death's ocean dark
Shall quench his life's expiring spark.

But Faith outshines his vision dim,
    And tells him God is good and just;
Tho' in life's vessel sorrows brim
    He'll bear them all in quiet trust:
But Faith like this is followed after
By sounds resembling devils' laughter.

The Sacrifice of Christ the strong,
    Is daily offer'd for his sins;
But jeering Cant and raging Wrong
    Laugh when the holy rite begins;
Make merry with their many friends
Whene'er the holy service ends.

Peer well into life's dark recesses,
    And there you'll find but darker guesses;
Probe these into the inmost kernel
    Within are mysteries eternal:
The gods laugh loud to find that man
Has reach'd the place where he began.

When Life's bright dawn the world was gilding,
　Man's infant mind went Babel building,
But want of knowledge man defeated,
　And left the work but half-completed:
For broadening powers of mind alone
Can climb upon God's highest throne.

And man, unshaken, still shall seek—
　Ignoring all the gods' derision—
To make eternal silence speak,
　To look behind life's hidden vision,
Till Thought may weigh and sift and scatter,
And mould again the life of matter.

November, 1905

G

Controversies

As early as 1914 a contemporary called O'Casey "a disgruntled fellow," and that is the way he has seemed to many comfortable and easy-going souls ever since. True, a superficial glance at his career suggests an unending broil and trouble. There was *The Silver Tassie* affair in which he lashed out at the grand poet Yeats. There was his stinging criticism of Irish politics and manners that appeared in his autobiographies and that polka-dot the last ten years of *The Irish Times*. There was his ferocious attack on Orwell, on Greene, on Coward, on Chesterton, on Heaven knows who else. There was his running feud with the Irish drama critics. There was his ruckus with the directors of the Dublin International Theatre Festival over *The Drums of Father Ned*. Remembering these typical forays, one might easily, if one were dense, dismiss him as an iconoclast, a misanthrope, and a querulous old curmudgeon.

"Sean was always a fighter," says his wife. That's true. A glance at his plays and essays shows it. But why was he? Simply, because he was a man of superb gifts born into conditions unfit for a criminal. Squalor, poverty, malnutrition, and manual labour were his lot, and by all odds so should have been an early death. He was the last of thirteen children, only five of whom grew to adulthood. "Man's inhumanity to man" was no meaningless phrase to him. He suffered it in a way that millions have, and that millions of others cannot conceive of. The opinions of O'Casey the man are strong because poverty, disease, and irremediable pain unforgettably dramatised them in his youth.

Because of his life in the Dublin slums he holds strong opinions which he expresses with force; because he is a writer of genius he also expresses those opinions with succinctness and flair. Bernard Shaw wrote in his Preface to *Man and Superman*:

. . . the main thing in determining the artistic quality of a book is not the opinions it propagates, but the fact that the writer has opinions. . . . He who has nothing to assert has no style and can have none: he who has something to assert will go as far in power of style as its momentousness and his conviction will carry him.

"I'm not quarrelsome," said O'Casey to me, "it's just that I express myself succinctly." It is easy to imagine why his companions might think such a succinct man disgruntled. As Shaw again wrote, in his Preface to *Immaturity*:

The truth is that all men are in a false position in society until they have realized their possibilities, and imposed them on their neighbors. They are tormented by a continual overweening. This discord can be resolved by acknowledged success or failure only: everyone is ill at ease until he has found his natural place, whether it be above or below his birthplace. The overrated inheritor of a position for which he has no capacity, and the underrated nobody who is a born genius, are alike shy because they are alike out of place. Besides, this finding of one's place may be made very puzzling by the fact that there is no place in ordinary society for extraordinary individuals.

This comment does much to explain the vigour, strength, and scorn of the attack against the labour columnist "Euchan" in the first controversy below.

It was not merely that O'Casey was in his wrong place in society; everyone in such a society was in his wrong place, for the society itself was meanly and barbarously wrong. The society which allowed the workers only starvation wages, which was entirely controlled by the business man, which sent its policemen out to bludgeon the workers on the street and used its power to starve them for months—as O'Casey had seen in the great Dublin Lockout of 1913—this society was most intolerably, most sinfully wrong.

This background made O'Casey a Communist. Recently, O'Casey's Communism has been somewhat whitewashed so that he might be more palatable to Americans. His Communism is held to be a highly individual belief, totally divorced from the principles and practices of the U.S.S.R., and hence only a harmless eccentricity. That view does injustice to the man's convictions, to his intelligence, to his whole work, and to his life. He is no Party-Liner, and he has said so, but he is no sentimental fellow traveller, clinging to a fuzzy vision of the good life.

I once asked O'Casey when he first began to think of himself as a Communist, and he replied, "Ah, Bob, I was born a Communist." That sentiment appears also in Shaw's Preface to *Immaturity* (and, indeed, one is struck when reading this preface with the similiar views of Shaw and O'Casey). "The born Communist," says Shaw, "before he knows what he is, and understands why, is always awkward and unhappy in plutocratic society and in the poorer societies which ape it to the extent of their little means: in short, wherever spiritual values are assessed like Income Tax."

The controversy with "Euchan" began early in 1913; already in January of 1914, in the controversy with James McGowan, O'Casey could smile at the narrow nationalism which even a few months before he had not entirely sloughed off. In 1913 he had said:

> We are out to overthrow England's language, her political government of our country, good and bad; her degrading social system; her lauded legal code which are blossoms on the tree which springs, not from the centre of the Dublin Corporation, nor from the Halls of Westminster, but which has its roots in the heart of the English race.

Now, in 1914, he reads James McGowan writing the same thing:

> That day shall . . . come when the Irish race, armed to the teeth, gives the signal that shall hurl the British Empire to eternal damnation unwept, unhonoured, and unsung.

And O'Casey could now chuckle in reply, that McGowan must be "a frequent visitor to the picture theatres."

By 1914 the narrow nationalist, who reportedly wore only clothes manufactured in Ireland "including his shoestrings," was gone. By 1914 O'Casey had found a broader struggle in the alleviation of the poverty of the workers of the world. He now writes, "in the hunger-cry of the nation's poor is heard the voice of Ireland." He now supports the Citizen Army with its membership drawn from the Transport Union, and not "the deluded wage-slaver Volunteers." He now exhorts the readers of Jim Larkin's labour paper to "yield allegiance to no movement that does not avow the ultimate destiny of the workers."

Ayamonn Breydon, the hero of O'Casey's play, *Red Roses for Me,* throws off the ties of nationalism, art, family, and love in order to assist the workers in a strike. Similarly, O'Casey came to direct his energies primarily into fighting the class war. It was not that he was less of a Republican or less of a Gaelic enthusiast, but that he was now more of a Communist.

In 1914 O'Casey criticised Madame Markievicz for remaining upon the councils of both the Citizen Army and the Volunteers and demanded that she resign from one organisation. Most of his colleagues upon the Citizen Army Council could see no contradiction in the lady retaining a foot in either camp. To O'Casey, however, the distinction was clear;

one organisation was for the worker, and the other was not. To the clear-sighted, logical, and fervent O'Casey, the view of Larkin and other labour leaders on this issue was but a half-hearted compromise that must have played a significant part in disillusioning him of the efficacy of the organised action of labour in Ireland.

To O'Casey, the Transport Union had fought its true fight, against Capital, in the Dublin Lockout of 1913. When, under the leadership of James Connolly, the Citizen Army became ever more involved in the fight for Irish freedom, it seemed to O'Casey that Irish Labour had become entirely deflected from its true purpose. When it became apparent that Connolly was leading the Army ever closer to the Rising of 1916, O'Casey regarded the whole affair as arrant folly, destined to end in failure. His view of the national struggles is well embodied in his criticism of Jack Clitheroe in *The Plough and the Stars,* but the same criticism appears with almost equal force in *The Shadow of a Gunman* and *Juno and the Paycock.*

Many of O'Casey's views were unpopular, but they were held honestly and emitted in a loud, firm voice. So, frustrated by temporizing and compromise—in Labour, in Republicanism, in the Gaelic League— O'Casey ultimately turned his abundant energies into the one channel in which he could express himself with freedom, into writing; and here, as an artist, he finally broke through and triumphantly made his mark.

Yet, though O'Casey became an artist, he did not forget his opinions. He merely expressed them with more cunning.

His opinion on the teaching of Irish in the schools appears several places elsewhere in this volume. The exchange with Liam O Rinn appeared after O'Casey's initial success as a dramatist. It shows him still a violently engaged writer and it shows him in an eminently practical light. Against the wistful vapourings of O Rinn, O'Casey appears at his most level-headed and clear-sighted. The argument demonstrates clearly his willingness to sacrifice what is desirable to what is necessary. He writes:

You cannot give a good education, either English or Irish, to a barely-nourished child—let that be a law unto itself; it is unassailable.

He had achieved such clarity only after controversy, disillusionment, and honesty. His vision of what was good was as firm as it had been when he had been more naive; experience and controversy had taught him the nature of folly.

Controversy and opinion are not O'Casey's weaknesses but his strength. If we accept O'Casey, it must be on his own ground, as a man burning with opinion. It would be, indeed, unfortunate if we came to regard him as many people have come to regard Shaw. To like him for his jokes, and to regard as whimsical and harmless eccentricities what those jokes are about, this is to know neither Shaw nor O'Casey.

A National Controversy

On FEBRUARY 1, 1913, in *The Irish Worker,* A. Patrick Wilson, a columnist who wrote under the pseudonym of "Euchan," wrote an article called
"The Labour Movement: Labour and Its Relation to Home Rule." The
gist of the argument was that, with Home Rule, Ireland would become
an even more commercial country, and that Labour must be then prepared for sterner struggles against "wealthy owners." If Labour would
combine and fight, Home Rule would help make the worker even more
prosperous. The article ended, "Home Rule is coming! Deo Gratias."

The paragraph to which O'Casey took exception was this one:

In its present position Ireland is comically pathetic. Its sub-
conscious mind is away back in glories of the past, while its conscious
mind is occupied in up-to-date political manoeuvring, with a sort of
pious hope that the glories of the past will be revived when the
political intriguing will be successful. The past, however, is for ever
past. Ireland can never again be the glorious nation it was. The present age is a commercial one, and all that the British political bosses
desire is that Ireland will become a cohesive, active and willing part
of the British commercial empire, and Ireland will undoubtedly
become so after Home Rule is established.

To this O'Casey wrote a letter which appeared on February 8:

To the Editor of
THE IRISH WORKER,
February 8, 1913

DEAR MR. EDITOR,

I would like to know what Euchan means when he writes
that "Ireland's sub-conscious mind is away in the glories of the
past." "The past, however, is past, Ireland can never be again

88

the glorious nation she was." What does the writer mean by
Ireland's sub-conscious mind, and what does he know about
Ireland's past? Can he see farther than the soldiers, the saints
and the sages of Eireann? Has he received this message from
Balor of the Evil Eye, or does he write the words whispered in
his ear by Manconan Mac Lir? Does Euchan think Labour will
lay a detaining hand on Ireland's shoulder? Is the hand of
Euchan about to write *ne plus ultra* on Ireland's soul? 'Twill
want to be steady and true, and very, very strong. How like
is Euchan's words to those written long ago which the Gael has
not forgotten: "The Gael is gone with a vengeance, Laus Deo!"
The Gael is here still, Euchan, stronger to suffer than Hell can
harm, and it is highly improbable that our hearts shall shake
before the words of Euchan. So the Labour Party is "not making pikes," but is "making intelligent voters." So, Euchan, you
sneer at the pike. It's not the first sneer that winked at the Gael
from the face of *The Worker*. The weapon only bruises the hand
that flings it. And we learn that new gods have come to
Eireann with gifts of intelligence in their hands, and Euchan is
one of them. Ah! I fear we Irish will prove unpleasantly un-
receptive. Attacks, ignorant and presumptive, upon our cher-
ished ideals will do no good to the Labour Movement. The
Labour Movement can afford to lose some of its friends; 'tis
wise to convert an enemy to friendship, who will dare to say
that it is wise to ignorantly offend a friend?

But we laugh at Euchan; "Ireland will never again be the
glorious nation she was," is comically equal to the statement by
the same writer,[1] "that Bobbie Burns was, perhaps, the greatest
of all Scots."—Perhaps he was, Euchan!

S. O'Cathasaigh

[1] In an article, "Robert Burns, Scottish Poet and Democrat," in *The Irish
Worker* on January 25, 1913.

"Euchan" replied:

Though I have read the letter with the gravest and greatest attention I can find nothing in it that is worth replying to. If my good critic would try to write less prettily and more logically I might endeavour to make something of his charges. As it is, I must say a suitable reply seems hopeless. If I say that Ireland's "past is past" I can't for the life of me see how I can be said to be laying a "detaining hand on Ireland's shoulder." Will my critic read the article again, without prejudice, in full and not in part, and then he may realise that I was discussing the commercial present and not the romantic past. If he reads the article as I suggest, he may also see that when I talk about "pikes" I am not sneering at them. Pikes have served their day, but their day is past, that's all.[2] When it comes to be a case of removing corrupt politicians from a nation's progress, I submit once more that intelligent voters are of more use than pikes. What does my critic think?

As to his closing remarks about Robert Burns, I am afraid I'm once more at a loss regarding my critic's meaning. It may be my density, or, again, it may be that the writer's logic has been lost amidst his flowers of rhetoric.

Briefly re-stated, the arguments of the article were:

(a) That the present is purely a commercial age.
(b) That the coming of Home Rule will bring Ireland into commercial line with its neighbours.
(c) That the battle of the future will be between Capital and Labour.
(d) That the workers of Ireland must prepare now for that battle.

An intelligent critic will either attempt to refute or to further these arguments in whole or in part. Would he mind writing again after he has READ the article.

EUCHAN.

[2]On this point O'Casey had the last word. See "The Man with the Pike" in his recent play, *The Drums of Father Ned*.

"Euchan" and Ireland, a Challenge to a Verbal Combat

'Tis man aspires
To link his present with his country's past
And live anew in knowledge of his sires.

SAMUEL FERGUSON

Are you ready, "Euchan"? On guard, then!

I asked "Euchan" some questions. He did not answer them. He says they were not worth answering. He stated "Ireland's past is past," and that "Ireland can never again be the glorious nation she was." I asked him what reasons he held for making such an assertion. But though probably reasons are, with "Euchan," as plentiful as blackberries, he will not give us one; the question is "not worth answering." The question will be answered for him. Surely "Euchan" did not think my brief letter was a criticism of his article. I therein asked for a fuller meaning of some astonishing announcements concerning the National faith of all Irishmen. "Euchan" should have READ my letter. Here are now my opinions on the various points raised by "Euchan": (a) "That the present age is purely commercial."

God forbid! This age has seen the rekindling of many nations; this age has witnessed in many lands the stirring of the dry bones of the toilers. Bohemia, which regarded more fondly her language and her literature than her linen and her glass, Finland and the Balkan States are all heaving in the throes of a National Revival. Nationalists are being hurried into gaol in Egypt for preaching Egypt for Egyptians; and Hindu and Mussulman, in India, are chanting Bande Bataram; in our own dear country Fleming, O'Growney and Rooney, among many have proclaimed that "the life is more than meat and the body more than raiment." Life is stirring everywhere; democratic States are appearing everywhere—even in China—but still the fountain remains unpure; the people still cling to the mire. In my opinion this is far from being a "purely commercial age," but is the age rather of an excitedly awakening democracy. Ireland never was, never will be the slave of Commercialism. Her glens and valleys will never be furnace-burned like the Vale of Dura. In the past, "Euchan," Commercialism was far from her shores; in the present, she, in her language, national and dramatic revival, has turned her back upon Mammon.

"Euchan" tells us that (b) "Home Rule will bring Eire into commercial line with our neighbours." Evidently, he thinks, too, Home Rule is the final settlement. Don't you think, "Euchan," the people have something to say to that? Ireland's soul is not symbolised by the buzz of Jacob's machinery, nor are her energies confined between the four walls of Irwin's paper mills (although Irwin once issued a Municipal election leaflet in Irish). Ireland's nearest neighbour is England. In language, industrialism or ultimate ideal Ireland will never be linked with her. Ireland will look for better things than an Old Age Pension, State Insurance Act, or Meals for Necessitous Children. Gaelic Ireland will have no room but a grave space for the persecutor and the oppressor. Our work will be, not to link our country with commercial England, but to make her feed as large a number of people as possible: making every sod productive, every tree a defence, and every son and daughter of our mother happy. "Euchan" further says (c) that "the battle of the future will be with Labour and Capital." Here again "Euchan" suggests that Home Rule is our final political settlement with England. Not so, "Euchan"—not so. And to supplement this "Euchan" adds that the Labour movement is the only rebel movement in Ireland, and "Euchan" is going to arm his rebels with votes. Good man, "Euchan"! but don't you think the revolution will be a tame one? But they'll have intelligence, too, says "Euchan." Aye, so had "O'F" and so had Richardson. Intelligence sometimes has its price and can be used against the very power it was expected to aid. Give me the men who simply did what's good, who'd hesitate to give the reason why; devotion to sacred principle is greater than acquired wisdoms. "Euchan" asks me if votes intelligently given are not more effective than pikes? I believe they are useless without power to resist their nullification. The votes of our Volunteers were useless when they handed up their arms; the votes of the French National assembly would have been choked in their blood were not behind them the people with arms in their hands. Ireland's future battle be, "Euchan," the continuance of the fight that has gone on since the thievish Normans came to Ireland with their English civilisation. We are out to overthrow England's language, her political government of our country, good and bad; her degrading social system; her lauded legal code which are blossoms on the tree which springs, not from the centre of the Dublin Corporation, nor from the Halls of Westminster, but which has its roots in the heart of the English race.

Now, "Euchan," place between the alphabetical points which constitute the analysis of your first article these phrases, which I suppose, as you say, are not worth answering: "Ireland's past is past"; "Ireland can never be again the glorious Nation she was." What are we to infer? Come, "Euchan," be honest as well as logical; add to this, "The Labour Movement is now the only Rebel Movement in Ireland." And what are we to think? Why, what else but that all our love for, and inspiration in Ireland's past is vanity, and that the glory of Ireland's future is framed in the Labour Party's pamphlet. You prate of logic, and you say that in your article you dealt with the Commercial Present and not with the Romantic Past. But you tell us, "Euchan," that Ireland's past, our past, is past, and thereby deal with our country's history in a way which we resent and which we challenge. You say that you dealt with the Commercial Present, and you add that "Ireland will never again be the glorious nation she was." Does this phrase not deal with Ireland's future? Aye, in a way that we resent and that we challenge. Past indeed! I tell you that where one ten years ago thought of Ireland's past, hundreds now are studying it. "Beidh tracht agus iomradh ar mo gniomhaibh fos,"[3] said Ireland's incomparable hero, and it is so. Sunday last the athletes of ten counties met in hurling and football to provide funds to erect a visible sign that a great Gael, whose life is now part of Ireland's past, is not forgotten. Now "Euchan" of the logic and the intelligence, I challenge you to debate with me that "this is purely in Ireland a commercial age"; "that Home Rule will link Ireland with her commercial neighbours"; "that Ireland's past is past" and "that she can never be the glorious Nation she was." You have already the advantages of intelligence and a logical mind; I will add to these: You can choose your own place— where you are most at home for preference—select your audience from the Transport Union Workers to whom, I presume, you are well known—I will not ask one of my friends to attend the debate—choose your own chairman—Jim if you wish—and behold, it shall be made manifest to-morrow (Sunday) week, the 2nd ulto, or that day week, or afterwards when you will, that the Faith of the Gael is even more potent than the prophecies of "Euchan."

With regard to the failure of "Euchan" to understand my reference to Bobbie, "the greatest of Scots, and the herald of democracy," which he attributes to his density or my rhetoric, I fear "Euchan's" failure is due to density and ignorance. If "Euchan" be a Scotsman his statement that Bobbie "was, perhaps, the greatest of Scots" proclaims him ignorant of the

[3]There will yet be comment and discourse on my heroic deeds.

history of his sires. It was not Burns of whom it was written, "Fortissimus heros Scotorum." The statement that he was the "herald of democracy," I leave to "Euchan" himself. His statements about Ireland manifest—if he be an Irishman—how ignorant an Irishman he is; but if "Euchan" be of the English breed, he is naturally trying to speak profoundly of things about which he knows next to nothing.

Ceangal[4]

The delivery of Ireland is not in the Labour Manifesto, good and salutary as it may be, but in the strength, beauty, nobility and imagination of the Gaelic ideal. I am one of those who has entered into the labour of our fathers; one of those who declare—by the fame of our forefathers; by the murder of Red Hugh; by the anguished sighs of the Geraldine; by the blood-dripping wounds of Wolfe Tone; by the noble blood of Emmet; by the death-wasted bodies of the famine—that we will enter into our inheritance or we will fall one by one. Amen.

The Irish Worker, February 22, 1913

On March 1, 1913, "Euchan" replied in a leading article called "The Good Old Past! 'Rip Van Winkle' Wakes Up." Most of the article is ferocious name-calling, and none of it really meets O'Cathasaigh's points. O'Cathasaigh had obviously gotten under his skin, for he rages for three columns. Some of his diatribe has considerable interest:

Judging by the article I would say that my critic is a dreamer— a man going about with his head deeply immersed in the mists of the good old past. We meet them from time to time, but not very often nowadays. The last one I met was in Sligo, and in his drunken enthusiasm he said just the sort of things my critic wrote. . . .

Poor old Rip Van Winkle shakes the fungus from his limbs and wants to fight. He is rather sorry that he has been awakened out of his dreams, but now that he is awake he will break a lance with "Euchan" who disturbed his slumbers, or if he cannot break a lance

[4]Envoi.

H

with him he will at least try to drown him in a flood of sentimentality.

Finally, in column three, "Euchan" returns to the issues, challenges O'Cathasaigh to "hit out as hard as he likes," and reaffirms his earlier arguments, adding the suggestion that O'Cathasaigh is "out to assail the Labour Movement."

On Saturday, March 8, 1913, O'Cathasaigh replied.

To the Editor of
THE IRISH WORKER,
March 8, 1913

I am seriously inclined by the promptings of Charity to say no more for Euchan's sake. I never anticipated that my few questions—which he has not answered, and my few remarks— could create such a hysterical commotion in poor Euchan's soul. But Truth is greater than Charity. I really wish Euchan would TRY to be logical. He says he said nothing derogatory of Ireland's History, and he heads his reply "The Good Old Past," and in the text he uses the phrase "motley collection of prehistoric red-herrings." What do these phrases mean? I wonder what does the writer of the "Coming of Cuchullain," Standish O'Grady, think of Euchan's opinion of Ireland's Past? Euchan says he bases his contentions principally on his BELIEF.

Upon what conditions, arguments and premises, does he base his belief? He may believe anything; he may say what he believes, but if he knew even the first elements of logic, he would realise that in no dispute or debate can belief be expected to carry conviction.

Does he expect all of us to fall down and worship when he chants his logical stanza, Credo Euchan! He still holds the "Labour Movement is the only Rebel Movement in Ireland."

This is only an opinion; let him prove it. I suppose he is still content to arm his "Rebels" with votes! If he armed each of them even with a halberd of an ancient man-at-arms, or the stick of a boy scout, they'd have a better chance of success. It was the rifle on Bunker Hill, not the VOTES of the American Representatives, that won American Independence. It was the same power that overthrew the French Monarchy.

To-day, even in the very ward where the Transport Union is strongest, the VOTES of the electors have declared that Jim Larkin is their councillor. What prevents him from sitting in the Corporation, Euchan? British Law. The votes were no use to him. Surely, these points are clear enough for you. You tell us that as a Labour Writer you are only concerned in Industrial History. But do you not know, Euchan, that you cannot separate the Industrial History of Ireland from their National and Political records?

James Connolly could give you some valuable information on this question. You say again that *The Irish Worker* is a labour paper, not a journal of historic research.

Your amusing mistakes have revealed that to me. I suppose it is because you have such a contempt for history in general that you make statements that historically are laughable, such as "He was the herald of Democracy," and "the greatest of the Scots," and that you try to hold up your beliefs by the arm with historical references, such as "Ireland's Past is Past," and "We are not Forging Pikes," etc.

I think your contention that *The Worker* is simply a Labour Paper is nonsense. The other week there was a long review of a recently issued volume of poetry, called "The Agate Lamp," which, according to Euchan, had nothing to do with Labour whatever. And the Editor recently, in a sub-leader, advised all his readers to go and see pictures exhibited in the Central Branch of the Gaelic League, which, according to

Euchan, had nothing to do with Labour. Are not the men of science and art and literature labourers, too? Ruskin says they are. What does Euchan think?

Euchan calls me a dreamer. I thank him for the word. He seems to think that the dreamer who lives in the inspiration of the past is a fool. This is another of Euchan's "beliefs." The dreamers were and are the salt of all nations. Ruskin was a dreamer; so was Burns, the "greatest of Scots—perhaps"; so was Robert Emmet; and only the other week, in one of his articles, The O'Grady said that without imagination nothing can be done. But the most amusing part of Euchan's "reply" is his anxiety about his miserable job. What a bold bad man I must be to try a Jacobean trick on "Euchan" and supplant him in the good opinion of Jim. Why, years ago I argued some labour and historical questions with Jim himself in Dumcondra, and though Jim in his reply said I "spoke straight and hit hard," he never expressed any fear of losing his job.

"Euchan" refuses to give any reasons for the various statements he has made, and is definite—very definite—in one point only—he won't debate with me. He is afraid. Along with the fear of losing his job, his other reasons are: "The hall could not contain the readers of *The Worker*"; "I would spend my time scouting in the history of two thousand years ago." Now, I challenge him again to debate these questions with me—one or all of them.

1. "That the Labour Movement is the only Rebel Movement in Ireland";
2. "That this is purely a Commercial Age";
3. "That the Coming of Home Rule will link Ireland with her Commercial Neighbours";
4. "That the Delivery of the Irish Workers is in the Labour Manifesto."

Now "Euchan," I will sign an agreement in the presence

of any witnesses you like that, in the eventuality of victory or defeat in a debate upon any one or all of the above subjects, I will not take your job from you; and if you do not wish Jim to behold your discomfiture—you know you never can tell—choose as your chairman the Labour Councillor for Kilmainham, W. P. Partridge. I am satisfied he will show no favour to either side.

If Liberty Hall cannot contain the readers of *The Worker*, the "old spot by the river" will do me equally well, or the Fifteen Acres if you like, for the matter of that; and I will further give "Euchan" a guarantee that my remarks shall not go back a thousand years, but will be confined to the incidents, facts, and history of the Present Generation.

Now, "Euchan," surely you need be afraid no longer, but give us an answer for the hope that is in you. "Euchan's" premises, which lead him to assert my criticisms were largely due to spite, are beneath contempt. His logical deductions consequent upon meeting in Sligo are equally contemptible. His passing remark that I either bought a copy of *The Worker* or got a LOAN of it, is another brilliant example of "Euchan's" arguments. His insinuation that a contributor who sent in a criticism over his true name was after his job is an example of his sense of fair play and of his courtesy.[5]

"Euchan" has already many obvious advantages. I have added all I could to these. It is his business now to accept my challenge and prove the things he says are or will be. It is an article of logic that no one can be called upon to prove a negative. This is my last word. If "Euchan" refuses then I declare that he is a poor, shadowy Labour writer, ignorant of history, unacquainted with the first elements of logic, unworthy to play a part in the Movement which he does not understand.

S. O CATHASAIGH

[5]Most letters to the Editor were pseudonymous, as were most articles in the paper.

On the same page "Euchan" replied, "I . . . am seriously inclined to think that the inflated sense of importance with which this relic of the past regards himself will be sufficient to carry him altogether off his feet some day, and then there will be more German airship scares when his swelled head is seen floating around in the heavens."

He adds that "no person outside a lunatic asylum could debate with this critic of mine" and that O'Cathasaigh is a "miserable hound!" He also accuses O'Cathasaigh of "trying to obtain a large advertisement for himself," suggests that if O'Cathasaigh wants "to knock the spots off the Labour Party why shouldn't he tackle one of their recognised speakers," adds that the "spiteful remarks about Burns . . . are beneath contempt," and ends by saying, "You've a big swelled head, Rip (the result of consorting with boys, possibly) but you have a very small mind. Take care that the mind doesn't sweep you off your feet some day."

On March 29, however, "Euchan" announced in his column that he was quitting the paper.

A Labour Controversy

An Open Letter to
Workers in the Volunteers

In a word, we demand Ireland for the Irish, not for the
gentry alone.

JOHN MITCHEL

Many of you have been tempted to join this much talked
of movement by the wild impulse of genuine enthusiasm. You
have again allowed yourselves to be led away by words—words
—words! You have momentarily forgotten that there can be
no interests outside of those identified with your own class. That
every worker must separate himself from every party—every
movement that does not tend towards the development of the
faith that all power springs from and is invested in the people.

The volunteer movement now shouts for the support of all
classes, but hopes to build its battalions from flank to flank and
from front to rear with massed bodies of workers.

Workers, do you not think it is high time to awake from
your sleep and yield allegiance to no movement that does not
avow the ultimate destiny of the workers. Ye stood by the
farmers in the Land War, by the Revivalists in the fight for the
Gaelic Language, largely by the Separatists in the Sinn Fein
Movement, and what have ye gained? Now you are cuddled
with dear words about Nationality and Country to devote the
power of reason and the force of energy to a movement
which silently disregards your claim to be anything but a slave
to a class that has always opposed, and will always oppose
National aspirations that may be opposite to their monetary and
commercial interests.

101

"To secure and maintain the liberties and rights common to all Irishmen"—they say they stand for this. We know the liberties and rights we enjoy.

The right to toil till the blood is dried in our veins; the right to bless the land that gives us what it thinks we are worth; the right to suffer starvation, and misery, and disease, and then thank God that such light affliction work an exceeding weight of glory! Workers, ye are fools to train and drill for anything less than complete enfranchisement, for the utter alteration of the present social system, for liberty to ensure the natural and absolute development of every Irishborn man and woman.

We, workers, know too, the rights that are common to many Irishmen; rights that are organised robbery and oppression; rights that give them the robber's privilege to enjoy exclusively by the wealth that was created for all.

Workers, the leaders of this movement will try to cajole you with terms of Wolfe Tone and Mitchel whom they never knew, or did not understand. They will impress upon you the will to pay from your hard-earned wages a weekly premium to support an organisation that may be used, subsequently, to preserve the so-called interests of the employing class—your enemies and your country's enemies. They will tempt money from you to deck you in uniforms of scarlet or grey, or green and gold, while they will ignore and cause you to forget the hundreds of your fellow-countrymen and country-women gliding through Dublin's streets naked and unashamed in sin, misery and want.

Workers, this movement is built on a re-actionary basis, that of Grattan's Tinsel Volunteers. Are you going to be satisfied with a crowd of chattering well-fed aristocrats and commercial bugs coming in and going out of College Green? Are you going to rope Ireland's poor outside the boundaries of the Nation? Do you know what Mitchel said of Grattan's precious

Parliament? This:—"This Parliament is a very fine thing to talk
or sing about; it has association of a theatrical sort, but no
Irish workman or Irish peasant will ever draw a trigger to
restore it."

They tell us, too, the Volunteers are for all classes. How
often have we heard that thrice-blessed statement before! Whenever we hear that we may know that the workers are welcome
so long as they are content to lie at the feet of others. It is stated
their manifesto is signed by a member of the Sinn Fein Executive, the U.I.L. Executive, and the A.O.H. Executive—a blessed
and impeachable political Trinity!

To you I would say, don't make d--- fools of yourselves!
Stand by no movement that does not avow the principles of
Tone and Mitchel and Lalor. Remember "equal citizenship" is
no use to us as long as we have to work day and night, year in
and year out, to avoid starvation for a pitiful wage in the workshop of another.

Use, or reserve for ultimate use, all your mental and physical energies towards the advancement of your own class.

The Irish Worker, January 24, 1914

Volunteers and Workers

> I wish to say I am more than ever convinced that the way I have
> been taking is the only true way to deal with the "Government," to
> right the wrongs of working men, and to achieve liberty for my
> country.
>
> MITCHEL in Newgate Gaol

James McGowan, standing proudly 'neath the fluttering
banners—I suppose they will have fluttering banners—of the
new Irish Volunteers, complains because the workers are beginning to dribble into public places, beginning to examine the

different banners of political parties; beginning to study the symbols thereon and ask their meaning; beginning to ponder these things in their hearts, if these things mean to them bread and life.

The cries and bitter interjections of hunger and disease and pain must always fall discordantly on ears closed to all sounds but honey'd words from Leaders dressed well and fed well by those who follow them in efforts that are bound to leave the workers' last state equally as bad as their first.

Does James McGowan mean to plead for a development of silent cowardice when the time has come to speak? Does he think that the stick which beats the workers now, will, in the hand of a Nationalist prophet, blossom and bear almonds like the rod of Aaron?

I am chided for using the name of Mitchel. I quote Mitchel because I am a Republican in principle and practice; because he denounced tyranny everywhere he found it, in the English Parliament, in the Irish convention; because he stood for the Irish worker against the English Lord and the Irish aristocrat, because tho' present day ranting extreme Nationalists conjure with his sacred name they ignore, I believe they deliberately ignore, the fact that he stood for, and fought for, the class they elect to despise and pass by.

James McGowan condemns the writer's criticisms because they may be calculated to upset the fraternal feelings of Volunteers recruited from various political societies, but he makes it clear he does not mean the "unity" so jealously guarded by the "Parliamentary humbugs."

Well, Mr. McGowan knows, I'm sure, there are humbugs that are not gilded with Parliamentarian glamour, and well he ought to know that the pretence of one is equal to the pretence of the other. He suggests there must be something wrong because I venture to criticise the Volunteers. There certainly is something wrong in the implied suggestion that we should receive all activities with acclamation, dumbfoundedly, that are heralded with the shrill bugle note of Nationality.

Is not this Unity, which seems like a king, to be hedged with an impenetrable divinity, another name for placid hypocrisy? How can there be any affinity of thought, any unity of action between a Republican and a member of the Board of Erin?

How can there be any semi-mutual understanding between a man starving, because he exercises a right that should "be common to all men," and an individual who denies him this right? Have not greater men than those who prance the National Stage of Ireland now, tried and failed to unite all Irishmen in a common bond? Davis tried and failed; so did Mitchel, and even O'Connell displayed at his meetings, on his breast ribbons of orange and green. The Gaelic League was to bring about this blessed consummation, and so was the Sinn Fein movement, and where all these failed we are asked to believe the Volunteer movement will succeed! There can be no unity amongst men save the unity engendered by a common heritage of pain, oppression and wage-slavery.

Picture the embrace of him who in the oath of allegiance bows lowly obeisance to an English king with the Separatist whose vision stretches to the grave of Wolfe Tone!

It has come to a nice pass when Nationalists declare that sweet is bitter and bitter is sweet. Well for you, Wolfe Tone, that you are in your shroud and safe!

James McGowan makes the point of declaring that national freedom surrounds social and intellectual emancipation. This statement would certainly be sublime if it were not ridiculous. He further alleges that had the workers always fought for their own interests they would never have recourse to the baptism of fire from the souls of such men as Tone, Mitchel, and Kickham.

For whom were they fighting in '98, '48, and '67? Will he answer us that? And were such men as Mitchel and Tone decorated with ribbons and stars and a' that? We toilers will welcome the help of all men who realise, as Mitchel realised, that "the life of one labourer is worth the life of one nobleman; no more nor no less."

This correspondent tells us that the Volunteers are "not modelled on the lines of the Volunteers of '82." Has he read the official organ of the society, which teems with detail regarding the formation, official government, apparel, and principles of the glorious soldiers of '82? Has he read the article contributed to the *Evening Herald* of blessed memory, by Arthur Griffith, holding up for the worship of Dublin's workers the kinemacoloured defenders of the privileged classes? Has he noticed the appeals in *Irish Freedom* to all Irishmen to follow in the steps of the men whom the aristocracy subsidised to repel the spread of Republicanism from France to Ireland? Maybe when he has read all these he will allow that there may be some justification for assuming that the inspiration of '82 is being used to make unfortunate men struggle to perpetuate the things they ought to destroy.

He says they are animated with a spirit identical with the spirit of '48 and '67. Does he think his readers are devoid of the rudiments of common sense? Fancy John McNeill or Laurence Kettle claiming kinship with the Fenians!

Picture the most Christian members of the Board of Erin tearing up the Pastorals that denounce Fenianism!

My critic reminds me "that Irishmen in general differ, not as to the end to be attained, but only in regard to the means to be used." Surely he ought to consider before he makes such a statement as this. Is it not clear that Irishmen differ very widely as to the end to be attained and the means to be used, and that on these points there can be no apparent or actual union?

There is a wide difference between Home Rule, a Republic, or a Co-operative Commonwealth. There was a wide difference even between the opinions of a Mitchel and those of Thomas Davis. There is an essential or unbridgable difference between Physical Force, Constitutionalism, Arrangement by Agreement and Devolution.

Personally, I hold the workers are beside themselves with foolishness to support any movement that does not stand to make the workers supreme, for these are the people, and without them there can be no life nor power.

The time is passing, and soon all workers shall realise that it is good to die for one's friend, but foolish to die for one's enemy.

This correspondent also ventures the statement that the presence of Tom Kelly, P. Macken, and P. H. Pearse in the Volunteers movement makes assurance doubly sure for the worker.

There seems to be a little of Browning's theory that "God's in his heaven and all's well with the world" in that statement. It provokes a smile to think of every wearer of the Red Hand being received into the Volunteer movement in the name of Pearse, Macken, and Kelly!

How is it that while Honest Tom Kelly held a high position on the Sinn Fein Executive the official organ slashed unmercifully at the workers in the throes of an industrial struggle?

Pearse is worse than all. When the workers of Dublin were waging a life and death struggle to preserve some of the "liberties" which ought to be common to all Irishmen, this leader of democratic opinion consistently used the trams on every possible occasion, though the controller of the Dublin tramway system was the man who declared the workers could submit or starve.

No sir; we have certainly made progress sufficient to be mentally independent on questions such as these, and beg leave to be allowed the common liberty we have been advised to practise, namely, to think for ourselves.

It is true that the British Government spilled the blood of the Dublin workers; it is equally true that the Irish mercantile Shylocks of Dublin created the conditions that gave the Government their sweet opportunity.

I have nothing to say regarding the observations made of myself. I challenge the officials of the Volunteers to tell us what they stand for. Is it for Home Rule? Is it for "the King, Lords, and Commons of Ireland"? Is it for a politically-free oligarchy? Is it for an Independent Irish Republic?

I challenge them to explain the meaning of "the liberties and rights common to all Irishmen." I challenge them to tell us if it be prudent to excitedly discuss the colours and distinctions of Volunteer uniforms, to beg for money to gratify their craving for pomp and show, while in Dublin alone twenty thousand families are wriggling together like worms in a putrid mass in horror-filled one-room tenements.

The preservation of one life is rather to be chosen than the decking of a thousand men in uniforms of green or scarlet and gold.

Not in the shouts of the deluded wage-slave Volunteers, but in the hunger-cry of the nation's poor is heard the voice of Ireland.

The Irish Worker, February 21, 1914

On February 28, McGowan answered with nearly three columns of fustian. Here is his peroration:

The evils of capitalism were unknown in free Gaelic Ireland, but they shall remain to blight our country and her people until the day when a revivified Ireland shall rise from the ashes of the past glorious, immortal and free, strong in the devotion of her daughters, invincible in the courage of her sons. That day shall only come when the

Irish race, armed to the teeth, gives the signal that shall hurl the
British Empire to eternal damnation unwept, unhonoured, and
unsung.

On March 7, O'Cathasaigh replied

Irish Workers and Irish Volunteers

Appearances to save his only care,
So things seem right no matter what they are.

At the risk of irritating *The Worker* readers, I venture to
send a last reply to James McGowan. My opponent justifies
his appeal upon the workers to fall into the Volunteer Movement by

Appealing to them to render allegiance to the principles of Tone, Emmet and Mitchel;

By the statement that it is "one of the most democratic
movements of our time";

By the belief that he holds that in the Volunteer movement is the power to evolve a Bond of Union for all
Irishmen;

By asserting the hope or belief that this movement will
hasten the day when "Ireland armed to the teeth, will hurl
the British Empire to eternal damnation!"

Because it is the only movement in our day that has
caused a "flutter in Dublin Castle!"

Yet neither from these beautiful flowers culled from Sligo,
and held like a nosegay to be smelled by the workers, nor from
any indication in official headquarters do we pluck a promise,
stated or implied, that this movement guarantees us any fuller
life, nor the bestowal upon us of that for which we are fighting
—the Moral and National Ownership of Ireland.

I venture to point out to James McGowan that the workers are, and cannot help being true to the pessimism of Tone and Mitchel.

As one of the leaders of the Volunteer Movements says in February's *Freedom*—"However the leaders may have failed, *the instinct of the people has always been unerring.*" At a meeting held in Navan recently, in answer to a question John MacNeill, one of the secretaries to the Volunteers, told us that the Volunteers would be under the supreme control of the Irish Parliament, which, according to Mr. J. Redmond, will be under the control of the English Imperial Parliament.

What do the Separatist and Republican members of the Volunteers think of that statement? Why, even the Chocolate Soldiers of '82 would not submit to such a bandaging, for they were independent of Grattan's property loving Parliament. James McGowan's time would be well spent in trying to insure that Tone and Mitchel were something more than useful games to the advanced Nationalists who are said to deny themselves so rigidly that they "have scarcely a second coat to put upon their backs!"

"The most democratic movement!" The same was said of the Gaelic League and Sinn Fein.

Will the officials of the Volunteers explain why, that while every National body, society and club, U.I.L., B.O.E.,[1] G.A.A., Sinn Fein received invitations to attend the initial meeting, held to start the movement, the Transport Union, that largest union of unskilled workers in Ireland, was ignored? That in a celebrated article entitled "The Coming Revolution," contributed to *An Claidheamh,*[2] before the founding of the Volunteers, P. H. Pearse expressed the wish to see every member of Sinn Fein, B.O.E., U.I.L., and the Transport Union armed; that subse-

[1] The Board of Erin, the descriptive subtitle of the Ancient Order of Hibernians.
[2] *The Sword.*

quently, dealing with the Volunteers in *Irish Freedom,* he mentions all these organisations but omits the Transport Union.

That while A. Griffith, dealing with the same movement in *The Irish American,* mentions the names of these organisations, but does not articulate the name of the Transport Union. Speaking some time ago to a prominent Volunteer, while criticising the principles of the new movement, he told me arrangements were being made to hold special drills for the leaders, who doubtlessly felt it would be injudicious to rub shoulders with the ordinary workers of Dublin.

Can the officials explain that, acting on a suggestion I made to Captain White, I myself wrote to a leading Volunteer with a view of possibly arranging for the use of the Dublin Halls at present engaged by the Volunteers, mutually by them and The Citizen Army, I received no reply to the communication sent?

Why is it that in the official organ reference was made in the speeches reported or articles contributed to every organisation in Irish National life, save and except the labour movement?

This canting cry of all creeds and all classes is worn to a ghastly shadow: it is the cry of all societies deaf to the appeals of the subject workers of the Nation: it is the long arm that chucks the aristocracy under the chin, who have always been in Ireland a selfish materialistic crew, exemplifying in their life that it is indeed a dangerous disease to eat too much cake. These people, whom the Gaelic League and Sinn Fein were, and whom the Volunteers now are afraid to shock, were the weakness and bane of every National movement. It was they who succeeded in preventing the Volunteers of '82 from opening their ranks to the then subject class, the Catholics of Ireland— and when new men with democratic ideals began to organise the enslaved Catholics, the patriotic Henry Grattan drew attention

I

to "the alarming drilling of the lowest classes of the populace. The old, the original Volunteers had become respectable, because they represented the property of the Nation; but attempts had been made to arm the poverty of the kingdom. They had originally been the armed property—were they now to become the armed beggary?" The modern Board of Erin and milk-hearted Republicans are apparently as anxious as Grattan was to maintain entire the respectability of the Volunteers and to prevent the inclusion of an armed beggary clamourous for the fuller exercise of human development and freedom.

I do not understand how Mr. McGowan's logical mind construed an appeal to the workers to have nothing to do with the Volunteers into a declaration that no physical effort should be made by them to fulfil the first law of nature—to act and fight for their self-preservation. If ever an Irish leader called upon the people to arm for themselves, that was Mitchel. Speaking of the movement which in his day "stirred thro'. Ireland from sea to sea," he says: "It is essentially not only a National movement, but *also*—why not admit it?—*a class movement.* Why should the gentry not join us? Why not lead us? Why? Surely because their interest is the other way—they know the end of British dominion here would be the end of them."

Arm indeed! Arm for what? Is it to preserve J. Redmond in the Cabinet Ministry of Ireland? Is it to "secure and maintain liberties and rights common to all Irishmen" which was denied and trampled upon by the very men who pose as leaders in the movement called together to secure and maintain them? Is it to preserve a system which compels thousands of our unfortunate fellow-slaves to rot in places declared by an unsympathetic Board to be unfit for human habitation? Let the Provisional Committee of the Volunteers give in their "Glorious Constitution," "The Rights of Man," an equal place with the "Rights of Ireland," and then the workers may have reason to disbelieve the statement that "National Liberty is not worth the shedding of a drop of blood."

Dealing with the question of the Union of all Irishmen, Mr. McGowan says, "that coming together we shall grow to know each other better." We already know some of the leaders too well, and beg to say that there can be no Union of Light and Darkness. My opponent says that my contention of the failure of Mitchel and Davis to unite all Ireland foreshadows a similar failure on the part of the Volunteers is not logical. Well, let him prove the affirmative.

Certainly, where men like Mitchel and Davis, progressive, turbulent, majestically minded nerves failed, it is hardly conceivable that reactionary, unprogressive baby-trained leaders will succeed. Mitchel declares the failure of Davis. When Davis joyfully hailed an article in the *Evening Mail* as an indictment of "the appearance in the sanctuary of the Orange Heart of the Angel of Nationality," Mitchel says—"He was too sanguine. In the sanctuary of the Orange Heart no angel dwells—of the better species." Mr. McGowan makes the point that the reasons of Mitchel's opponents' failure was that he was transported before his policy had time to wash the people. But in *Irish Freedom* for March, 1913, "Lucan," a well-known contributor, remarks that "Mitchel's gospel went thro' Ireland like lightning; the people loved it and forced their leaders to adopt it."

But my opponent perhaps is right. Mitchel failed not, but the other timid-soul'd leaders failed to grasp at the greatness of the class war Mitchel preached, and to-day the Volunteer leaders aim at a union with a class that has nothing in common with Ireland and ignore the masses that contain the will and the power to make Ireland, not a Nation in name, but a Nation in spirit and in truth.

I fear the Ezekielian vision of our friend of "the British Empire being hurled by the 'Irish Race' armed to the teeth to eternal damnation," conjures up, in my mind, that he is a frequent visitor to the picture theatres.

Mr. McGowan sings the praises of the Volunteers because "it is the only movement in our day that has caused a flutter in the dove-cotes of Dublin Castle."

Still trusting on the fame of the workers' sentimental imaginations, of which we begin to tire: we ask for bread and they give us a stone.

But dealing with the point: Who were they who caused the Castle Authorities to imagine they saw recently in the streets of Dublin the Birth of a Revolution? Who were they who were charged with sedition and conspiracy to disturb the Peace of His Majesty's subjects? Were they the leaders of the Volunteers? Dublin Castle again sleeps in peace; the Revolution was still-born. But then, it is still in the hearts of the people; as Newman says—"a whole wherever it is, unapproachable and incapable of being grasped, as being the result of causes far deeper than political or other visible agencies, the spiritual awakening of spiritual wants."

I challenge again the leaders of the Volunteers to explain their constitution; to tell us if Eoin MacNeill's statement be true; to declare if they stand for Home Rule, Grattan's Parliament, or an Irish Republic; to give in their constitution the Rights of Man an equal place with the Rights of Ireland, as the United Irishmen did; to tell us why they allow a paternal welcome to those who have attempted to prevent workers from preserving the elemental right to join the union of their choice.

Let them cease to rave about the principles of '98 and '67. Let them demonstrate unmistakably that they are not afraid to realise that Tone and Mitchel stood for something more than a politically free Ireland. That these men saw that the People were greater than the pride of power and the influence of Property. Let the leaders of the Volunteers have the courage to tell us which they prefer—The Aristocracy and the propertied Class, or the long-suffering but all-powerful People. Leaders of the Irish Volunteers! Why halt ye between two opinions; choose ye to-day whom ye shall serve!

The Irish Worker, March 7, 1914

On March 14, McGowan fired a parting shot aimed directly at his opponent rather than at the argument:

The whole tone of his letters is evidence of the spite which frustrated ambition engenders. In them is reflected the narrow-mindedness, the shallowness and the pessimism which are the chief characteristics of the cynic and the sceptic.

A Language Controversy

O'Casey's story, "Irish in the Schools," was but one instance of the frequent discussion about Gaelic in the pages of *The Irish Statesman*. As A.E. wrote on December 6, 1924, in answer to a letter by Mary Mac-Swiney, "The Editor . . . has allowed Joseph O'Neill and other advocates of the revival of Gaelic to argue their policy freely and at length, just as he has allowed Senator Yeats, Sean O'Casey and others to stress other aspects of the controversy."

On the same page as A.E.'s comment there was this reply to O'Casey's story:

> To the Editor of the *Irish Statesman*.
> A Chara,[1]—I take it that the contention Sean O'Casey seeks to prove by means of his crude and long-drawn sneer in last week's *Irish Statesman* is that a child who is starved in body should also be starved in mind.
>
> Mise,[2]
Liam O Rinn

To this letter, on January 10, 1925, O'Casey answered:

To the Editor of
THE IRISH STATESMAN
January 10, 1925

Dear Sir,—I have been often advised to read Mark Twain's *Innocents Abroad,* but good patriot as I am, I am satisfied with the intense amusement derived from the antics of our own dear innocents at home. They are sprinkled everywhere, in the political parties, in the Dail and the Senate, and some have re-

[1] Dear Sir.
[2] I remain.

116

cently been chirruping at the Conference of the Catholic Truth Society about the saintly lives of the poor in the tenements.

They have turned Ireland into a huge crystal ball in which they see visions, and over which they dream dreams.

And not the least of the innocents of Ireland is Miss Mac-Swiney, of Cork, and 'Iliam O Rinn, of Dublin of the Golden Goblets and the slums. 'Iliam asks me if it be my contention that because the body is starved that the mind should be starved as well. For the sake of the child—yes. How can a half-starved child be educated? The torture of semi-starvation is bad enough, but 'Iliam wants the mind in the half-starved body to be tortured as well. I have no hesitation in saying that I am against the torture of animals, even though it be done "for the glory of God and the honour of Ireland." Our half-starved children are a shame and a reproach to the State, and *is* and *'ta* are not even the shadow of equivalents for bread and butter. Man doth not live by bread alone, but, all the same, he lives by bread. If he thinks this view demonstrates a contempt for the education of the workers' children, he is very simple indeed; it is because of the importance of education (after life) that I stress the necessity of food.

But there are other reasons that induce me to oppose the teaching of Irish, compulsory or voluntary, to the children of the working-class. One is that the attachment to Irish on the part of the elders of the nation is a fancy fraud and a gigantic sham. They know it to be a sham, and, consequently, wish to give it the semblance of reality by forcing it down the throats of the defenceless children. This view is supported by an Irish-Ireland Moses and many of the prophets. In the issue of this week's *Fainne An Lae* we are told by "Cu Uladh"[3] that in the recent election in Tirchonaill the election literature of both parties was written exclusively in English; and that all the official

[3]Hound of Ulster.

work was wholly performed in English. He tells us that in the districts where English was known those that listened to the speakers became impatient when Irish was spoken for more than a few moments. He tells us that English is used in all the activities of the law, politics, commerce and trade; he says that the young everywhere are turning to the English. "Cu Uladh" complains that he heard that Irish isn't spoken by the clergy in two of the most Irish of the Tirchonaill parishes, and ejaculates that "this is an insufferable and a damned scandal!"

He plaintively tells of having met a man, twenty years younger than himself, who couldn't ask in English for even a half-glass of whiskey, and how he felt that he could have fallen on his neck and kissed him. Perhaps it's just as well he didn't, for the man might have decided that English was the safer if it wasn't the better tongue of the two.

Recently in a Dublin weekly there was a discussion on the force and quality of the dramas by Synge by two contributors, one of whom, I presume, wears the Fainne[4] (undoubtedly he is qualified), the other a native speaker. The discussion, up to the present, and I think it has almost concluded, has been written wholly in English, save for a quotation by one of the contributors from Geoffrey Keating. Now, why, if the desire for Irish be what it is said to be, should this discussion between two Irish speakers be carried on in English? The reason is obvious: one wished the readers of the paper to understand her attacks on Synge, and the other wished them to appreciate his defence of the dramatist, and the English language served admirably for both purposes.

Out of thirty-four advertisements in *Fainne An Lae*, three are in Irish, and the rest are in the much-abused but ever serviceable English.

Why, the very teaching of the Irish in the schools, in spite

[4]Emblem indicating proficiency in Irish.

of the fierce blasts on the Barr Buadh,[5] is, perhaps, the biggest
sham of all. The compulsory learning of Irish is as detestable to
the teachers as it is to the children; I'll venture to say that the
unhappiest days of a teacher's life (the most of them, anyhow)
are those on which they crowd together to read, mark, learn
and inwardly digest some of the textbooks that have added
copiously to the thorns that are so lavishly scattered in the way
of poor Kathleen Ni Houlihan. Of course, they all pretend to be
supremely happy, and at the end of the session present a peace-
offering to their Irish teacher in the shape of a bangle or a fountain pen. But their efforts, I fear, are like the efforts of Sisyphus,
the stone they roll up during the session slips away from them
during the rest of the year, and they have to grapple with the
stone again, till, I feel sure, some of them wish the Stone of Destiny had never come to Ireland.

And if the teachers find it difficult to learn the language,
how can the children find it easy? They don't learn it, and the
time spent trying is, in my opinion, a criminal waste. Only a
few months ago I had in my room a hardy specimen of a worker's son, red-headed and bare-footed. He had been attending
Phibsboro School for some years, and had been learning Irish
half an hour a day for twelve months. He is a particularly
bright and vivid boy, yet all he knew were a few sentences and
the numerals up to ten.

And there is one thing certain even if the rest be lies, and
that is that the parents of these children don't care a damn
about the Irish language, for they have something else to think
of. Let 'Iliam O Rinn on his way from Sackville Gardens to the
town call to the tenements in Summerhill, in Hutton's Lane, in
Gardiner Lane or Middle Gardiner Street, knocking at every
door and entering every room; let him speak to the people
there of the glories of Brian the Brave, and I can tell him he
finds, as far as these people are concerned, that the days of that

5Victory horn.

hero are o'er. And let him remember that these places form but a tiny portion of the multitude of the Dublin tenements.

Let us take the question of culture pure and simple: what is the teaching of the Irish in the schools going to do for culture; what can it do? In this manner culture can come to the children only through the teachers; and they, forlorn enough as they are in English, a language which they know, how can they excel in Irish, a language which they don't know?

Supposing, however, that the circumstances of our Dublin children were as comfortable and as reassuring as they ought to be, and that the teachers were able effectively to teach the things that belong unto their peace; are we blindly to believe that

A Thomaisin an cheoil, ciacu is fearr leat an bhean Chriona no
    an bhean og?
Is fearr liom an bhean chriona mar 'si thugan an bainne beirithe
    dhom,[6]

and the like, are any better than "Casabianca" or "Under a spreading chestnut tree the village smithy stands"?

Even if teachers and pupils were, after many years of study, able to read the ancient Irish classics, would they be able to understand and enjoy them, or would they know them in the fashion of those that have won honours in the Intermediate?

We have had twenty-five years of "The Gaedhilge, the Gaedhilge," and we have no modern writer of Irish—with the happy exception of Padruig O Conaire—worth reading. The best book of the day—*The Black Soul,* by 'Iliam O Flaherty—written by a Gaelic speaker, has been written in English.

Miss MacSwiney, with a vigorous push of her gentle hand, hurls all who are opposed to the compulsory teaching of Irish

[6]Thomas of the music, which would you prefer—the old woman or the young woman?
I prefer the old woman because she gives me hot milk.

into the shadowy Limbo of howling hypocrites. Oh, Miss Mac-Swiney, Miss MacSwiney, what about your own collection of noisy camp followers? Have we not often had to run like hell from the valiant green-plumed knights, galloping hither and thither, trying to prod our backs with their lances, and forced, when caught, to read the mystical pennant scroll of "A chara, agus is mise le meas mor."[7]

While we are waiting for that Irish Government that "will rigidly insist on the restoration of the Irish language to its proper place," will Miss MacSwiney insist on the restoration of the Irish language to its proper place among her own young Republican soldiers? She durst not; for her life she durst not.

And we have the G.A.A. vehemently resolving (a few years previously) that the Irish language would be the language of the 1917 Convention; when, as a matter of fact, the Convention of 1924 is as (or more) English than ever.

We learn that, out of seven thousand members of An Fainne, only five hundred forwarded their yearly subscription of one shilling, and that this is not an occasional but an invariable omission. Perhaps it would be well for Miss MacSwiney to know that "the fairy tale" of opposition to compulsory Irish by the Ard Fheis[8] of Sinn Fein has been exploited by some other than those whom she is pleased to call hypocrites.

In *Fainne An Lae* for December 27th, the editor, complaining of the weakening of the Gaelic League for the current year, stresses the sharp necessity for the continuance of the movement on account of what is happening every day under the Free State Government, *and of what recently happened at the Ard Fheis of Sinn Fein.*

Unable to force the big people, Miss MacSwiney and the rest of them are determined to make national Atlases of the little

[7] A gabble of rudimentary Gaelic, rather like a first-year Latin student repeating, "Amo, amas, amat."
[8] High Council.

ones, bearing up what she is pleased to call the nation on their frail little backs.

In conclusion, I wish to say that, while I believe my knowledge of the circumstances of the children of the Dublin workers to be greater than that of 'Iliam O Rinn, I am convinced that his sympathy with them and for them is no less than mine—I remember the collection he made for us in the Gaelic League during the lock-out of 1913—but he must try to forgive me when I laugh, for the rash humour my mother gave me makes me occasionally forgetful.—Yours faithfully,

SEAN O CASEY

The Irish Statesman, January 10, 1925

On January 24, 1925, O Rinn replied at length in Gaelic. The editor, A.E., commented, "We insert the letter in answer to a challenge, but it must not be taken as a precedent. Though we believe in a bi-lingual country, bi-lingual journals are irritating to those who subscribe to them." The last sentence, though alleging fidelity to the Gaelic, inadvertently underscored the futility of its widespread adoption.

On February 7, O'Casey returned to the fray.

To the Editor of
THE IRISH STATESMAN
February 7, 1925

DEAR SIR,—'Liam O Rinn by writing in Irish gives an additional proof of the fragile hold of the language in the actual life of the people, for his views probably remain unread by 95 per cent of the readers of the *Statesman,* just as the readers of a contemporary probably pass by the articles of Father Dinneen without even waiting to ask themselves what they may be all about.

I did not say, nor did I mean to say that the writers arguing around the works of Synge should have written in Irish. That is an ancient method of attack of which I have grown weary. I said it was strange that two Irish speakers wrote in English; asked why, and gave myself the reason, namely, that they wished their views to be understood by as many as possible, so writing in English, they demonstrated the enormous strength of the English with the weakness of the Irish language.

'Liam, abhorring the fact that great numbers of school-going children are improperly and insufficiently fed, argues that since they must attend school, the education received there should be good and strongly Irish. "Throw the Irish language," says he, "out of the schools, and the hungry children will be hungry still."

Agreed. But at least they will escape a torture and a strain their circumstances will not allow them to bear. You cannot give a good education, either English or Irish, to a barely-nourished child—let that be a law unto itself; it is unassailable. But, since they are forced, ill-fed as they are, to go to school, I hold that the efforts required of them, and the calls upon their impoverished energy should be as few and as bearable as possible, so as to leave them some of the resisting force necessary to withstand the physical dangers surrounding them. We see when any epidemic is rife how weak this resistance is, for the schools are usually the places most likely to be flooded with its havoc. We can again see its weakness in the Dublin Eye and Ear Hospital, in the various Union Dispensaries, and in the country Sanatoria. And this addition, if it weakens the resistance of the children to the diseases that are always flourishing around them, is an added burden to their parents, and what this burden is only a poverty-stricken woman with an ailing child can know. Then, with all respect to 'Liam O Rinn and his comrades, neither he nor they have any right whatsoever, to do anything calculated to add to the already almost intolerable hardships of their more unfortunate brothers and sisters.

That it is easier for the children to learn English than it is for them to learn Irish seems to be painfully obvious to me. They have a good knowledge of it before they begin to go to school. The fundamentals of geography are learned by the locality of the places connected with the street in which they live; of arithmetic by the counting used in their games, and the division of money when sent on messages for their parents, and, by the use of pencil and chalk, they learn the elements of writing. I would venture to say that a teacher who had gone through two or three sessions of intensified study of Irish, would have an infantile grip of the language, compared with the grip of English a child of ten would have on the day of its entering school for the first time in its life.

While the learning of the language may be difficult to older people, admits 'Liam, the learning of it by the children, he contends, is a comparatively easy task: "To my own children," he goes on, "I have spoken nothing but Irish since the day on which they first saw the light; and, though English is spoken to them by their mother and all those who speak to them during my absence, they readily understand everything I may say to them."

That is, I presume, the children of 'Liam speak Irish to the one and English to the many. If they speak English to their mother and to every, or almost every, other individual whom they know, then, I think, their ultimate current of thought will, in the nature of things, be a flow towards an English, an ebb away from an Irish influence.

Again, what comparison can there be between a family group of children to whom Irish only is spoken by the father and the tens of thousands of family groups to whom only English is spoken by father, mother, sister, brother, and all others with whom they live and have their being? Does 'Liam think that these children will, does he think they can, make use of whatever of the "teachers' Irish" they can remember in the homes in

which not a word of it is understood? One would think that
the appalling impossibility of the thing would shake the confidence, if it didn't undermine, the faith of the most fanatical
Gaelic Leaguer.

I can hear 'Liam crowing when he says that never did he
meet Gael, Gall or Jew who, having learned a little Irish did
not like it. Of course; we all like it; but this interesting fact
is what astronomers would call a "light year's distance" from
the difficulty of making the Irish language the living tongue
of the plain people.

'Liam cannot agree that the teachers are against the
language, and says that the few who have written to the
papers against the compulsory teaching of Irish are not representative of the rest. I think they are, and, what is more,
I think that the clamour of the few is not half so eloquent
as the silence of the many. Their jobs grip them by the throat,
and, to use a phrase of the common workers, "when the gaffer
laughs we all have to laugh." The first prostrate consent to its
imposition may have been due to the hidden thought that their
love for the glory of Ireland would deliver them from a reduction in their salaries. The teachers have yet to learn that the
Labour Movement is something more than affiliation with the
Trades Union Congress. It would be interesting to examine the
mind of the teachers through a secret ballot.

'Liam introduces a comrade who teaches a teacher's class
through the post; we are told that the class has a high knowledge
(Ard-eolas) of the language and of its literature, and love for
both. The high knowledge of and the love for the Gaelic is really
becoming as comic as

> Eileen alanna, Eileen asthore,
> Faithful I'll be to the colleen I adore—

but what else would the comrade say: did anyone ever hear of a correspondence school that wasn't at least an inch or two above perfection?

I am advised that if I speak to the residents of the tenements of the poetry of Yeats, of Milton, or of Shakespeare, I will find that there isn't, never has been, and never will be, a surrender to their beauty, power, and inspiration. Exactly; one can hardly look for the blossoming of roses in these sun-forgotten places. It isn't a question of English or Irish culture with the inanimate phantasies of the tenements, but a question of life for the few and of death for the many. Irish-speaking or English-speaking, they are what they are, convalescent homes of plague, pestilence, and famine.

I should be delighted to know that little lad that is such a devil for Irish that he "nearly ates his Irish book, and then rams it under the pilla goin' to bed, so as to be at it the first thing in the mornin'," and who, probably, in the meantime, dreams of Deirdre and the Children of Ua Uisnuigh.

'Liam is kind enough to think that I am not using the hungry children of the tenements as a buckler to hide an attack on the teaching of Irish, but this expression seems to suggest that others do. My sympathies were always with the rags and tatters that sheltered the tenement-living Temples of the Holy Ghost. Years ago I was at a gathering of these in a huge hall— probably once a stable—lying at the back of the Grenville Street tenements, organised by some friends from Trinity College. A number of Gaelic Leaguers were present to entertain the little ones. I see still the slim little shadows violently prancing through the Waves of Tory and the Walls of Limerick; I can hear a young lady telling the heap of atrophied life before her of the strength and glory of the Hound of Ulster; I laughingly listen still to a little, ragged elf trolling out a terribly smutty song, that shocked the Leaguers, causing one of them to shake over us all the incense of "Sing O hurrah, let England quake, we'll watch

till death for Erin's sake." I see Miss Nelli O Brien dancing a
jig on a kitchen table amid the dignified applause of the visitors
and the wild cries of the little savages of the slums. And Grenville Street is here to-day, a little older, but as ugly and as horrible
as ever.

I am worried that if I continue the criticism of the language
that I will separate the sympathies of the Leaguers from the
children of the tenements: Well, God's will be done! If they
harden their hearts to the misery of the places where the language
is dead, let them soften their hearts to the misery of the places
where the language is living.

I am urged to cease blathering, and to put forward a plan
that will make the tenements fall like the walls of Jericho;
'Liam says he is willing to blow a blast on one of the ram's
horns. I am sure he would, but the days of the ram's horns
are over. Each of us, from President Cosgrave to Mr. de Valera,
is woven into the fabric of responsibility for the continuance of
the slums. Conscious or unconscious of it, they have corrupted
each of our souls with a spot of their own leprosy. It is a National
problem that cannot be solved by a conjuring trick.

The question of the general revival of Irish must be left
to a future letter. It would be well if we tried to determine
whether the panel we seek is of such value that it is worth the
sale of all the others we possess.

I have gently but determinedly set aside 'Liam's invitation
to continue the discussion in Irish. It is strange that Irish should
be defended by the English language; but it is only natural, for
Irish as a defence to itself is only a toy sword. But it would be
ridiculous to defend the English in the Irish tongue, for we
would be looking at a huge giant, armed, not with a weapon
like a weaver's beam, but with a wisp of straw that would only
tickle when it strikes.

K

If 'Liam decides, like Roderick Dhu, to throw away his target, then he must take the consequences of additional wounds from a rapier held in a hand that thrusts indifferently at friend or foe.

Yours faithfully,
SEAN O CASEY
The Irish Statesman, February 7, 1925

Songs

"THE GRAND OUL' DAME BRITANNIA" was probably O'Casey's most popular song. The first printing of it that I can find was in James Connolly's *The Worker's Republic* for January 16, 1916, where the poem was signed with O'Casey's pseudonym "An Gall Fada." On the title page of O'Casey's *Songs of the Wren,* published in 1918, was "By Sean O'Cathasaigh, Author of 'The Grand Oul' Dame Britannia.'" And although Lady Gregory did not know the author, she printed a version of the poem in her *Kiltartan History Book* in 1926. O'Casey printed what may be considered the final version of the poem in *Windfalls* in 1934. The version printed here is the one from *The Worker's Republic* which differs from the *Windfalls* version in many minor ways, and which contains one more verse.

In the Preface to *Windfalls* O'Casey wrote this of the poem:

Many hot and weary days of activities in various National and Labour Organisations followed. This was the time before the symbol of Irish Republicanism had blossomed out into the now well-known flags of green and white and orange, but was represented by little tiny bows of these colours worn by the stewards in charge of the gatherings held in the Mansion House or in the Rotunda, to celebrate the memories and deeds of Wolfe Tone or of Robert Emmet. Finally came the crash of the guns in the Great War, and England's hurried and agitated recruiting campaign in Ireland calling on Irishmen of goodwill to go out and fight a fight for little Catholic Belgium. Then "The Grand Oul' Dame Britannia" was written, printed as a "nix job" by friendly printers, and circulated among the various National Societies.

The other songs are a selection from the two "Wren" pamphlets. O'Casey would put words to well-known airs, for he enjoyed singing the songs to his friends in the O'Toole Club. The satiric songs frequently comment upon World War I, for O'Casey regarded Britain's part in it and Britain's attempt to recruit in Ireland with a cold and satiric eye. The sentimental songs are not notably original, but neither are they cloying. I have heard O'Casey sing snatches of them, and as songs they are lovely. I have printed the melody with them so that no one will train the blockbusters of criticism upon them. As songs, they were not meant to withstand the ferocious scrutiny that contemporary criticism thinks necessary for poems. As songs, they can still give pleasure.

131

In another intellectual climate it might be unnecessary to defend the sentimentality of the songs or, for that matter, the sentimentality and its obverse, the melodrama, of O'Casey's mature plays. Many critics would prefer an O'Casey without the sentimentality and the melodrama. The tone of some of these songs and the tone of the Thomas Ashe pamphlet in the next section show that these qualities were always in O'Casey and suggest that they are integral.

The use of sentimentality and melodrama by a major artist does not suggest that he is without judgement; it suggests that he is committed to a portrayal of feeling more intense than that usually shown by such playwrights as Eliot or Graham Greene. Actually, sentimentality and melodrama do not exist apart from tragedy, but on a continuum with it. In many plays by the Greeks and the Elizabethans, it is impossible to make any nice distinction between the tragic and the melodramatic.

"The trouble," O'Casey said to me recently, "with writers today is they're wringing the emotion out of literature. Well, the emotion is in life, and you can't wring it out of that."

The Grand Oul' Dame Britannia

Air — "The Bonnie Bunch of Roses, O!"

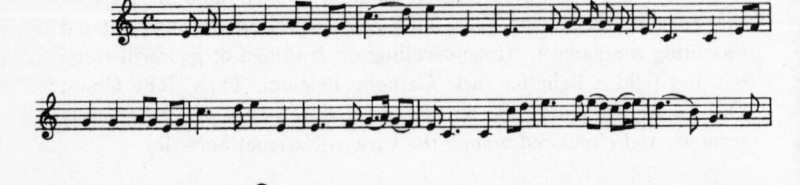

Och! Ireland, sure I'm proud of you—
    Ses the Grand Oul' Dame Britannia,
To poor little Belgium tried and true,
    Ses the Grand Oul' Dame Britannia.
Ye've closed your ear to the Sinn Fein lies,
For you know each Gael that for England dies
Will enjoy Home Rule in the clear blue skies,
    Ses the Grand Oul' Dame Britannia.

Ah! Casement! Damn that Irish Pig,
   Ses the Grand Oul' Dame Britannia,
We'll make him dance an English jig,
   Ses the Grand Oul' Dame Britannia.
But Redmond's here—the good and great—
A Pillar of the English State—
Who fears to speak of "Ninety-eight"—
   Ses the Grand Oul' Dame Britannia.

The Castle's now an altered place,
   Ses the Grand Oul' Dame Britannia,
It's the Drawin' Room of the Irish Race,
   Ses the Grand Oul' Dame Britannia.
John Redmond to the Throne is bowed
'Mid a frantic cheerin' Irish crowd—
Sure it's like the days of Shane the Proud,
   Ses the Grand Oul' Dame Britannia.

For Redmond now Home Rule has won,
   Ses the Grand Oul' Dame Britannia,
An' he's finish'd what Wolfe Tone begun,
   Ses the Grand Oul' Dame Britannia.
Yet rebels thro' the country stalk,
Shoutin' "67" and "Bachelor's Walk,"—
Did ye ever hear such foolish talk?
   Ses the Grand Oul' Dame Britannia.

Ye want a pound or two from me!
   Ses the Grand Oul' Dame Britannia,
For your oul' Hibernian Academy!
   Ses the Grand Oul' Dame Britannia.
Don't ye know we've got the Huns to quell,
And we want the cash for shot and shell;
Your Artists—Let them go to Hell!
   Ses the Grand Oul' Dame Britannia.

Ah! Scholars, Hurlers, Saints an' Bards!
   Ses the Grand Oul' Dame Britannia,
Come along an' list in the Irish Guards,
   Ses the Grand Oul' Dame Britannia.
Each man that treads on a German's feet
'Ill be given a parcel—tied up neat—
Of a Tombstone Cross an' a Windin' sheet,
   Ses the Grand Oul' Dame Britannia.

Be jabers! Redmond, you're the Bhoy!
   Ses the Grand Oul' Dame Britannia,
Shure you're Ireland's pride and England's joy,
   Ses the Grand Oul' Dame Britannia.
Like a true born Gael he faced the Hun,
Then he jumped around an' fired a gun—
Faix, you should have seen the Germans run!
   Ses the Grand Oul' Dame Britannia.

Sure I spoke to-day with Inspector Quinn,
   Ses the Grand Oul' Dame Britannia,
An' he told me straight we were bound to win!
   Ses the Grand Oul' Dame Britannia.
What mean these deafenin' newsboys' yells—
What tale is this the Paper tells—
A British retreat from the Dardanelles!
   Ses the Grand Oul' Dame Britannia.

The Worker's Republic, January 16, 1916

Songs of the Wren —
Humorous and Sentimental

Merrily, merrily, all the day,
   Merrily, over the stile, a
A merry heart goes all the way—
   A sad one tires in a mile, a.[1]

The Bonnie Bunch of Roses, O!

Dear England, now we'll take a walk,
   Says the Bonnie Bunch of Roses O.
An' we'll have a quiet little talk,
   Says the Bonnie Bunch of Roses O.
An' I'll show you places in the land
Where the stroke of your soft, gentle hand,
Ruled—for our good—you understand?
   Says the Bonnie Bunch of Roses O.

The Church that stands here in this place,
   Says the Bonnie Bunch of Roses O.
Looked down on Emmet's noble face,
   Says the Bonnie Bunch of Roses O.
Just here his sacred blood was shed—
I hear now what the hangman said:
"Behold the shameless traitor's head"—
   Says the Bonnie Bunch of Roses O.

[1]Probably a rendering from memory of the song at the end of Act IV,
scene iii in *The Winter's Tale*:

Jog on, jog on, the footpath way,
   And merrily hent the stile-a:
A merry heart goes all the day,
   Your sad tires in a mile-a.

135

Now, isn't this a lovely scene?
   Says the Bonnie Bunch of Roses O.
With its trees an' grass an' rath serene,
   Says the Bonnie Bunch of Roses O.
This place links up our country's past—
No wonder, now, you stand aghast—
For there's blood on the slopes of Mullaghmast,
   Says the Bonnie Bunch of Roses O.

The Jail of Newgate once stood here,
   Says the Bonnie Bunch of Roses O.
Why do you shake like that with fear?
   Says the Bonnie Bunch of Roses O.
Before me visions sadly float;
'Twas here poor Eire's heart you smote,
When you cut poor helpless Wolfe Tone's throat,
   Says the Bonnie Bunch of Roses O.

We're walkin' now, along the Quays,
   Says the Bonnie Bunch of Roses O.
I hope, dear friend, my words will please—
   Says the Bonnie Bunch of Roses O.
When Mitchel answered Ireland's call
He passed in chains down this North Wall—
We've forgot all this? Oh, not at all—
   Says the Bonnie Bunch of Roses O.

This place we're in is Limerick Town,
   Says the Bonnie Bunch of Roses O.
Ah, England, dear, why do you frown?
   Says the Bonnie Bunch of Roses O.
For here your word was overthrown,
When Sarsfield left the land alone—
Ah, a teacher great is the Treaty Stone!
   Says the Bonnie Bunch of Roses O.

Strong Labour here his vigil keeps,
  Says the Bonnie Bunch of Roses O.
O'er the place where Connolly calmly sleeps,
  Says the Bonnie Bunch of Roses O.
His teachings true in Ireland soon
Shall flourish like the flowers in June—
I'm afraid they'll hasten on your ruin—
  Says the Bonnie Bunch of Roses O.

Conscript the Gael is now your cry,
  Says the Bonnie Bunch of Roses O.
Ah! listen to our calm reply,
  Says the Bonnie Bunch of Roses O.
Tho' the country be with soldiers crammed,
Tho' every street with guns be jammed—
Conscription, ay! an' you be damned!
  Says the Bonnie Bunch of Roses O.

If the Germans Came to Ireland
in the Mornin'

Air — "I'm Off to Philadelphia in the Mornin'"

There are men in this 'ere Nation without any education—
  An asylum ward they ought to be adornin'—
For they tell us—Holy Moses—life ud be a bed o' roses
  If the Germans came to Ireland in the mornin'!

To capture, sure, they're eager, each United Irish Leaguer,
   In Home Rule Sauce to give them all a cornin';
An' the men that serve king Billy, they'd be fed on Popish skilly,
   If the Germans came to Ireland in the mornin'!

Now, the noble men that lade yez, they'd imprison in bird cages,
   An' make them whistle God Save Ireland, out o' scornin'—
Oh! the Germans are such damn rogues, they'd destroy our
        harps an' shamrogues,
   If they came and landed here now in the mornin'!

In our noble secret service the peelers now are nervous,
   For they'd kill these gentle creatures without warnin'—
Every peeler on his beat, sir, they'd cut off his little feet, sir,
   An' make submarines of his boots, then, in the mornin'!

Sure as God made little apples, they'd demolish all our chapels,
   An' our grand homes in the slums that we were born in—
With their big guns firin' shrapnel, well—God help poor
        Charlie Chaplin—
   If the Germans came to Ireland in the mornin'!

Now take heed to what I'm sayin', they'd destroy potato
        sprayin' —
   Sure with indignation sore my heart is burnin'—
An' what would happen, pray, sir, to the Sinn Fein rainbow-
        chaser—
   If the Germans came to Ireland in the mornin'!

Mary Is Faithful to Me

Air —"Has Sorrow Thy Young Days Shaded?" [2]

Tho' Fate fills with lavish profusion
    My Chalice of Life with woe,
And shatters the shining illusion,
    That youth is all pleasure and glow;
Yet Life's lonely womb's bred a blessing,
    And fate has dealt kindly with me—
For the sweet truth my soul is caressing
    That Mary is faithful to me.

Tho' the future's broad sky that is o'er me
    Is dark, with a darkness drear;
And in Life's winding pathway before me
    No symbol of Hope is near;
Yet bright as the sun's beaming splendour
    Soft as gentle star-shine on the sea—
Is the gleam of thy love, true and tender,
    That lightens Life's roadway for me.

I know, dearest love, that thou carest
    For me in my woe and pain,
And for this fearless love, that's the rarest,
    I'd bear all my sorrows again.

[2]The actual name of the air to which Thomas Moore's poem "Has Sorrow Thy Young Days Shaded?" was set is "Sly Patrick."

Let troubles and cares come thronging,
For now they are nothing to me—
Losing all that's to Pleasure belonging,
I find a joy deeper in thee!

The Demi-Semi Home Rule Bill

Air — "The Wearin' o' the Green"

The struggle now is over, oul' Ireland, sure, is free,
An' if you don't believe it—well, just you wait an' see!
For the fruits of th' Irish Party—the Sinn Feiners say they're
nil—
Is a demi-semi, semi-demi, demi-i-i-i-i-i-i-i-i-Home Rule Bill!

With knives an' forks stuck in them the pigs will run about,
And when they see a green flag "who'll eat me" they will shout;
An' each fish'll come to the land and use his tail as a writin' pen,
An' they'll write on all the rocks an' trees "A Nation Once
Again"!

The peelers then will meet us with forces mild and bland—
Instead of batons each'll wave green shamrocks in his hand;

'Twill be a thing of joy to meet them as they march along the
    street,
For they'll all look like fairies—if it wasn't for their feet!

To make us saints an' sages will only take a week,
An' we'll all be speakin' Latin, Esperanto, ay, an' Greek;
Every hungry man an' woman will then eat an' drink their fill,
When in the Statute Book they'll send along the demi-semi
    Home Rule Bill!

Oh! the Force of Evolution may be workin' in the land;
An' Dunraven's Devolution, yet, may get the upper hand;
Or a Sinn Fein Revolution may be brewin' here—but still,
We'll know no peace in Ireland till we get the Home Rule Bill!

[The last of the first verse may be sung as a chorus.]

As I Wait in the Boreen[3] for Maggie

Air — *"Cnochainin Aerach Chille Mhuire"*[4]

— Songs of the Gae

[3]A lane.
[4]The Airy Wee Hill of Kilmurray.

A bright Autumn evening now darkens its hue,
    And the wild flowers are wearily sleeping.
With her rich fragrant moisture, the life-giving dew,
    The green mantle of Nature is steeping;
So enters love into souls—silent and still—
    Giving hope to each heart and new force to each will,
And here in the twilight I feel its dear thrill,
    As I wait in the boreen for Maggie.

The noble and rich may be happy and proud,
    With their parks and fair places of splendour,
But the poor little spot with fond memories crowd,
    Of dear meetings and happiness tender;
The leaves whisper a name as they bend to and fro,
    The birds lilt of love as home flying they go,
And I hear a soft voice in the brook's gentle flow,
    As I wait in the boreen for Maggie.

In the arms of the strong hedge the winsome wild rose
    Is quite calmly and safely reposing;
While her fair, fragile face with love tenderly glows,
    In a manner both coy and imposing;
When rough winds of trouble strive hard to molest,
    So I'll gather my girl to my sheltering breast,
And I'll tell all that love on my heart has impressed,
    When I meet in the boreen with Maggie.

And I told her if me she would venture to wed,
    That I honour and cherish her highly;
Tho' keen, ah! but few were my moments of dread,
    For she answered, yes, softly and shyly;
Should Fortune abandon and leave me alone,
    And woe destroy seeds of hope, joyfully sown,
I'll dare bravely the future, tho' dark and unknown,
    As I go thro' life's boreen with Maggie.

We Welcome the Aid of Japan

Air — *"Twenty-Four Strings to my Bow"*

"Japan is the last hope of the Allies."—*The Daily Mail*

At first, for the sake of small nations,
    We ran an' we took down our gun,
For our heart was in wild palpitations
    When we thought on the strength of the Hun.
For Religion and Truth, sure, we fought, too,
    An' the Rights an' the Freedom of Man—
To a frazzle we're bet—but we'll carry on yet
        With the help and the aid of Japan!

Chorus:

With the help and the aid of Japan,
    We'll accomplish the freedom of man:
An' we'll still rule the waves, while the workers are slaves,
    With the help and the aid of Japan!

Poor Belgium, like a little goose, sir,
    Answered quickly fair Honour's loud call,

L

But Germany's strength was let loose, sir,
 And, faith, she soon ended them all;
And now our poor Belgium is numbered
 With horses that then also ran—
Sure, that's just as well—let her now go to hell,
  For we've captured the aid of Japan!

     Chorus:

On Russia for years we depended,
 But their tidy and trim apple-car
The merciless Huns soon upended,
 And, now, we've no use for the Czar!
And the Bolshevicks fierce had destroyed, too,
 Our nicely developing plan—
But now we don't care for the great Russian bear,
  For we've collared the aid of Japan!

     Chorus:

Roumania, all caution and cunning,
 Came out on the side of the Right,
But, faith, sure, I hear they are running—
 They never had stomachs for fight.
And these gilded chocolate soldiers
 Finished up well before they began;
But we've got to, now, keep our hands to the plough,
  So we welcome the aid of Japan!

     Chorus:

Now, Ireland is blighted with Sinn Fein—
 Tho' we thought that she'd give us her aid—
For they're all thinkin' now of their own gain
 By diggin' up plots with a spade.

But if ever we get a good chance, boys,
  Her obstinate hide we will tan,
For she didn't act fair—Ah! but still we'll get there,
  With the much welcome aid of Japan!

Chorus:

Tho' Providence helped us before, boys,
  In the great days of Nelson and Drake,
I'm afraid that she'll help us no more, boys,
  For she thinks that we're out on the make!
But now we can well do without her,
  And we laugh at her pitiful ban—
For we don't care a damn, now, for Bible or psalm,
  For we've captured the aid of Japan!

Chorus:

The Japanee may be a haythen—
  A bloody and villainous tyke—
But when we're at war we're not playin',
  And that's just the thing that we like!
For Civilisation needs, now, boys,
  The help, sure, of every man,
And the Savage, we find, is a help to Mankind—
  So we welcome the aid of Japan!

Chorus:

The Girl From the County Kildare

Air — "*Twenty-Four Strings to my Bow*"

Whenever the plough I am driving
  Into Mother Earth's passionate breast,
My own heart I'm thinking I'm riving
  With sharp thoughts that give me no rest;

For, faith, I am sorely entangled
  In Love's wide, unbreakable snare—
And I'd rather be dead if I am not to wed
  The sweet girl from the County Kildare!

Chorus:

  The girl from the County Kildare—
    In my heart Love has lighted a flare,
Oh, I am the lad would be joyful and glad
    With the girl from the County Kildare.

Dear maid, when the valleys are blazing
  With wild flowers of many a hue,
They seem to be pensively praising
  The much sweeter beauty of you.
For the fairest of all the fair flowerets
  That are splendidly blossoming there,
Would not dare say to me, I'm fairer than she—
  The sweet girl from the County Kildare.

Chorus:

  The girl from the County Kildare,
    Sure, the wild flowers in chorus declare
That the gems of the field in their beauty must yield
    To the girl from the County Kildare.

When the sun in his rapture's arraying
  The morn in a ravishing dress,
To my mind every beam is displaying
  The glow of each radiant tress;
The rich flame of the sun cannot equal
  The gleam of her shimmering hair—
When she stands near the stile the sun seems to smile
  On the girl from the County Kildare.

Chorus:

> The girl from the County Kildare—
> The sun whispers now everywhere,
> There's no stars in the skies like the bright flashing eyes
> Of the girl from the County Kildare.

Bright joy in my bosom is dancing,
    And Hope builds a nest in my soul,
For my heart in its task is advancing
    To rob hers, now, for mine that she stole!
And soon I'll have courage to ask her,
    If the rest of her life she can spare,
To give a poor boy a long life-time of joy,
    With the girl from the County Kildare.

Chorus:

> The girl from the County Kildare—
> Sure Life will not muster a care,
> When at home by the fire sits my heart's one desire,
> The sweet girl from the County Kildare.

We've Captured the Cave of Machpelah

Air—"The Ould Orange Flute"[5]

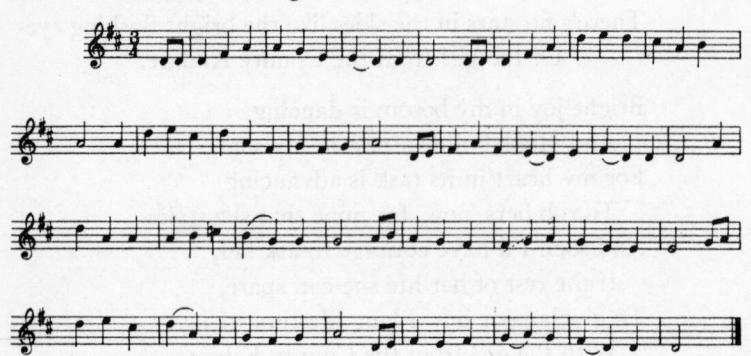

"The British arms have scored a great victory by the capture of Hebron, which contains the Cave of Machpelah, the tomb of Abraham."

—*The Daily Mail*

In the fight for Poor Freedom against the Huns,
    We've lost thousands and thousands and thousands of guns;
But still in the struggle we're givin' them tons.
        An' we've captur'd the Cave of Machpelah!

Chorus:

Hurrah! for John Bull and for Uncle Sam—
    We're losin' the war, but we don't care a damn,
For we've taken the tomb of poor Abraham,
        An' we've captur'd the Cave of Machpelah!

To triumph they'll carry the Union Jack—
    Our warriors bold, brown, red and black

[5]The air to which O'Casey originally intended these verses to be sung was "Under the Willow Tree." When I was unable to locate this air, I asked O'Casey if I might substitute "The Ould Orange Flute." He replied, " 'The Ould Orange Flute' is as good as any and better than a lot; by all means adopt it." I have made a few slight changes in the tune to make it fit O'Casey's words.

The Germans hit us, but we're hittin' them back—
   An' we've captur'd the Cave of Machpelah!

Chorus:

With Joy an' with Pride, now, our bosoms thrill!
   Tho' we're losin' each dale an' we're losin' each hill,
But we're givin' the bloodthirsty Germans their fill,
   For we've captur'd the Cave of Machpelah!

Chorus:

Wirrastrue, Wirrastrue, we have lost Trieste,
   An' the Germans are reignin' in Bucharest—
But these losses are now but a mighty jest,
   Since we've captur'd the Cave of Machpelah!

Chorus:

We're proud, aye, we're proud of our British pluck,
   That fought against Hope an' the hardest of luck,
We've won all we want an' we've settled Von Kluck,
   For we've captur'd the Cave of Machpelah!

Chorus:

Mackensen may brag and the Kaiser may blow
   About Russia's and Italy's overthrow,
But they'll soon change their tune when they get to know,
   We've captur'd the Cave of Machpelah!

Chorus:

Since Maggie Went Away

Air—"The Auld House"

No more I'll stroll, no more I'll stroll along the boreen,
Or see the scarlet poppies flame amid the corn green;
No more beneath the hedge I'll watch the butterflies at play—
For my heart is fill'd with woe, with woe, since Maggie went
    away!

The sweet wild-rose, the sweet wild-rose, that lov'd to see us
    there,
And seem'd to bid us hope, now droops and tells me to despair;
The linnet sings his song unheard, perched on a leafy spray—
Ah! my heart is fill'd with woe, with woe, since Maggie went
    away!

The gentle flowers, the gentle flowers, their happy charm is fled,
And now they seem like blossoms strewn above the silent dead;
They're symbols now of sorrow deep and life's swift sure decay—
Ah! my heart is fill'd with woe, with woe, since Maggie went
    away!

The heartless Sun, the heartless Sun, with splendour gilds the
    skies,
And mocks with smiling beams a heart that now can only sigh;
Shine on bright Sun, shine on, while I could curse thy proud
    display—
Ah! my heart is fill'd with woe, with woe, since Maggie went
    away!

Then welcome grief, then welcome grief, man's warm true-
      hearted friend,
For tho' all things be false, thou still art faithful to the end;
And now I'll walk alone with thee, till life turns into clay—
For my heart is fill'd with woe, with woe, since Maggie went
      away!

The Divil's Recruitin' Campaign

Air—"*Sergeant Willy Baily*"[6]

I suppose you've often heard, now, of the place that lies below—
      Too all tooral, ooral, ooral, ooo!
A public meeting there was held not very long ago,
      Too all tooral, ooral, ooral, ooo!
'Twas the Divil that presided, and soon it was decided
  That the only way to see the matter through,
An' to keep the British Nation at its present elevation,
  Was to hasten on Conscription, tooral ooo!

Ses the Divil, "Things in Ireland, now, they will not do at all—"
  An' he spoke in tones of thunder, tooral ooo!
"All the men that's left in Ireland, now, will have to hear the call
  To get out and to get under, tooral ooo!"

[6]The air to which "Sergeant Willy Baily" is set is an older one called
"Smith of Bristol."

Ses his Secretary, "Look, sir, Home Rule's on the Statute Book,
     sir;
And we've only just another thing to do:
The Duke of Connaught swear in as the great High King of
     Eireann,
     And we'll get recruits in thousands, tooral ooo!"

Ses the Divil, "In our Empire things have reached a pretty pass,
     Tooral, ooral, ooral, ooral ooo!
With their air raids, submarines an' all their latest poisoned gas,
     Tooral, ooral, ooral, ooral ooo!
But I wouldn't still be carin' if it wasn't now for Erin,
     And the doings of the silly Sinn Fein crew;
I'm beginnin' to feel queer, oh! with this cursed De Valera—
     Tooral, ooral, ooral, ooral, ooo!"

An' the Divil sent his agents out to gather in recruits,
     Tooral, ooral, ooral, ooral ooo!
To preserve the Saints in England an' destroy the German Brutes,
     Tooral, ooral, ooral, ooral ooo!
"You'll get a welcome hearty from the gallant Irish party—
     Tell them to spread an' preach what isn't true—
'Twas written by St. Kevin that no Gael could enter Heaven,
           Unless he dyed the green, red, white and blue."

After years an' years of work his agents all came back,
     Tooral, ooral, ooral, ooral ooo!
They carried an old man nicely tied up in a sack,
     Tooral, ooral, ooral, ooral ooo!
"We could only get just one, sir, to put the Khaki on, sir—
     Tho' we search'd an' search'd the country through an' through;
He'll join the British Awmy, but the doctors say he's bawmy—
           Tooral, ooral, ooral, ooral, ooo!"

A Lament

In 1918 O'Casey published *The Sacrifice of Thomas Ashe,* a lament for his friend, the Irish patriot who had died in Mountjoy Prison. But long before 1918 O'Casey had come to see the struggle for Irish Nationalism as but a skirmish in a much broader, international struggle for liberty. For, as he wrote years later in *Inishfallen, Fare Thee Well:*

Two fierce fights were going on for liberty: one on the little green dot in the world's waters, called Ireland; and the other over a wide brown, grey, blue, and scarlet expanse of land, later to overflow into the many-coloured, gigantic bloom of the Soviet Union. The first for a liberty of the soul that was to leave the body and mind still in prison; the other for the liberty of the body that was to send the soul and mind as well out into the seething waters of a troubled world on a new and noble adventure. Dublin was astir, for many were busy in its secret places hammering out in thought the iron nature of an ironic people into a shape of an Irish Republic. Young men, in slum and shady avenue, were concerning themselves with the idea of giving up any comfort they had, and risking their lives, that they might be numbered among them who would be remembered, if not forever, for awhile anyhow. Some had died already, and Thomas Ashe was dead now. Killed through the rigours of forcible feeding. In Mountjoy Jail, one of Eire's golden boys was changing into dust.

Sean had written two laments for Thomas Ashe, for he had been an old friend of his when both had been pipers; and now, with a Fergus O'Connor, who had published the two laments, he was on his way to the prison to get news as to when the body of the dead man would be allowed out for burial. This most handsome man, Ashe, six foot tall, straight as a standard, with a leonine head, bannered by a mass of hair that was almost golden, this most handsome man was dead. Turning into the long avenue leading to the prison, with a few birds still twittering on the languid trees, the entrance gate looked like a toy fort in the distance, with a few tiny black figures before it, waiting permission to go in to a toy dead brother, a toy dead son. But the gate grew rapidly larger as they came closer, and beside it, then, the thing towered high over them all, fitting and frowning the figures now into the look of sad humanity, waiting to go forward and endure the last act of reluctant charity of burying their beloved dead.

In silence, there they stood, Sean in his old clothes his broken cap pulled sullenly down over his eyes; O'Connor in well-cut Irish

155

tweeds and costly cap; and the relatives in solemn black, stood before the heavy, dull-brown gateway, with its subsidiary wicket to one side for admission of privileged persons on business bent; silently praying, the lips of the black figures moved slightly in an unheard murmur, of *Eternal rest grant to him, O Lord, and let perpetual light shine upon his brave soul;* acting as a chorus to O'Connor chanting in a low whisper Sean's lament for the dead man, the pity in it forcing the tears to trickle down his cheeks before the high and heavy oaken gateway, braced with many a thick and unbreakable iron clamp.

The "two laments" are *The Story of Thomas Ashe* and the later *The Sacrifice of Thomas Ashe,* which is printed here. The second pamphlet is a revised and slightly expanded version which does not greatly differ from the first.

It is foolish to apply the standards of cold evaluation to writing so strongly hammered out in the forge of emotion. By fashionable literary standards, *The Sacrifice of Thomas Ashe* appears awkward and melodramatically overwritten. Yet *Thomas Ashe* is one of those documents which arise with disconcerting frequency to bowl over academic niceties and distinctions.

It would be easy to dismiss the pamphlet as a crude work of genius. But it would not be so easy to explain why, despite all the strictures one might make of it, the pamphlet is yet moving.

The key, of course, lies in the style. O'Casey was saturated with the eloquence of the Elizabethan dramatists, and the tone of the pamphlet is that of the impassioned soliloquy. The speaker addresses Ashe directly; in his foreboding comments he sets the stage; he is almost a chorus without a play: in sum, the pamphlet has the vital directness of dramatic speech.

O'Casey was saturated with the English poets, particularly with the nineteenth-century Romantics, and his style ever strains to leap up from the pedestrian matter-of-factness of prose to the freedom of full-throated lyricism.

O'Casey was saturated with the English nineteenth-century prose writers, with Ruskin and Carlyle, whose rolling periods are the antithesis of modern prose. Let us, then, call his style melodramatic. Melodrama is not greatly to the modern taste. But we must remember that taste fluctuates from age to age; intrinsic value does not.

I make no extravagant claims for the style of *Thomas Ashe.* Compared to O'Casey's mature style in the autobiographies, it is indeed naive.

But we must not mistakenly compare it to the style of Orwell or Hemingway.

At its best, even this early style has its moments:

Oppression of the Bloody Hands, you cannot put a rope around the neck of an idea; you cannot put an Idea up against a barrack-square wall and riddle it with bullets; you cannot confine it in the strongest prison cell that your slaves could ever build.

We cannot wish for much more than irreducible eloquence.

The Sacrifice of Thomas Ashe

Tom Ashe is a man.

JIM LARKIN

His life was gentle, and the elements
So mix'd in him that Nature might stand up
And say to all the world "This was a man!"

SHAKESPEARE

What danger singly if I stand the ground,
My friends all scattered, all the foes around?
Yet wherefore doubtful? let this truth suffice:
The brave meets danger and the coward flies;
To die, or conquer proves a hero's heart;
And knowing this, I know a soldier's part.

POPE

Lament for Thomas Ashe

The breasts of the mountains with anger are heaving,
   Swift rivers of tears down their rugged cheeks flow;
Their mantle of heather the wild wind is reaving,
   And their proud heads are capp'd with a storm cloud of woe,
Why gathers the gloom in a manner appalling—
   What causes the sunshine in terror to flee?
The mountains of Erin are plaintively calling—
   Thomas Ashe, Thomas Ashe, we are mourning for thee!

The wild mountain glens are now silent and lonely,
   And Grief on their bosom has laid her poor head,
Here thoughts of new life have no place, for now only
   The green woods are wrapped in dear thoughts of the dead!

The leaves from the trees, sadly sighing, are falling
  And form a bronze pall for the once flower'd lea,
The winds rustling thro' them, are plaintively calling—
  Thomas Ashe, Thomas Ashe, we are mourning for thee!

In the ears of the coast Erin's grey waves are beating
  A curse on the Power that his life would not spare,
And mingle a prayer in their gloomy retreating,
  With a caoine[1] for the soul that had courage to dare!
The grey restless waves are all rising and falling—
  Oh! a sorrowful breast is the breast of the sea—
And her waters, uneasy, are plaintively calling—
  Thomas Ashe, Thomas Ashe, we are mourning for thee.

Shall we then to Nature's sad, heart-broken grieving
  Our own Gaelic Nature in apathy close?
Ah! No! To our hearts this dear sorrow receiving
  We'll send in a shout to our circle of foes!
Your thoughts, Thomas Ashe, now, shall shortly be ours—
  As you fought the good fight so we'll fight to be free.
'Gainst all the vain pomp of their princes and powers,
  Made strong by the thought of dear vengeance for thee.

Foreword

Lispole, Dingle, County Kerry, was the cradle of Thomas Ashe. Here, with the purple, blue and golden-tinted shadows of the mountains colouring his thoughts, the sound of the Kerry sea sounding in his ears, breathing the heather and gorse scented airs of his country, Thomas Ashe spent his days of youth, which were the days of joy, and his soul was gradually steeped in the rich and fragrant, and now all too rare incense of an Irish life.

The Irish Language opened to him the inner, secret and enchanted recesses of the Irish nature, and he understood Ire-

[1] A keen, dirge, or lament.

M

land as none but an Irish speaker can understand Her. With the passing of boyhood's years his broad heart became broader as it opened to receive the desire of freedom for his native land —desire that was nourished by the lessons taught by the sweep of the Kerry skies, the boldness of the Kerry mountains, and the untrammelled surge of the sea on the Kerry coast. And nature went on, adding strength to the body, culture to the mind and grace to the soul, so that in years to follow the whole man became a rich and ripe sacrifice for the Cause of Human Freedom and for the Cause of Ireland.

At last his march towards the goal of an Irish Republic brought him to Ashbourne, where, on the Thursday of Easter Week, he and his little band of Republican friends gave an unmistakable answer for the Hope that was in them. The victory of Ashbourne seems to have created the necessity in the mind of the British Government of placing on the brow of this dangerous man, the brand of a political Cain. And of a military tribunal, armed with the Heavenly Authorities of Khaki Suits, Sam Browne Belts, and divers Ribands and Stars, sentenced this young Republican to death, which other Authorities of costlier Ribands and Stars, commuted to penal servitude for life.

Released, under the general Amnesty of June, 1917, we find Thomas Ashe again in his natural element of Hope, Endeavour and Activity. Full of thoughts for the future of his country, he laboured on sowing the seed of Human Liberty in the hearts of the people, conscious that the seed was at last beginning to fall on good soil; half-conscious that a merciless enemy dogged his steps; waiting an opportunity to dash the seed from the hand of the sower, or to remove him from the field of his labour; and this brings us now to the first of the few last chapters that formed the last tragic days in the life of this purehearted worker for Ireland.

Chapter I

The Arrest

Unfortunate young man, which way now guides thee—
Guides thee from death? The country's laid around for thee.

An Autumn Evening—O'Connell Street—A Few Friends—
Death's Parchment Order—By the Grace of God—To Prison—
The Curragh—Mountjoy

The sun with ardent autumn affection poured his rich rays over the City of Dublin on the Saturday, the 18th of August. O'Connell Street shared his kindly attention, and the gaunt and ruinous remains of her principal buildings shone and glistened with a glow which reminded one of the way in which they had been dappled with light of a very different kind some few months ago, when men fought and fell with the glow of burning buildings on their faces, and the glow of enthusiasm lighting their hearts in the effort to establish an Irish Republic.

Two men strolled along the broad thoroughfare, passing alternately into the sunshine and the shadow—so typical of human life—their thoughts possibly re-creating the stirring scenes that had been enacted here, and shaping, in the visions of their ideals, the new and greater Ireland that would inevitably arise out of the creative energies and perseverance of the Irish people. The shops held their wide mouths open catching customers, taking all they could from them; the air was full of the concentrated activities of thousands bent upon their own particular work of maintaining and developing their grip upon life, paying no attention to the young men that passed them by; unaware that, in a few short weeks, a last and tragic episode in the life of one of them would stir the pulse and move the heart of the Irish People from one end of Ireland to the other.

On they walked, till, reaching the few tall hoardings that showed where once the firm of Clery's carried on a thriving trade, they were met by two comfortable looking men who paused in front of them, looked keenly in their faces, and approaching to their side, tapped the taller on the shoulder and said: "Thomas Ashe, the R.I.C.[2] want you." "When," asked Ashe. "Now," said the detective. "Do you mean I'm arrested," said Ashe. "Yes," replied the detective—and which of the Irish People realised then that the little parchment scrap of paper authorising the arrest of Thomas Ashe, with all the pompous power of a "Defender of the Faith," accompanied with the "Grace of God," would, by its malignant power, hand over the young Republican's life, not only to a temporary deprivation of activity between the walls of a prison cell, but would consign his life to the long and unbreakable durance of the grave? And this ominous power hurries Thomas Ashe to the Bridewell, whence, after a stay of a few days, he is taken in a motor car to the Curragh, brought back to Mountjoy Prison; subsequently removed thence to Ship Street Barracks, before a Military Tribunal, formed by a Power that is organising the Earth and calling upon Heaven to help it in its effort to crush under a most human and democratic heel the militarism of other Nations which have no prerogative from God—as England has— to keep other small Nationalities in subjection.

The sentence of the Courtmartial, Thomas Ashe, is that you serve two years penal servitude for presuming that you have a free soul and that your soul is Irish. But Thomas Ashe is hopeful; it will not be a long confinement; soon he will be free again—it is but a small cloud, no bigger than a man's hand, that appears in his sky; but bigger and heavier will gather this cloud, Thomas Ashe, till it wholly envelopes you in the impenetrable darkness of death!

[2]The Royal Irish Constabulary.

Again the motor car spins along the streets from Ship Street Barracks, passes thro' Dublin, and swings into the gloomy, dreary avenue leading to the prison gate at Mountjoy. Heavily and ponderously the massive gate rolls open to admit another of the Sons of Ireland to suffering and final martyrdom.

Thomas Ashe, Thomas Ashe, take a last look at the Irish sky, for when these grim gates open to let you forth, your strong body will be limp and helpless, your brave heart will faintly beat in a final effort to live for the people, and your eyes will be too dim to see clearly the kindly Irish skies that have watched your life-long efforts to free your Country and to uplift Her People. The gate closes: Thomas Ashe is separated forever from his relatives, his friends, and the Irish People—when once more they look upon him they find him dead!

Chapter II

The Struggle Against Oppression

When you see a people loaded with irons and delivered to the executioner, be not hasty to say this people is an unruly people that would trouble the earth, for peradventure it is a martyred people which suffers for the salvation of humanity.

LAMMENAIS

Criminals—The Fight to Be Treated as Prisoners of War—
The Answer of British Justice—The Raid on the Cells

Criminals according to the British State and Constitution this was the designation of Thomas Ashe and his comrades. Criminals they were not, but criminals they must be made. The upholders of the British State and Constitution forgot—for it was necessary to forget—that when the American Colonies rose against the tyranny of the Home Government in the reign of

George the Third, and their rifles rang a challenge in the face of oppression on Bunker Hill, that the then British Government treated these "rebels" with all the courtesy and kindness extended to prisoners of war. Courtesy and fair treatment to captured COLONISTS were *permissible lenities,* but what sensible and statesmanlike English Politician could possibly acquiesce in similar treatment being extended towards a revolutionary of the Historic Gaelic Nation? What sensible English Statesman could regard seriously the Hague Peace Conference scrap of paper that declared all that "carried arms openly, were commanded by responsible leaders, had a fixed distinctive sign recognisable at a distance, that conducted operations in accordance with the laws and customs of war, should be recognised as prisoners of war and treated as such." No! Thomas Ashe and his comrades were criminals according to the English State and Constitution, and that State and that sacred Constitution must make them criminals in spite of the protests of the Irish People, and in face of the declaration of civilised humanity!

The methods are clear though they are cruel. Strange way to make poor criminals honest, and pure, and noble. Sure way to humiliate nobility of nature and greatness of heart. Bolts and bars, rules and regulations, and the servants of Justice, dressed in silver and blue to fix the bolts and bars and to enforce the rules and regulations. Hiding the blue of the heavens from the eyes and the voice of human communion from the ears; erasing the sacred function of Baptism, and fixing on the Irish Rebel, by the Grace of God, and to defend the faith, a number, instead of the name branded by Holy Chrism on his brow by a Christian Priest. What are the elevated thoughts of a noble soul to the dignity and sanctity of a British prison rule book? What is a human life even to the unsightly smudging out of one of its immutable phrases? What is the indignation of Thomas Ashe to the ruffled pomp and power of Max Green, Chairman of the Prisons' Board? And if we peer closely into the pages of the prison rule book, we find that the ink reddens, and becomes the darkened and faded imprint of human blood. But Thomas Ashe and his comrades are lower even than criminals.

A letter had been sent by Thomas Ashe, who, at the time, had not even been tried, to one of his friends asking for a visit and for food, and detailing the way in which food might be brought and visits received; this letter and its contents was initialled by the prison authorities; but when the food was brought, Ashe's friend was then informed that the hours mentioned in the letter were wrong, and that visits must be regulated in accordance with the rules. The letter was passed, its mistakes ignored to cause pain to his friends and disappointment to the prisoner.

But Tom Ashe dared to assume that he was not a criminal. He was amiable, honest, cultured, brave and humane, and he thought these virtues. But the stamp of virtue must be bought from the British Government, and as Ashe refused to pay the price, he must be branded as a criminal.

The British Government strikes first, hiding its face under the mask of power possessed by the prison officials, the English Government sends her hired servants to help them in their holy work of overthrowing Brute Force in the world. The prisoners' cells are suddenly entered. Because the prisoners have protested against the deprivation of their usual exercises they are to be punished. And the servants of the Champion of Little Nationalities take away by force the plank beds, the mattresses, the covering, the scanty cell furniture, the few, but necessary cell utensils, and, still unsatisfied, the prisoners are held down by warders, and the boots are forcibly removed from their feet. Then they are left to themselves to reflect upon this latest effort of Her Most Britannic Enemy of Brute Force to stamp upon their broad, clean souls the loathsome mark of criminal. Now the young Republicans exert the only power of protest and opposition they have, and the Hunger Strike begins. A few brave hearts against the whole British State and Constitution.

The clouds are gathering heavier and darker around your life, Thomas Ashe. Death has been summoned by the Government to help in your subjection. The doctors are gathering to show him how to do his work.

Thomas Ashe, your last great fight will soon be fought!

Chapter III

The Torture of Thomas Ashe

> I was ever a fighter, so—one fight more,
> 　　The best and the last!
> I would hate that death bandaged my eyes and forebore,
> 　　And bade me creep past.
> No! let me taste the whole of it, fare like my peers
> 　　The heroes of old,
> Bear the brunt, in a minute pay glad life's arrears
> 　　Of pain, darkness, and cold.
>
> 　　　　　　　　　　　　BROWNING

The Hunger Strike—The Examination—The Gag—Strapped to the Chair—The Tube—Sir Arthur Chance and Sir Thomas Miles—Dr. Lowe—Naked and Cold—The Lord Mayor of Dublin—Sir John Irwin—Duke—Green—Ashe's Fifty Hours of Loneliness—Release

The Hunger Strike has lasted some days and Thomas Ashe is led in once more, weak and faint, to undergo the terrible torture of forcible feeding. The veil of the British Temple of Isis has been lifted at the inquiry held on the death of Thomas Ashe, and Irish eyes have seen some of the horrid rites practised upon their now dead comrade. The doctors hurriedly see if his heart still beats, and finding him, as they think, strong enough to bear another blow, Ashe is seated in the chair by the warders —who must do their duty—his mouth is forced open, and a gag is fixed firmly between the lips, that were guilty of proclaiming their owner's love for Ireland. The strong limbs are securely strapped to the chair. He feebly resists, but the warders—who must do their duty—overcome him, and the victor of Ashebourne is bound and helpless. The doctors—who must do their duty—now prepare the instrument of torture—a tube of three feet in length, with a funnel through which the food would be forced down into the stomach—the tube, which had previously been used on ten other sufferers, was dipped in hot water by one of the warders, and this was forced past the gag, down the gullet and into the stomach of the fettered prisoner. As it passed his throat, the prisoner sickened, and the tube was withdrawn, and inserted again, and the slow and dreadful operation was continued. Sometimes particles of food clogged the tube, which had then to be withdrawn and cleansed, to be again shoved down with sickening effect into the stomach of the helpless prisoner. Sir Arthur Chance, one of Ireland's greatest surgeons, proclaims the operation, even with skilful treatment, to be highly dangerous; but what is that to Dr. Lowe—who must do his duty, for which he receives from the British Government five guineas a week—and the operation is carried on again making weaker the hourly weakening frame of Thomas Ashe.

Sir Thomas Miles, another of Ireland's famous surgeons, declares he is opposed to forcible feeding—but what is that opinion to Dr. Lowe, who must do his duty—and get his five guineas for it. Weaker and weaker grows the once muscular body of the young Republican, the curly head falls helplessly on the shrunken shoulder, and the once red lips are rapidly turning blue. The tube is quickly pulled out, and Thomas Ashe's tortured stomach vomits forth some of the food that has been forced into it. The straps are unbound, and the tortured prisoner falls limply forward in a state of collapse. Dr. Lowe tells the warders to lead him forth and to leave him down quietly on his bed—he had done his sacred duty and has assuredly earned his five guineas.

But worse suffering is to follow. The bedding, the miserable cell furniture, the plank bed which had previously been removed, in violation even of the brutal prison rules, and without the consent of any of the doctors, had not been restored; and a punishment, dreadful and inhuman, that had never been inflicted before upon any prisoner during the grim history of Mountjoy—never even upon the vilest thief, burglar, or prostitute within its walls—continued, and Thomas Ashe was left weak—aye, dying—almost naked, on the cold, hard flags of the prison cell. The only method that could be thought of by the humane authorities—who had to do their duty—aye, and more than their duty—to relieve his sufferings, was to administer a dose of Epsom Salts, which had been mixed with the food forced down his throat!

Hours passed and Thomas Ashe lay, cold and sick, breathing away his young life on the cold floor of the cell. Ah! the loneliness and horror of it all!

Then came the Lord Mayor of Dublin, accompanied by Sir John Irwin, J.P., and they looked down on the bruised body of the prisoner. How full of sympathy was the Lord Mayor, and how he almost wept as he told the story at the inquiry! But why did you not, Lord Mayor, proclaim from the house-tops *then* the inhuman treatment of Thomas Ashe? But, like the Levite, he passed by the suffering man, and hastened down to Cork to join the Convention, "Throw the Dart," and attend the subsequent Banquet, and the shadows of the evening fell; colder and colder grew the shuddering frame of Thomas Ashe, and nearer and nearer Death crept to him. And down in Cork the Lord

Mayor of Dublin, his fair round belly with good capon lined whiled away the time appealing for some kind of Home Rule.

Ashe struggled to his feet, gasping for breath, and smashed the cell window that he might have more air, and lay down again in the cold and the silence; and Sir John Irwin, J.P., Chairman of the Visiting Justices Committee, warmed himself, and went to his well-stocked and comfortable bed, and doubtlessly, slept the sleep of the good and just man; and the night passes quickly to those, slowly to the prisoner lying on the cell floor, and the dawn trickled through the broken window pane; and Death crept nearer still to Thomas Ashe.

And Mr. Duke, Chief Secretary for Ireland, took his breakfast in his Lodge, and looked out at the Autumn Sun gilding the bronzing face of leafy nature, and Max Green, Chairman of the Prisons Board, sat in his snug office, looked over his official papers, and wondered when would the soul of Thomas Ashe bend to the baseness of his rules and regulations; and the inert and almost lifeless form of the young Republican, stretched on the cell floor, answered silently, but immutably: Never! And Death crept nearer, nearer still to Thomas Ashe.

Fifty hours dragged themselves slowly over the prostrate form. Fifty hours of cold, of loneliness, of pain, of bodily misery and mental anguish, with never a friend near to lay a hand on the cold brow nor to whisper a word of encouragement to the brave, though fainting heart of Thomas Ashe.

Then came the prison doctor, who, after a hasty examination, pronounced him dangerously ill, and forwarded the following report: "I have to report that I am of the opinion that the illness of prisoner Thomas Ashe may terminate fatally before termination of his sentence." And then they let the young Republican pass out into kinder hands, having done their duty to the best of their ability to God—and to the English Government.

Again has the veil of the Britannic Temple of Isis been lowered. Max Green refuses to answer the questions put to him by the Counsel for the relatives of Thomas Ashe. There are things in the Temple that this High Priest cannot, dare not, reveal, and he claims privilege, privilege, privilege!

Glorious privileges are yours, Max Green. Happy, singular and ennobling privileges to possess. Privileges that almost deify you, but which savour not of Heaven but of Hell!

Chapter IV

Death of Thomas Ashe

My native land, good night!

BYRON

On the 25th day of the month of September, 1917, there was a stillness about, around, and in the Mater Hospital that had never been felt before.

Thomas Ashe, weak, wan, and worn was painfully surrendering himself a captive to Death. The doctors had abandoned hope, and, watched by the sympathetic Sisters of Charity, the young Republican's soul struggled for release from his battered body. Dimmer and dimmer grow the bright eyes; rigidity begins to creep into the once muscular but now lean, emaciated limbs; colder and colder becomes the broad, humane brow of the soldier and democrat; fainter and fainter are the beats of the heart that once throbbed so strongly and so fervently for Ireland and down-trodden man. Ah! how those who were near him then must have felt the horrors of a power that had no mercy on such a man.

Fainter, fainter still are the heart beats—Ireland is losing thee, Thomas Ashe—Ireland is losing thee. What is the use of tears—what is the use of cursing? The heart has stopped—no not yet, not yet—Ah! now, it is still, and Thomas Ashe is dead!

Thou has said farewell to Ireland, Thomas Ashe, but Ireland will not part with thy soul. What can we think of the Power that robbed us of the life of this dear dead man?

Frangas Non Flectes[3]

Oppression has broken Thomas Ashe, but she could not bend him. His brave soul has overflowed into the soul of the Irish People. He is dead! His Ideals are alive and flourishing!

Oppression of the Bloody Hands you cannot put a rope around the neck of an idea; you cannot put an Idea up against a barrack-square wall and riddle it with bullets; you cannot confine it in the strongest prison cell that your slaves could ever build.

Thomas Ashe's body, to-day, is covered with Irish mould, but his principles are surging into stronger life within the minds of the Irish Proletariat, the Irish Scholar, and the Irish Worker. Death has won a poor victory! Labour has lost a champion; Irish-Ireland has lost a son; Militant Ireland has lost a soldier; but all have gained a mighty and enduring inspiration. Ashe died that Human Liberty might be vindicated and that Ireland might live.

To your soul for awhile we all murmur farewell!
    And we take the dear gift that you gave:
For your great life stamp'd out in the cold prison cell,
    Shall be potent our own slavish nature to save—
Tho' your body we leave in the drear hidden gloom of
        the grave.

[3]You may break, but not bend.

The Jury's Verdict

Out of thine own mouth will I judge thee, thou wicked servant.

Luke 19:22

Let us examine well what the court, held under the auspices of the Power that was responsible for Thomas Ashe's death, thought and declared respecting the horrible treatment the young Republican received: the Jury empanelled according to the "law of the Statute made and provided," presided over by a coroner, created by the same Statute of the British State and Constitution—listened to the damning evidence, and after due deliberation, these servants under the Statute of the British State and Constitution declared:

"We find that the deceased, Thomas Ashe, according to the medical evidence of Professor M'Weeney, Sir Arthur Chance, and Sir Thomas Myles, died from heart failure and congestion of the lungs on the 25th September, 1917, **caused by the punishment of taking away from the cell bed, bedding and boots, and allowing him to be on the cold floor for 50 hours,** and then subjecting him to forcible feeding in his weak conditon after hunger-striking for five or six days.

"**We censure the Castle Authorities** for not acting more promptly, especially when the grave condition of the deceased and other prisoners was brought under their notice on the previous Saturday by the Lord Mayor and Sir John Irwin.

"**That the hunger-strike was adopted against the inhuman punishment inflicted and a refusal to their demand to be treated as political prisoners.**

"We condemn forcible and mechanical feeding as an inhuman and dangerous operation, and which should be discontinued.

"That the assistant doctor called in, having no previous experience, administered forcible feeding unskilfully.

"We find that the taking away of all deceased's bed, bedding, and boots was an unfeeling and barbarous act, and we censure the Deputy-Governor for violating the prison rules and inflicting punishment which he had no power to do.

"That we infer he was acting under instructions from the Prison Board and Castle, which refused to give evidence and documents asked for.

"We tender our sympathy to the relatives of the deceased."

So that even the British State and Constitution condemns itself and stands forth before all men as the first of oppressors and the prince of hypocrites.

Fergus O'Connor, Publisher, Dublin, 1918

A History

T he Story of the Irish Citizen Army was published in 1919 by Maunsel & Co., Ltd. It was a 72-page paper-back booklet that sold for a shilling, and it was the first writing which O'Casey was paid for. In the chapter "Mrs. Casside Takes a Holiday" in *Inishfallen, Fare Thee Well,* O'Casey tells of the bitter experiences that he had in attempting to cash his cheque. As that account is too long to print here, the following version from *Lady Gregory's Journals*[1] must suffice:

> *June 8* [1924]. Casey grieves for his mother. She, 89, died in 1919. He had lived all his life with her, the others of her children had died or gone away. "She had a strong sense of humor, could always see the humorous side of human life. I did everything for her, she did not like to have anyone else about her. I had written a little story. The publishers promised me £15 for it, and after it was published I wanted the money and went three times for it but could never get it. Then when my mother was so ill I had to go again to press for it, and I did get it, but when I came back she was gone. I made arrangements for the funeral, but when the day came the undertaker said that if I did not pay at once he would take it back again and there would be no funeral. It had to be put off until I could get change for the cheque. I thought I should have to go to the bank, but I went to the Rector and he cashed it. I felt the treatment of the undertaker very bitterly, he was a Labour man, I a Labour man, and I had helped him and worked in the movement, worked for them all, and that is how I was treated."

O'Casey wrote that *The Story of the Irish Citizen Army* was "intended to be historical rather than critical . . . the simple and concise narration of the facts as they occurred." Whatever was intended, the little book, like all of O'Casey's work, is saturated with opinion. It is true that he does present some incidents, like his censure of Madame Markievicz, with a terse objectivity; but his major opinions about Labour and Nationalism and about Connolly's defection from the aims of Labour clearly pervade the whole book. "E. O'D," possibly Eimar O'Duffy, writing in *The Irish Statesman* for July 12, 1919, disapprovingly but accurately thought that, "The actions and attitudes of the national movement are judged, or misjudged, entirely in reference to their bearing on the labouring section of the nation; and the worth of each and every prominent

[1]Lennox Robinson (ed.), *Lady Gregory's Journals* (New York: The Macmillan Co., 1947).

Nationalist is estimated from his attitude towards the social and economic views held by Mr. O Cathasaigh."

Through most of the book, the opinions are phrased less forcefully than O'Casey had earlier expressed himself in *The Irish Worker*. He knew that the manuscript, to pass the British censor, must be fairly temperate; even so, the book did not escape unscathed. O'Casey wrote me on July 7, 1960:

> Regarding material you think of collecting: THE STORY OF THE I. CITIZEN ARMY was much bulkier in the original—I wish I had the Ms now—, if I remember right . . . it was slashed by the then Competent Military Authority (Censors); went to another Censor who marked with red pencil what he deemed must come out from among the green marked parts; then this went to the final Censor who confirmed what must finally be deleted by blue pencil enclosures—the Ms was a sight!

In another letter, on March 28, 1961, he added:

> The I. Citizen Army: Don't know who has the copyright. Anyhow it isn't the book I wrote. Ms had to be put before a military Censor. . . . You should have seen it! This Ms would be priceless now, for it was all written in longhand, and had all my attempts to get around the forbidden passages. It came back to me three times!

The Maunsel company, which published the booklet, went out of business in the 1920's, and I have had no success in my inquiries about the manuscript, which is probably irretrievably lost. The published version, reprinted here, is, then, considerably muted in tone; and to realise the full force of O'Casey's opinions, one should compare this book with some of the articles and letters in *The Irish Worker* which are published below.

Some of the other shortcomings of the booklet can probably also be attributed to the Censor. For instance, the booklet is a little lopsided in content. The early years of the army are treated at length, but the story of the army's part in the Rising of Easter Week appears more scantily. Partly the disproportion exists because O'Casey knew the early events at first hand and was in the hospital during the Rising; but mainly, I think, the Censor demanded that the more recent and inflammatory events be treated discreetly.

Because he was writing a history, O'Casey perhaps wanted to be more impersonal and objective. That attitude, coupled with the restraints of censorship, would explain why the booklet is less suffused with his own personality. From time to time, however, that personality breaks ebulliently through; and for a moment we glimpse his excitement at Larkin addressing a meeting, or his pleasure at a recruiting jaunt into the country, or his pensive mood at dusk while camping with the army in Croydon Park.

These furtive glimpses of personality that spasmodically flash across the pages of the book, suddenly light up a whole scene with the glow of life, and for a second we have a convincing glimmer of real people. For a second the shadowy names and figures of people long dead come alive, breathe, and have flesh and blood. In these seconds we are given the recreation of history that only art can give us.

In contrast, Bulmer Hobson's *History of the Irish Volunteers,*[2] published the year before, is only a dull and lifeless compilation of facts and documents. O'Casey's book is not a good one, but it is not a dead one.

As a sidelight, it is interesting to note that, while O'Casey's history of the Citizen Army frequently refers to the Irish Volunteers, Hobson's history of the Volunteers never in its first volume refers to the labour army. In fact, despite Hobson's frequently stressed contention that the Volunteers' "aim was not to secure adherents for their own views on party questions, but to bring into being a national force composed of men of all parties," he refers to organised labour only once. In describing the great enlistment meeting that the Volunteers held at the Rotunda Rink on November 25, 1913, Hobson writes:

> The audience was unanimous in its support of the Irish Volunteers, but an unpleasant scene was created by an organised crowd from Liberty Hall, the headquarters of the Irish Transport Workers' Union, who refused L. J. Kettle a hearing, on account of some episodes in the then recent labour troubles in Dublin. Kettle read the Manifesto, but the din created by the Liberty Hall men made his voice inaudible.

Adding his voice to that din was an obscure, opinionated, and bright-eyed railroad labourer named O'Cathasaigh.

[2]Bulmer Hobson, *A Short History of the Irish Volunteers* (Dublin: Candle Press, 1918).

The Story of the
Irish Citizen Army

Preface

Sec. Citizen: Answer every man directly.
First Cit.: Ay, and briefly.
Fourth Cit.: Ay, and wisely.
Third Cit.: Ay, and truly, you were best.

Julius Caesar (III, iii)

The author ventures to hope that this humble attempt to reveal some of the hidden things correlative with the origin and development of the Irish Citizen Army will prove interesting to all who participated actually or sympathetically in the motives which inspired its creation, and, indeed, even to those who viewed its activities with suspicion and mistrust.

By many the budding Citizen Army, that struggled for expression and expansion in Dublin's streets, was a subject for amusing jokes and quiet laughter, and its actions were almost entirely ignored till the bud flowered redly on the second morning of Easter Week. Incidents are generally recorded as they occur, and few attempts are made critically to consider the circumstances that evolve them. The author hopes that the materials, carefully gathered together from original manuscripts in his possession, from notes recorded during the organising period of the Army, and from the contemplation of events in which the author participated, will be of use for incorporation in whatever history may be subsequently written around the events which culminated in the dramatic rising of Easter Week.

The author wishes, gratefully, to acknowledge the assistance he has received in the writing of the last chapter of this unpretentious work by Captains McCormack and McGowan, of the Irish Citizen Army.

It is impossible yet to say whether the events of Easter Week will achieve a Democratisation of Irish Nationalism, or whether the latter influence will deflect itself towards the broader issues of the Irish Labour movement.

Present events point to the probability that Jim Connolly's earlier ideals will be covered by the ever-rising tide of a militant Nationalism, though it also seems certain that the younger and more progressive elements of National thought will endeavour to associate with National advancement the upliftment of the Irish working class.

It appears certain that Nationalism has gained a great deal and lost a little by its union with Labour in the Insurrection of Easter Week, and that Labour has lost much and achieved something by its avowal of the National aspirations of the Irish Nation.

We can only hope that Nationalism, in its new-found strength, will not remain deaf to the claims of Irish Labour for a foremost place in the National Being, and that the sacrifices of Irish Labour through the Citizen Army may not be forgotten by those who are working towards the regeneration of our common country.

Chapter I

The Founding of the Citizen Army

The people were waitin' in thousands there,
An' you couldn't hear stir nor breath.

The Man from God Knows Where

Discontent had lighted a blazing camp-fire in Dublin. The ruddy light of the flame was reflected by an earnest and ominous glow in the face of every Dublin worker. Men, full of the fire of battle, thronged in dense masses the wide, expansive area facing Liberty Hall. The city was surging with a passion full, daring, and fiercely expectant; a passion strange, enjoyable, which it had never felt before with such intensity and emotion. It was felt, unconsciously, that this struggle would be the Irish Armageddon between Capital and Labour. The workers were exuberantly confident that the unparalleled spread of the sympathetic strike would overthrow the moneyed hosts of Midian. Did you not hear it? It was true, many great scholars had declared in their favour, and even now Captain White, the aristocrat and gentleman, was with their beloved Leader, and had signified his intention to throw in his lot with his socially humbler brothers, abandoning the privileges of position, ignoring the remonstrances of friends, choosing freely and bravely to stand by the people now in their hour of need.

And the eager, toil-worn, care-lined faces of the workers now turned with concentrated uneasy patience towards the window on the left-hand side of Liberty Hall, waiting for it to be raised, that they might listen to this nightly message of hope, progress and encouragement from those Leaders, whom they were convinced would guide them safely through the heavy ordeal that each man must share that there might be preserved to all the elemental right of the workers to choose their Union, and to follow the Leaders in whom alone they placed their whole confidence and trust.

The disappearing Artist Sun had boldly brushed the skies with bold hues of orange and crimson, and delicate shades of yellow and green, bordered with dusky shadows of darkening blue, which seemed to symbolise the glow of determination, the delicate hues of hope, and the bordering shades of restless anxiety that coloured the hearts and thoughts of the waiting, watching masses of men that stood silently beneath the oriental-coloured panoply of the sky.

Suddenly the window is raised, and the tense, anxious feelings of the men crowded together burst out into an enthusiastic and full-throated cheer that shatters the surrounding air, and sends up into the skies a screaming flock of gulls that had been peacefully drifting along the sombre surface of the River Liffey. Louder still swells the resonant shout as Jim Larkin appears at the window, with an animated flush of human pride on his strong and rugged face, as he brushes back from his broad forehead the waving tufts of dark hair that are here and there silvered by the mellowing influence of Time and the inexorable force of issuing energy from the human structure. Again the cheers ring out, and Larkin quietly waits till the effort to demonstrate their confidence and affection will give place to the lustful desire to hear what he has to say to them, while hidden under the heavy shadows of the towering Custom House a darker column of massive constables instinctively finger their belts, and silently caress the ever-ready club that swings jauntily over each man's broad, expansive hip.

Rumours had been circulated that Jim Larkin had forged a new weapon for the workers, some plan which, when developed, would make their resisting power irresistible, a power that would quickly change their disorganised, clumsy, incohesive units into a huge, immovable, unbreakable Roman phalanx.

Hope's ruddy flame was leaping in their hearts: this day would be an historic one in the unhappy annals of the Irish Labour Movement.

Perhaps this lovely autumn sunset would be followed by the dawn of their social emancipation.

And the lusty cheers died away to a droning echo, which was followed for a few moments by a silence that was so strangely sincere that the mass of people resembled the upright figures of an assembly in the shady and silent regions of the dead.

And then, with a sweeping gesture of his arm, that seemed to pass around that tremendous gathering and make them one with himself in thought and hope and action, Jim Larkin began to speak.

In rugged, passionate, vitalising phrases he told them that "they were engaged in the fight of their lives; that every conceivable combination had united its forces against the workers; that it would be a long and bitter fight between the Titans of Capital and the Titans of Labour.

"Therefore, the workers must become disciplined, organised, made of the one stuff in thought and action, so that in all that they would essay to do for themselves there would be a spontaneous unity of pressure and a hardened and impenetrable unity of resistance. The men must get to know each other. They must no longer be content to assemble in hopeless, haphazard crowds, in which a man does not know and cannot trust the man that stands next to him, but in all their future assemblies they must be so organised that there will be a special place for every man, and a particular duty for each man to do.

"They knew to their cost that a few determined men, determined because they were imbued with the force of discipline, led by men whom they looked upon as their leaders, could scatter, like spray before the wind, the largest gatherings of men, who, untaught and loosely strung together, would always be dominated by the possibility of fear and panic.

"If they would not agree to bring themselves under the influence of an ordered and systematic discipline, then they could never hope to resist the efforts that were being made to prevent them assembling peaceably to discuss affairs of their Union. By order and discipline only could they hope to secure for themselves the recognition of the sacred heritage bestowed by Nature upon every man born into the world—the right to live. All this must be changed, and he, with the help of Captain

White, who would soon address them, was determined to begin the work now that would bring about this much-desired improvement in the strength and mutual combination of the various sections of the workers.

"Labour in its own defence must begin to train itself to act with disciplined courage and with organised and concentrated force. How could they accomplish this? By taking a leaf out of the book of Carson. If Carson had permission to train his braves of the North to fight against the aspirations of the Irish people, then it was legitimate and fair for Labour to organise in the same militant way to preserve their rights and to ensure that if they were attacked they would be able to give a very satisfactory account of themselves.

"They were going to give the members of their Union a military training. Captain White would speak to them now and tell them the plans he had to create from among the members of the Labour Unions a great Citizen Army. Captain White would take charge of the movement, and he trusted that the various Trades Unions would see to it that all their members joined this new army of the people, so that Labour might no longer be defenceless, but might be able to utilise that great physical power which it possessed to prevent their elemental rights from being taken from them, and to evolve such a system of unified action, self-control and ordered discipline that Labour in Ireland might march at the forefront of all movements for the betterment of the whole people of Ireland."

Like the loud rolling of a multitude of drums the cheers broke out again. This was what was long wanted—a Citizen Army! What could not Labour accomplish with an army trained and disciplined by officers who held the affection and confidence of the workers! Now they would get some of their own back; and vivid visions of "Red-coats and Black-coats flying before them" floated before the imaginative eyes of the

Dublin workers filled with and almost intoxicated by the wine of enthusiasm.

And once again the cheers rang out as the tall, athletic figure of Captain White appeared, and his boyish face was aglow with gratification as he listened to the cheers that seemed to proclaim to him a ready realisation of the schemes he contemplated towards the disciplined consolidation of the lower orders in the battalionised ranks of an Irish Citizen Army.

Captain White told them that the work would commence immediately. He told them to attend the very next day at Croydon Park, Fairview, where they would be marshalled, divided into battalions, sub-divided into companies, and put through the elementary stages of military training. "This was a day of Hope for the workers," continued Captain White, "the definite result of their plans depended now on the efforts and sincerity of the workers themselves. The Irish Citizen Army would fight for Labour and for Ireland." He asked all those who intended to second their efforts by joining the army and training themselves for the fight for Social liberty, to hold up their hands.

Almost every hand was silhouetted out against the darkening sky, and a last long deafening cheer proclaimed the birth of the Irish Citizen Army.

Chapter II

Renaissance

Everything indicates—the smallest does, and the largest does;
A necessary film envelops all, and envelops the Soul
    for a proper time.

WALT WHITMAN

For some time the enthusiasm engendered at the great meeting held in Beresford Place, "the old spot by the river," flamed hotly in the hearts of the workers, tens of thousands of whom were then on strike in Dublin. Imposing drills were held in Croydon Park, the picturesque suburban headquarters of the Transport Union, and thousands of working-men zealously endeavoured to learn "the soldier's glorious trade." It was certainly inspiring to watch the stalwart workers marching in column of company formation from Croydon Park back to Liberty Hall under the command of the indefatigable Captain White. Everything looked promising; the rank and file were representative of every shade of thought and every degree of national feeling. Here was the clerk, the artisan, the labourer, the United Irish Leaguer, Republican, Sinn Feiner and Gaelic student. These were the fat days of the Irish Citizen Army, but, alas, lean days were soon to follow. The people of Ireland were not ripe enough to be shaken from the green tree of Nationalism into the wide basket of an Irish Labour Army. A Citizen Army can only be formed from a class-conscious community of workers, and the Irish workers still slumbered on in the dark shade of unawakened thought. And the Irish Labour Leaders were forced to devote all their attention and thoughts to the difficulties which the mighty labour upheavals were hourly creating, and they could not surrender to the Citizen Army that regard which was essential if the movement was to be made a permanent and ever-growing success. Nightly meetings in Beresford Place; rallies in all the districts in which the men had declared war on their employers; midnight meetings in Liberty Hall, meant that energy and force, which would have preserved the initial imposing proportions of the Citizen Army, were employed for other purposes, more pressing, and calculated to overcome the terrible pressure that the employers were using to crush forever the effort the exasperated workers were making to assert the elemental liberties and rights of their class. Entertainments were organised in the Dublin Theatres to provide food and clothing for the wives and children of the locked-out workers; the food distribution entailed an enormous amount of organised attention; the municipal elections, in which Labour endeavoured to exert its influence on Civic affairs, exacted a further contribution of time and energy, and all these activities, which were urgent and necessary, robbed from the organisation of the Citizen Army that application and support which alone would have made it the success that many believed, from first appearances, it had already achieved.

But the principal events which most injured the progress and shook the stability of the Irish Citizen Army at this time were the frequent arrests of the Labour Leaders; the gradual and humiliating weakening of the workers' resistance to the pressure of the employers; the malignant penalising of the Irish Transport Union by the hierarchy of commerce; and the establishment in the Rotunda Rink on the 25th October, 1914, of the Irish National Volunteers. Hundreds of men began to dribble back to work, and this meant that they had very little time to spend in the training that Captain White still carried on, in spite of all difficulties, in Croydon Park, in Liberty Hall, and in the Fianna Hall, Camden Street, which was placed at the disposal of the Citizen Army by the Countess Markievicz.

The penalty of dismissal which the united employers of Dublin held over the heads of the workers if they continued to remain members of the Transport Union caused, naturally, hundreds of men to abandon their connection with the Citizen Army, though comparatively few, happily, evinced the slavish weakness to respond to this threat by severing their connection with the Union itself.

The creation of the National Volunteers was one of the most effective blows which the Irish Citizen Army received. Thousands that had originally attached themselves to the Citizen Army passed over into the more attractive and better organised camp of the Volunteers.

Many, no doubt, preferred Caithlin Ni Houlihan in a respectable dress than a Caithlin in the garb of a working woman. Many also realised that the governing body of the Volunteers was eminently influential, and that the ban which was over the Citizen Army, like a dark cloud, because of its arterial connection with the Transport Union, was not to be chosen as a shelter, when they could radiantly enjoy the National halo that glittered around the whole structure of the National Volunteers. The old lingering tradition of the social inferiority of what were called the unskilled workers, prompted the socially superior tradesmen to shy at an organisation which was entirely officered by men whom they thought to be socially inferior to themselves.

And in spite of the fact that the most prominent members of the Executive of the Volunteers were those who had done all they could to snatch from the workers the right to join the Trades Union of their choice; in spite of the fact that many of those who controlled the local requirements or occupied a position on the local Executive had locked out their employés because they had ventured to assert the first principles of Trades Unionism.

It is difficult to understand why the workers chose to join an organisation which was largely controlled by their enemies rather than one which was guided and governed by the men who were their elected leaders in the social war against economic tyranny and oppression.

Looking back on this surprising anomaly, it becomes obvious that because of the undeveloped comprehension by the workers of the deeper meaning of the Labour movement, the call of the National Tribe appealed to them more strongly than the call of the Tribe of Labour. Years of National propaganda overcame the influence that had been exercised upon their minds by the fierce teachings of Jim Larkin and the quiet but equally effective reasoning of Jim Connolly. But the Volunteer movement enjoyed other less attractive, but equally real and tangible, advantages. They had, comparatively, unlimited funds with which to equip their members, while the money that Labour collected had to be devoted to the work of providing food for the workers, that these might live and not die.

The National movement, too, had, practically, the monopoly of all the available halls in Dublin and elsewhere in which systematic drilling could be carried on. An effort was made by the Citizen Army Council to induce the Volunteer movement to allow them the use of these rooms on a few nights each week, but the Volunteers were, evidently, determined to maintain their advantage in this respect, for every request was answered by a polite but very emphatic refusal to help the Citizen Army to overcome this important and embarrassing difficulty.

The leaders of the Volunteers were also in the enviable position of being able to devote all their energies and their whole time to the one work of organisation, an advantage that told forcibly in favour of their efforts, while the Labour leaders could only now and then snatch a hasty moment or two in which to pay a little attention to the fast vanishing companies of the Labour Army.

For some months Captain White worked gallantly, trying to do the work of ten men, and making superhuman efforts to organise, drill and equip an army single-handed, furnished with no help, and receiving very little encouragement. But the inevitable happened; the drills became irregular, the numbers continued to decrease, and, finally, the Captain found himself reduced to the command of one Company of faithful stalwarts, who, in spite of all obstacles, had remained as a sure and trustworthy nucleus of the Irish Citizen Army.

Then Captain White began to lose hope. He seemed to be building on foundations of sand. He had no outlet for his energies. If Labour failed to rise to the opportunity that presented itself, what good purpose could it serve for him to be eternally trying to accomplish the impossible?

About this time the Labour organisation began to retire to their trenches. The strike had waned, and, finally ended, and Labour engaged again in the work of re-organisation, making strenuous efforts to recover lost ground and rehabilitate the forces that had been scattered in the great social offensive of 1913.

It was then that the writer of this little work, in an interview with Captain White, suggested that definite steps should be taken to form the Citizen Army into a systematic unit of Labour; that a Constitution should be drafted and submitted for approval to a general meeting of workers; that a Council should be elected to see after the revival of systematic drills, to open a fund for equipment purposes, to arrange for public meetings, to form companies of the army wherever Labour was strongest, and to generally take steps to improve and strengthen the condition and widen the scope of the Irish Citizen Army. Captain White enthusiastically welcomed the suggestions, and promised that he would recommence the work with redoubled ardour if a strong committee could be got together to second his efforts. A preliminary meeting of sympathisers and members was then arranged for a following night, and Sean O Cathasaigh was deputed to make out an agenda and draft a Constitution, so that the meeting could decide definitely upon a determined and regular course of action.

The meeting was duly held in Liberty Hall, and amongst those present were: Jim Connolly, Countess Markievicz, W. Partridge, P. T. Daly. Captain White presided, and Sean O Cathasaigh acted as secretary to the meeting. The proposed Constitution was the item principally discussed, and its formulas were generally approved of and tentatively accepted. On the motion of Jim Connolly, seconded by P. T. Daly, it was unani-

o

mously decided to hold a public meeting in the Concert Room, Liberty Hall, on March 22nd, 1914, to invite the workers of Dublin to attend, and to ask Jim Larkin to preside over the meeting, as it was felt by all that the Chief of the Labour movement should know all that was recommended before it was finally approved of.

The general meeting of Dublin workers assembled and filled the Concert Hall, and at 12:30 Jim Larkin commenced the proceedings. Before calling upon the secretary to the meeting to read the proposed Constitution, he expressed the hope that all members of the Transport Union would immediately become members of the Irish Citizen Army. He told those present that steps would be taken to provide a standard uniform for the army, as this feature would tend towards keeping the men together and infuse them with a sense of dignity that would be lacking if they were dressed in the nondescript garments of civilian life. A member would be sent to England to secure accoutrements, and he asked those present to co-operate in every possible way to make the Army of Labour an effective and lasting success. Tents would be procured, and during the summer months night camps would be held in Croydon Park, which would be a source of pleasure and healthful recreation for their members. He counselled them to be careful as to whom they would elect to the Council of the Citizen Army. He was certain that attempts would be made to influence or capture their organisation, or to wean it from its first attachment to Labour Ideals, and, therefore, it was necessary for them to take every precaution so that the army might always continue to work for the principles which it had originally adopted, and not be set aside from its path by any outside or subsidiary considerations.

He then called upon the secretary to read the proposed Constitution, which would be considered and discussed, clause by clause, each of which would be approved of, amended or rejected as the meeting cared to decide.

The Secretary to the meeting explained that this was the initial effort to lift the affairs of the army from the unsatisfactory condition in which they at present were, and to begin work in a systematic manner to consolidate and improve the conditions of the army so that it might become an influential fighting force in the ranks of Labour.

The proposed Constitution was then read, discussed clause by clause, and unanimously accepted by the vote of the members present.

Its principles were as follows:

1. That the first and last principle of the Irish Citizen Army is the avowal that the ownership of Ireland, moral and material, is vested of right in the people of Ireland.
2. That the Irish Citizen Army shall stand for the absolute unity of Irish nationhood, and shall support the rights and liberties of the democracies of all nations.
3. That one of its objects shall be to sink all differences of birth, property and creed under the common name of the Irish People.
4. That the Citizen Army shall be open to all who accept the principle of equal rights and opportunities for the Irish People.

Jim Larkin then asked one of the members present to propose the following clause for inclusion in the Army Constitution:

"Before being enrolled, every applicant must, if eligible, be a member of his Trades Union, such Union to be recognised by the Irish Trades Union Congress."

This clause was then proposed by the Countess Markievicz, seconded by Thomas Healy, put to the meeting, and carried unanimously.

The election of a Provisional Committee, to hold office for six months, was then proceeded with, and the following were elected to positions on the first Army Council of the Irish Citizen Army:

Chairman: Captain White, D.S.O.

Vice-Chairmen: Jim Larkin, P. T. Daly, Councillor W. Partridge, Thomas Foran, F. Sheehy-Skeffington

Hon. Secretary: Sean O Cathasaigh

Hon. Treasurers: Richard Brannigan, Countess Markievicz

Committee: Thomas Healy, Michael Mullin, John Bohan, T.C.; P. Morgan, T. Burke, T. Blair, C. Poole, J. McGowan, T. Kennedy, P. O'Brien, F. Moss, P. J. Fox, John Shelly, P. Coady, P. Fogarty

The following notes relative to the meeting appeared in the following issue of the *Irish Worker:*

"On Sunday, March 22nd, the first steps were taken to fortify and extend the claims of the Irish Citizen Army upon the Irish workers by the framing of a Constitution and the election of an Army Council.

"Steps will be taken immediately to form companies and provide drill-halls.

"District meetings will be held to select officers and elect suitable district committees. All Irish workers should join the Citizen Army, which is prepared to explain and define its Constitution upon any platform in Ireland. Let the workers keep clear of Girondin politicians, who will simply use the workers as the means towards their own security and comfort. Let others who may prate about 'the rights and liberties common to all Irishmen.' We are out for the right to work and eat and live. As John Mitchel says:

" 'Let the canting, well-fed classes shout and rave as they may. Where you see a respectable, fair-spoken lie sitting in high places, feeding itself fat on human sacrifices, down with it, strip it naked, and pitch it to the devil.'

"We have a few of these things to pitch to the devil; so we ask the workers everywhere in which these few words are read to prepare for the advent of the Irish Citizen Army; to take the names of all who would be willing to join; to secure the advice and services of ex-army men, and to write for all particulars to the Honorary Secretary, Citizen Army Council, Liberty Hall, Dublin."

And so the Irish Citizen Army was changed from airy nothing, and made solid, and given a local habitation and a name, and it immediately began to forge its way into the stormy centre of Irish politics, giving no mercy and receiving none from those organisations whose operations were similar, but between which there was fixed, apparently, an impassable gulf of Ideal and Principle.

Chapter III

Reorganisation

What we believe in invites no one, promises nothing, sits in calmness and light, is positive and composed, knows no discouragement, waiting patiently, waiting its time.

WALT WHITMAN

The reorganisation of the Citizen Army began immediately, and though zeal at times outran discretion, good and permanent work was done.

Two splendid companies of picked men were formed as the nucleus of the City Battalion. Captain White gave an order to Messrs. Arnott for fifty uniforms of dark green serge, and the men eagerly awaited their arrival. For the time being the rank and file wore on their left arms broad bands of Irish linen of a light blue colour, and the officers a band of crimson on the right arm.

In a short time a consignment of haversacks, belts and bayonets arrived, and for a few nights following there was a terrible scene of polishing, oiling and cleaning, in which work Jim Larkin showed an enthusiasm worthy of a young boy with a new toy.

The army was divided into units of half-companies; the Dublin Regiment was divided into three sections, the 1st City Battalion, the second North County Battalion, and the third South County Battalion.

Drills were held twice weekly in Croydon Park, which were conducted by Sergeant-Major Fogarty and Captain Mac-Dowell, under the supervision of Captain White. These officers were ably assisted by Lieutenants C. Poole, Fitzpatrick and O'Byrne.

Finally the uniforms arrived, and then there was a scene that certainly rivalled some of the tragic episodes depicted in Dante's Inferno.

The Council decided that no man could be allowed to bring his uniform home till he had fully paid the cost, but the confusion of undressing and redressing whenever a parade took place finally convinced the Council that there was no other alternative possible but to permit the men to whom uniforms had been allocated to bring them home and to come to all assemblies and parades in full marching order to save time and ensure military punctuality.

The two first companies certainly looked picturesque and imposing in their dark green uniforms and broad slouched hats of the same hue, most of which were jauntily turned up at one side, the leaf being fastened to the side with the ever-popular badge of the Red Hand.

The Citizen Army made great progress in drilling during the summer months, for splendid facilities were provided for extensive manoeuvring in the capacious grounds of Croydon Park, Fairview, then rented by the Irish Transport Union. But when the winter arrived, the accommodation in Liberty Hall was limited, and an effort was made to secure the use of the rooms used by the National Volunteers for a similar purpose. But it was evident that the Executive of this organisation were unwilling to give any encouragement to the Citizen Army. Several applications were completely ignored, and a written request to the Secretary of the House Committee of the Gaelic League premises, 25 Parnell Square, elicited an answer in Gaedhilge, the translation of which was as follows:

> THE HOUSE COMMITTEE
> 25 PARNELL SQUARE, DUBLIN
> April 12th, 1914

I received your letter concerning our hall last night. It is engaged now every night, except Saturday, and on this night it is occasionally wanted for a social. The Volunteers use the hall on Tuesday and Sunday nights, and *I don't think* the Committee would give it to *any other organisation* for drill.

The caretaker has now a good deal of work to do, and the women, also, who are engaged to keep the hall clean. However, I will put your letter before my Committee at their next meeting, which will not be held till the beginning of next month.—Yours,

> G. IRVINE, *Secretary*

In fact, it was plain that, as far as encouragement and support were concerned, the workers would have to rely upon themselves, but it is certain that the lack of suitable places in which to carry on systematic drill materially interfered with the progress and growth of the Citizen Army.

A manifesto to be sent to the various trades bodies in Ireland was drafted, and, having been submitted to the Army Council, and approved of by them, it was dispatched to labour organisations in Cork, Belfast, Derry, Sligo, Limerick, Kilkenny, Waterford, Dundalk, Galway and Wexford. This manifesto declared the principles that the Citizen Army stood for, and asked the secretaries of the Trades Union to make preparations for public meetings in their several districts, which would be addressed by the Labour Leaders when an opportunity presented itself. The manifesto pointed out that all political organisations were preparing for serious eventualities; the Ulster Volunteers in the North; the National Volunteers were establishing companies everywhere in Ireland, while the lazy Hercules of Labour was content to lean on his club, indifferent to the stirring of all around him. "Would it not be a shame," declared the manifesto, "if the forces of Labour alone were content to believe all things; endure all things; to starve rather than to take; to be stricken and not to strike back?"

The manifesto was partially successful in arousing an interest in the work and objects of the Citizen Army. Efforts were made to respond to the appeal in various places, but, on the whole, the battle went with the strong, and the National Volunteers effectively held their advantages almost everywhere, outside of those places in which the Irish Transport Union still carried on the fight for human emancipation.

The first definite meetings held to establish a company of the Irish Citizen Army, outside of Dublin, were held in Lucan and Clondalkin, on Sunday, April 12th, 1914. Announcements had been made that meetings would be held in these districts, and early on the Sunday morning the Countess Markievicz, Captain White, P. T. Daly, and Sean O Cathasaigh proceeded to Lucan in the Captain's motor-car to commence the shaping of the definite destinies of the Irish Citizen Army.

It was a happy spring day, and everything in nature seemed to laugh quietly at the querulous efforts of man to solve the complex human problems with which he was surrounded. We had no thoughts to spare on the loveliness that peeped at us out of every corner as the car swung towards Lucan, and our eyes were closed to the bursting buds, and our ears stopped to the singing of the birds, for in our hearts were commingling thoughts that painted pictures of the hope of success and the fear of defeat.

When we reached Lucan things looked far from promising, for we were silently and curiously received by a few stragglers, that stood here and there about the village, and seemed to be in no way desirous of helping in the promotion of anything that Labour stood for. After a very pleasant tea in a local restaurant, the Captain motored to a suitable place in the vicinity of the village, and, standing on the car seat, waited a few moments, while a shy and obviously timorous crowd of about five hundred people slowly gathered around the car, and displayed a demeanour of such ominous quietude that plainly revealed to us that the Irish Citizen Army had a long and energy exhausting struggle in front of it before the rural workers would become sufficiently class-conscious to understand the elementary principles of Labour thought and aspirations.

Captain White opened the meeting, and told them that necessity itself should force them to make an effort to safeguard their interests. P. T. Daly and the secretary followed, but much more interest was evinced in the passionate and nervous eloquence of the Countess Markievicz. During the progress of the meeting twenty names were taken by the secretary, and these were authorised to hold a subsequent meeting to elect officers and arrange for drills, and, in the centre of a rousing and sincere cheer, the motor-car sped out of the village of Lucan on its way to the more distant village of Clondalkin. The residents in and around Clondalkin evinced the same diffidence in coming together, and stood afar off for quite a long time, gazing fixedly towards the Captain's motor-car as if it were some dangerous machine calculated, if approached too closely, to upset for ever the quiet rhythm of the pastoral life of Clondalkin's inhabitants.

After some hours of waiting our patience was rewarded and a fairly successful meeting was held, over which Michael Costello, the Transport Union delegate for the district, presided, and after its conclusion the car was turned head homewards, and we arrived shortly afterwards at Liberty Hall, by no means satisfied at what we had achieved, but fully conscious that we had bravely faced enormous difficulties and thoroughly convinced that the work of building up the Irish Citizen Army would be a long, arduous and painful task.

On Sunday, April the 19th, 1914, meetings were held in Coolock and Kinsealy, at which Jim Larkin, Daly and O Cathasaigh spoke, and in Swords, on the same day, a further meeting was addressed by these speakers, ably seconded by Captain White, who had proceeded to Swords after a parade in Croydon Park. A poster had been previously issued which called upon the "Men of Fingal! to join the Irish Citizen Army, that stands to defend the fair and just claims of the workers for opportunities to live honest, upright and cleanly lives."

On Friday, April the 24th, an enthusiastic meeting was held in Finglas, over which Frank Moss presided, and the speakers were M. O. Maolain, J. Magowan and S. O Cathasaigh. So in spite of many difficulties the Irish Citizen Army was making steady progress, and companies now had been formed and were actively drilling in Clondalkin, Lucan, Swords, Finglas, Coolock, Kinsealy and Baldoyle. The Irish Citizen Army had been officially recognised and approved of by the Trades Council on the 6th of April, 1914, and the delegates present gave a very warm welcome to the earnest appeal for

their support and co-operation made by the Countess Markievicz and Richard Brannigan on behalf of the objects and aims
of the Citizen Army.

Difficulty followed difficulty, but still the Army Council
refused to realise that anything could permanently withstand
the onward march of the army. The Council had to fight the
vindictive hostility of the puffed-up employers, who had succeeded in plucking many useful feathers from the growing wing
of Labour; they had to regard the silent but relentless antipathy of the officials of the National Volunteers; they had to
consider the shattered courage of the Dublin workers that created a condition of secret determination never to be openly
identified with Liberty Hall; and, last of all, they had to passively
submit to the irritating indifference of the Transport Union
officials to the work that needed the help of every available
man. P. T. Daly spoke at many meetings, but, with the one
exception of Councillor Partridge, no other official of the
Transport Union or of the Labour movement in Dublin, stirred
a hand in the development of an organisation which they all
sincerely, we feel sure, hoped to see the pioneer guard of the
militant Irish Labour movement.

Many a time members were prompted by the feelings of
hopeless endeavour to take their hands away from a heavy
plough that seemed to be ever ploughing the sand.

Chapter IV

The Quarrel With the National Volunteers

> *Plantagenet:* The truth appears so naked on my side
>   That any purblind eye may find it out.
> *Somerset:*   And on my side it is so well apparell'd,
>   So clear, so shining and so evident
>   That it will glimmer through a blind man's eye.
>
> *1 King Henry the Sixth* (II, iv)

A sharp, definite and lasting antagonism was born during the night on which the National Volunteers were established between the official controlling power of that body and the Labour movement in general.

Some of the most prominent speakers at the initial meeting, held in the Rotunda Rink, Dublin, on Tuesday, November the 25th, had been, and indeed were then, intimately associated with the effort to smash the Labour movement, and violent opposition was manifested by a large section of the audience towards these as they were advocating the reasons for Irishmen to unite in the Volunteers for the maintenance of the "Liberties and Rights common to all Irishmen."

It was generally concluded at the time that this disturbance was deliberately organised by the Irish Citizen Army, but the facts are that the army or its officials had nothing whatever to do with the occurrence, nor did any of its officers ever suggest that such an action would meet with their tacit consent or definite approval.

Efforts were made frequently by Captain White and by the Secretary to promote co-operation in the use of halls for drilling purposes, but no concession whatever in this respect would be granted by the Volunteers to the Citizen Army. Their original manifesto had been signed by members of the Hibernian organisation and by a member of the United Irish League, two movements that were bitterly and implacably opposed to the interests of Labour. Every political movement had received an invitation to attend the preliminary meeting, while Labour was silently ignored. In *Irish Freedom* every political body was welcomed into the National Volunteers, but no mention was made of the workers' organisations.

At a meeting held in Navan Mr. John MacNeill had announced that the National Volunteers would be under the control of the Irish Parliament, which Mr. Redmond had declared would be subservient to the English Imperial Parliament, and these incidents and declarations filled the mind of Irish Labour with so much mistrust and suspicion that definite and organised hostility began to be displayed by the Irish Citizen Army towards the efforts of the National Volunteers to induce the Irish workers to join its ranks. A vigorous discussion was carried on in the *Worker* by Seumas Mac Gabhan, a well-known Sligo Volunteer, and the Secretary of the Citizen Army. An effort was made by the Volunteers to form a company in Swords, a stronghold of the Irish Transport Union, but the meeting, which was kept secret till the last moment, was attended by officers of the Irish Citizen Army, who proceeded to Swords by car, and a strong company of the latter organisation was formed from those workers who had gathered together to hear the speakers sent to Swords by the Executive of the National Volunteers.

The Volunteers were asked if John MacNeill's statement was true; to declare if they stood for Home Rule, the principles of Grattan's Parliament, or an Irish Republic; to give in their Constitution a declaration in favour of the Rights of Man as well as the Rights of Ireland, as the United Irishmen did; and to refuse a welcome to those who attempted to prevent the workers from asserting their elemental right to join the Union of their choice.

At the suggestion of Jim Larkin, the Secretary of the Citizen Army sent to the Secretary of the Irish National Volunteers the following challenge:

TO THE PROVISIONAL EXECUTIVE OF THE IRISH NATIONAL VOLUNTEERS:

Whereas, the Provisional Executive of the Irish National Volunteers have claimed from public platforms and in the Press the support of the Irish workers; and, whereas, the rank and file of the movement are almost wholly composed of members of the working class; and

Whereas, the conviction is growing stronger in Labour circles, owing to the ambiguous principles of the Volunteers' Constitution, and the class basis of the Provisional Executive, and the Ladies' Auxiliary Committee, and the strong elements co-operating with the movement, which have been consistently antagonistic to the lawful claims of Labour:

We the members of the Council of the Irish Citizen Army, representative of Organised Labour, now challenge the Executive of the Irish National Volunteers to public debate in which to justify their appeal for the sympathy and support of the Irish working class.

Details of debate to be arranged by three members of the Volunteers' Executive and three members of the Council of the Irish Citizen Army.

(Signed) SEAN O CATHASAIGH,
Hon. Sec., Irish Citizen Army

The following reply, written in Irish, was received from Mr. John MacNeill:

19 HERBERT PARK, DUBLIN

DEAR SIR,—I received your letter last night at the Volunteers' Headquarters, and I gather from its contents that you think that there is a distinction being made by the Volunteer

Executive between the noble and the obscure, the rich and the poor, and that you wish to discuss the matter in public debate.

I am ignorant of the existence of such a distinction. I never heard much or little of it till I read your letter. It is impossible for me to enter into a discussion upon a matter about which I know nothing.

Sincerely yours,
EOIN MacNEILL

THE SECRETARY, IRISH CITIZEN ARMY

This letter was succeeded by a reply subsequently received from Mr. Gogan, Assistant Secretary to the Irish National Volunteers, which ran as follows:

THE IRISH VOLUNTEERS
206 GREAT BRUNSWICK STREET, DUBLIN
May, 1914

DEAR SIR,—With reference to your challenge to public debate, the Provisional Committee regret to say that they cannot see their way to participate.

Fraternally yours,
THE HON. SECRETARIES
(Per L. G. GOGAN, *Assist. Sec.*)

THE SECRETARY, IRISH CITIZEN ARMY

The following comment on these letters appeared in an issue of the *Irish Worker* dated June 13th, 1914:

We venture to draw the attention of the readers of the *Worker* to the fact that the challenge was first answered by Mr. MacNeill himself without consulting his Executive—a singular action—and also that the subsequent letter from the Assistant Secretary includes the rejection of the suggestion of a conference between the members of each committee to discuss the whole question. Is it any wonder that Labour

looks dubiously upon a movement which is afraid or unwilling to give an answer for the hope that is in it? These
replies are eloquent testimonies to the workers that the
National Volunteers' attachment to Democracy is built upon
foundations of hay and straw and stubble.

It is singular to relate that notwithstanding the acute feelings of antipathy that existed between the official elements in the
Volunteers and Labour, the cordial relations between the rank
and file of both organisations remained warm and apparent. It
was a pleasure, when the Citizen Army accidentally encountered
a body of Volunteers on the march, to see how eager both were
to do honour to each other in an earnest and brotherly salute.

It was also strange that the Labour Leaders were always
enthusiastically received everywhere, though their speeches were
usually punctuated with sharp and penetrating criticisms of the
Volunteer movement.

At a meeting held in Bray, on April the 15th, 1914, outside
of the Town Hall, which had been let to the Volunteers to hold
an organising meeting, but which was refused to the Citizen
Army, though its use had been sought for the same purpose, the
greater part of the audience consisted of members of the Volunteer movement. Yet Jim Larkin and Captain White got a rousing
reception, and Larkin's impassioned appeal to all to follow the
principles of Wolfe Tone and John Mitchel, in spite of the backboneless Volunteer Executive, was received with a loud and an
earnest cheer. Jim advised all the workers to identify themselves
with the Citizen Army, and reminded them that to suffer for
Ireland and for humanity was to enter into a brighter and fuller
heritage.

The antagonism of the official element in the National
Volunteers was painfully demonstrated by the following an-
nouncement which appeared in the *Irish Worker* from the
Labour Day Committee, May, 1914:

Judging by the number of delegates present at last meeting, the celebration of Labour Day this year promises to eclipse anything held in recent years, notwithstanding the fact that the National Volunteers have organised an opposition demonstration for the same day.

One day while the Secretary was preparing an agenda for a Council meeting, a messenger arrived who told him Captain White was very eager to speak with him on the telephone. The Secretary answered the call and was astonished to hear Captain White say that he had received an astonishing letter from Mr. MacNeill; he went on to tell the Secretary to summon a Council meeting at once, "for," said he, "the Lord has delivered John MacNeill into our hands." It was explained at the Council meeting held that night that Captain White offered the Volunteer Executive two companies of fully uniformed and equipped men, if the Executive would allow them to remain an independent though affiliated body. This offer, with which the Citizen Army Council had nothing to do, and about which they knew nothing at the time, was made subsequent to the celebrated encounter which Captain White had with the police while leading a few hungry men to the Mansion House with a view of protesting against the organised attempt to intensify unemployment in Dublin, that the men might continue to suffer for their temerity in resisting the tyranny of the employers. The letter which was sent by Mr. MacNeill, and which was read to the Council, rejected the Captain's offer, and explained that the National Volunteers could have no association with an organisation that had recently been in conflict with the police. Several members urged that this letter should be immediately published, but it was finally decided that, as the Citizen Army had no intention of amalgamating with the Volunteers, the wiser course to adopt was to pass the incident over.

P

Looking over past events now in the calm of new thought, it is painful to reflect upon a division that perhaps could not have been avoided but might indeed have been less bitter. The men in the National movement who understood and sympathised with Labour might have been more tolerant, and probably would have been so had those in the Labour movement who understood National Ideals been more forbearing.

During the whole controversy Captain White and Countess Markievicz separated themselves from and frequently opposed the antagonism displayed towards the National Volunteers. And it is most probable had any indication been given by the Executive of the Irish National Volunteers to promote an amicable understanding between two bodies who had so much natural affinity with each other, that the influence of these two Leaders of the Citizen Army Council would have evolved a working basis of genuine and useful unity between the two organisations, with results that would have materially benefited and strengthened the objects for which both were ostensibly and actually working.

But there was one man whose voice was seldom heard, whose personality was little known in the Labour movement, but who was almost worshipped in the National camp, that silently but effectually opposed any corporate union between militant Nationalism and Labour. It was only when the star of this genius began to fade, which happened after his attempt to hand over the National Volunteers to the guidance of the Parliamentary Party, that a definite spirit of evident comradeship began to manifest itself between the Volunteers and the Irish Citizen Army. This man's persistent attitude towards Labour was the attitude of the witches towards the intrusion of Faust and Mephistopheles:

"Who are ye? What would ye here? Who hath come slinking in? The plague of fire into your bones!"

This man was Bulmer Hobson, whose warmest appreciation of all things appertaining to Labour was a sneer, and whose influence, which was powerful and potent, even with those whose sympathies were undoubtedly with the working-class, was always directed towards the prevention of an understanding between the forces of Labour and the militant power of young-hearted Nationalism.

But during all this unfortunate strife the Citizen Army was painfully developing its strength, adding to its members slowly, but surely, till, at a meeting of the Army Council, it was at last announced that the roll-book showed that the Citizen Army in the City and County of Dublin numbered a thousand men.

Chapter V

Pilgrimage to Bodenstown, 1914

Oh! sweet 'tis to think that such faith can remain
To the Cause and the Man so long vanquished and slain.

DAVIS

On June the 26th, 1914, a pilgrimage was made to Bodenstown, under the auspices of the Wolfe Tone Memorial Committee, and the Citizen Army Council decided to participate. Vigorous preparations were accordingly made for a full muster of members, for we all knew that Jim Larkin had expressed his determination to visit the grave of Theobald Wolfe Tone. The Secretary visited the Wolfe Tone Committee to procure tickets; and though some of the Wolfe Tone Executive doubted the wisdom of encouraging the Citizen Army to participate, because of the differences between them and the Volunteers, who were to attend in full strength, the Chairman, Mr. T. Clarke, warmly welcomed the suggestion, and personally undertook to be responsible to the Wolfe Tone Executive for the good and earnest intentions of the Irish Citizen Army.

On the Saturday previous to the day on which the pilgrimage was to be held, the President of No. 1 Branch of the Transport Union came to the room where the members of the army were assembled, and appealed to them to abandon the enterprise, as it was essential that every available man should be present at the general meeting which was to be held the following day in Croydon Park to consider the resignation of Jim Larkin from the position of General Secretary to the Transport Union.

A messenger was hastily despatched to discover if Jim was determined to carry out his intention of accompanying the pilgrimage to Bodenstown, and upon an answer in the affirmative being brought back by the messenger, upwards of two hundred men declared that they would accompany their chief. The first and second companies, headed by the Fintan Lalor Pipers' band, marched from Liberty Hall to Kingsbridge, and were met there by Jim and his eldest son, Seumas. The members were at first somewhat diffident as to the reception that would be extended to them, but their doubts in this respect were shortly set at rest by the kind and cordial welcome given to them by Tom Clarke, who appointed a special orderly to look after the Citizen Army, secure particular carriages for the members, and provide a special apartment for Jim and the members of the Army Council. The march to Bodenstown was a memorable one; large crowds lined the narrow streets of Sallins, and Jim Larkin, "the great Labour Leader," was the observed of all. The march past, in a field contiguous to Bodenstown graveyard, was an impressive spectacle, and certainly, without expressing any undue partiality, the members of the Irish Citizen Army, in appearance and in technical movements, left little to be desired.

At a subsequent meeting, held around the grave, it was gratifying to see that the committee in charge made every possible effort to give equal honour to all. The Fianna formed an inner ring around the grave, and the outer ring was formed by alternate members of the Volunteers and units of the Irish Citizen Army.

On the return journey a desperate attempt was made in Sallins by a great crowd of villagers who had assembled together to induce Jim to deliver a speech, but this he refused to do, because, as he said, he was the guest of the Wolfe Tone Memorial Committee, and all arrangements were in their hands, and he could not possibly allow himself to interfere with the arrangements that had probably been made weeks before the date fixed for the Pilgrimage.

It was a journey never to be forgotten, for it heralded the possibility of a closer unity and a fuller understanding between the Irish Citizen Army and the National Volunteers.

It was the first time they had stood side by side, the first time they had received and taken orders from a common commander, and this drawing together was possibly a symbol of a union that would be finally cemented together with the blood of both organisations.

From the issue of the *Irish Worker* succeeding the Pilgrimage, the following extract from an article that appeared in that journal is taken:

At the meeting, held in a field contiguous to the graveyard of Bodenstown, we were advised to regard the points of agreement between different sections of Irishmen rather than the points of difference between them.

We venture to suggest that the Republicans should act upon their own counsel and take into consideration the points of agreement between themselves and the workers' organisations. If they took time to consider this over, they would discover that all workers are, through the force of necessity, potential rebels. Wolfe Tone held no foolish hopes of the union of all classes. He hated the aristocracy and thoroughly despised the propertied class and the merchants. He saw that these served only their own interests, and looked with affection, not upon Ireland, but on the stake they had in the country and the business they carried on in Ireland. He passed by the members of the Ascendancy Church, and linked up the oppressed Catholics with the equally oppressed Presbyterians. This union created the Society of United Irishmen.

To-day the only possible union that Republicans can hope for is a union between themselves and the workers, whose principles are practically identical with their own.

It seemed that the fraternal association of Citizen Army soldiers and Volunteers around the grave at Bodenstown had started in the breasts of both organisations a desire for closer communion in thought, principle and action.

Chapter VI

The Social Side of the Army

Wi' merry songs and friendly cracks,
I wat they did na weary;
An' unco' tales an' funny jokes,
Their sports were cheap an' cheery.

ROBERT BURNS

The daily and nightly routine of the Citizen Army was sensibly relieved by many merry events which lightened the dull gloom of monotonous organisation. In a great marquee which had been erected in Croydon Park during the summer months, every Sunday evening, popular concerts were held, at which the members of the army, their sweethearts, friends and relatives held high revel. Dancing, singing and piping kept the night perpetually young, and, after a hard week's work of drilling, parading, and routine duties, these gatherings were a welcome change, when discipline was relaxed, and the officers remembered they were human and joined hilariously in the fun and frolic of the moment.

Jim Larkin was the life and soul of these gatherings, and frequently the audience would imperiously demand "a song from Jim," who, after some coaxing, would, like the shy boy he sometimes was, sing in a hoarse, tremulous voice, amid a tense and reverent silence, the "Red Flag" or "The Risin' o' the Moon." And the deafening applause, that would make the stained flaps of the marquee shake with terror after the song had terminated, would have gladdened the heart of even Caruso.

During this time Jim Connolly was busy writing Labour Songs, and "Freedom's Pioneers," "The Call of Eireann," and "The Watchword of Labour" shortly became favourite melodies during the many route-marches of the Army.

Many striking and original festivals were held in the beautiful grounds of Croydon Park. Features were introduced into these that were never seen before in Irish-Ireland Aeridheachteanna. The first event held was an astonishing and most embarrassing success. It had been splendidly advertised, and the crowds attending were so enormous that most of the items on the programme had to be abandoned, and it was only by the kind and herculean efforts of Messrs. Burke and Harty, of the Gaelic Athletic Association, that the committee succeeded in running the five miles Marathon race, which event provoked the wildest enthusiasm of the onlookers. It was amusing and humanly tragic to watch the despairing efforts of the stewards to evolve order out of hopeless and irremediable chaos. Everybody was looking for everybody else; no systematic communication could be kept up between different workers, for between each was always a dense, surging and impassable crowd. Bands played, artistes sang, and children danced desperately at the same moment. Jim Larkin hurried frantically about from place to place, threatening the stewards that if they did not do something he would send the people home; and the gallant Countess Markievicz tried frequently to be in ten places at the one time. By superhuman efforts the "Citizen Army's Attack on a Cowboy Stockade" was carried through, and this spectacular event, with the advancing army taking cover and firing as they advanced, the little stockade fringed by swaying trees, from which came sharp and savage fusillades, the closing in on the defenders, and their ultimate capture from the midst of the blazing stockade was a scene that was rapturously acclaimed, and well repaid the disordered tedium of the early evening; and when the Park was emptied of its huge assembly, tired stewards crept towards Croydon Park House, and in the deepening shadows began to count the gains of the day, ever and anon ejaculating, "Thanks be with God that it's all over!"

During the summer Croydon Park was used by groups of the workers as a night camp, and this practice gave to the army life a realistic emotion that was pleasurable to many natures. The rank and file slept in the huge marquee, beside which were pitched two small tents, one for the Commandant, Jim Larkin, and the other for the use of the Council officers that elected to spend the week-end in that way.

Each member was charged a shilling, and for this on Sunday morning he received at 6 a.m. a substantial bowl of milk and porridge, to be followed at eight by a satisfying breakfast of bacon, eggs, butter and tea.

Though situated well within the boundaries of the city, Croydon Park was singularly pastoral and peaceful. Here indeed one could rest at ease "far from the madding crowd's ignoble strife," and its restful influence had a powerful potency for good in bringing the workers closer to the warm, beautiful, pulsing heart of Nature.

It was beautiful to sit at the door of one of the tents on a camp stool, and dreamily survey the surrounding scene: The fading May-blossoms, the petals of which strewed the grass like confetti on the shimmering wedding garments of Summer. The tarnished gold of a laburnum tree, that gleamed redly in the rays of the declining sun. The tall chestnut trees whose waxy blooms, like fat and fairy candles, now "'gan to pale their diminished fires," and to view, here and there, beneath the sheltering arms of the lusty hedge, the ruby saucer-like blooms of the scarlet poppies as yet untouched by the childish vandals of the Irish Transport Union.

The surrounding trees were swaying clumps of melody which sprang from the swelling throats of numerous finches and linnets, and, sometimes, one was forced to ask the question, was all the strife with which man's life was coloured a shining light or a gloomy shade?

At times the stillness would be so strange that one would wonder if it were not death to again associate with man's noisy, selfish effort to explain and manifest human existence.

Ah, this book of Nature is the best Bible from which to learn charity towards all men and love towards all things.

> Now fades the glimmering landscape on the sight,
> And all the air a solemn stillness holds,
> Save where the beetle wheels his droning flight,
> And drowsy tinklings lull the distant folds.

Here, with one's head in the bosom of Nature, to what a small compass shrinks even the Constitution of the Irish Citizen Army! How horrible is a glistening, oily rifle to one of the tiny daisies, that cowers in a rosy sleep at my very feet, happy in itself, and giving to the world to which it has been born the fullest beauty and fragrance that its simple nature has to give.

And then rings out with exasperating shrillness, the bugle-call declaring that it is time to retire, and as discipline is very strict in the night-camp, and the officer of the watch will shortly go his rounds to see that all is well, we leave the presence of the still redly-tinted sky, and withdraw to our tent, stretch ourselves upon the stretcher-bed, pull the blankets over our bodies, and try to go to sleep—to sleep—perchance to dream, and to wait till the loud notes of the Reveille wake us up at six o'clock on Sunday morning to make ready for the morning church-parade.

Chapter VII

Some General Events

For in and out, above, about, below,
'Tis nothing but a magic shadow's show,
Play'd in a box, whose candle is the sun,
Around which we phantom figures come and go!

OMAR KHAYYAM

For some time Captain White had expressed dissatisfaction with the members attending the various parades, and finally signified his intention of resigning if conditions were not improved. But the difficulties surrounding the assemblies of the Citizen Army were so great, owing to the singular hours of the men's employment, that no appreciable improvement could be maintained, and in 1914 Captain White definitely severed his connection with the Citizen Army, and Jim Larkin was elected to the vacant position.

It is only fair to say that a quiet reflection of past events convinces the writer that Captain White did not obtain the ready and affectionate co-operation his nature craved for.

His efforts to understand the mysterious natures of working-men were earnest and constant, and were never fully appreciated by those amongst whom he spent his time and a good deal of his money.

But we feel sure that he will never be forgotten by those who knew him and worked by his side for many months.

He was a gentleman according, as Mitchel says, "to the British State and Constitution," but he was also a gentleman according to the kindly and benevolent law of Nature, and those who sat with him on the Council, and differed from him most, now wish to express their sincere affection for one who honestly and unselfishly endeavoured to use his gifts, natural and acquired, to lift the workers to a higher plane of usefulness and comfort.

Event succeeded event in the progress of the Citizen Army. The banner, the idea of which was given by a sympathiser, and executed by Mr. McGahey, was generally admired, and its symbolic design of the Plough and the Stars was indeed strikingly original. The tallest man in the army was selected as banner-bearer, and he was always proud of his work, though the carrying of the flag, which was of large dimensions, was no easy task, particularly upon a breezy day.

A rifle-range was erected in Croydon Park, and in the evening Volunteers and members of the Citizen Army vied with each other in trying to demonstrate the peculiar skill of their several organisations. The summer evenings in Croydon Park were peaceful no longer, and as the Park was approached, the cannonade of the terrible Howth guns smote the ear, and formed the impression that the place was the practice ground of batteries of heavy artillery.

In 1914 an elaborate plan had been sketched by Jim

Larkin for the organisation of all Ireland, and he spent some weeks designing a suitable travelling caravan, which was to consist of a living room and two small bedrooms, in which he and a few chosen followers were to tour the country, and to form companies of the Army in every hamlet and village in Ireland. It was a pity that circumstances prevented this scheme from being definitely carried out, for it would have given to the Irish Labour Movement a strength and a cohesion which was sadly needed, and the results would have been tremendously more effective than even those attained by his celebrated "Fiery Cross" campaign throughout England.

For many years to come the Irish people will follow leaders rather than principles, and in Larkin Labour had a leader for whom the Irish rural workers were waiting.

But the proposed scheme never materialised, and the Labour Movement and the Citizen Army were left to flourish as best they could in the industrial districts and the rural parts of county Dublin.

The divided difference in Ideal still flowed freely between the Volunteers and the Citizen Army, though on many occasions fraternal minglings testified of the deeper mutual understanding that existed between the two organisations. The incidents that took place during the celebrated episode of the Howth gun-running[3] had engendered a fellow-feeling between the rank and file of both movements, which was very near akin to comradeship.

At the funeral of the victims that took place in Dublin, subsequent to the unfortunate shooting in Bachelor's Walk,[4] the guards of honour around the funeral corteges were composed of alternate units of members of the Citizen Army and Volunteers.

[3] The Irish Volunteers openly landed a cargo of rifles and ammunition at Howth on July 26, and were engaged in skirmishes by police and soldiers at Clontarf.

[4] This shooting occurred on July 26, when a contingent of Scottish Borderers shot into a crowd, wounding thirty-two civilians and killing three.

Chapter VIII

Marking Time

In such a time as this it is not meet
That every nice offence should bear his comment.

Julius Caesar (IV, iii)

By their action in surrendering to the demand of the
Parliamentary Party for the inclusion of a large number of
nominees upon their Provisional Executive, the Volunteers made
the cleavage of principle between themselves and the Citizen
Army deeper than ever. By this inexplicable action the last link of
tacit sympathy and union was broken. Whatever hope Labour
had of the evolution of a progressive policy from the Volunteer
movement was now utterly abandoned, and the Citizen Army
was forced in defence of the aims of militant Labour to become
more antagonistic in thought and action towards the Volunteers
than ever before.

Trenchant articles denouncing the compact appeared in
the Labour Press from the pen of Jim Larkin, and biting car-
toons illustrative of the situation were drawn and published by
"E. K." pictorially ridiculing the union of opposite forces. All
hope of an eventual junction between the Citizen Army and the
Volunteers was shattered, and, day by day, it became increas-
ingly evident that in aim and objects the two forces were marching towards opposite poles. The National Volunteers, through
the action of their Executive, had definitely joined hands with
Labour's bitterest enemies, and Labour's only attitude could be
one of bitter suspicion and militant opposition towards the
results that were expected from the new amalgamation.

But the new situation which had so unexpectedly been
created caused a division in the Council of the Irish Citizen Army
itself.

A special meeting of the Council was summoned by the Secretary to discuss the possibility of members of the Council being allowed to continue an active and sympathetic connection with the Volunteer Movement. This thrust was aimed purposely at the Countess Markievicz, whom the Secretary knew to be actively sympathetic with the Volunteers, and to hold an official position on the Committee of one of the branches of Cumann na mBan, the women's auxiliary movement, to advance the cause of the Volunteers. The Council assembled, and there were present: Countess Markievicz, Richard Brannigan, S. Rogan, J. Fitzpatrick, P. O'Brien, J. O'Leary, T. Blair, T. Healy, P. J. Fox, J. McGowan, H. Broderick, T. Foran, M. Mullen, Sean Shelly, who presided, and the Secretary, S. O Cathasaigh.

The following was the motion moved by the Honorary Secretary:

> Seeing that Madame Markievicz, was, through Cumann na mBan, attached to the Volunteers, and on intimate terms with many of the Volunteer leaders, and as the Volunteers' Association was, in its methods and aims, inimical to the first interests of Labour, it could not be expected that Madame could retain the confidence of the Council; and that she be now asked to sever her connection with either the Volunteers or the Irish Citizen Army.

The Secretary briefly pointed out the reasons he had for bringing forward the resolution, and remarked that he felt it was the most honest course to pursue, to state frankly to the Council and to Madame Markievicz the thoughts that filled his mind respecting her connection with an association with which the Irish Citizen Army differed so widely.

The resolution was vigorously opposed by Messrs. Fox, Foran, Brannigan, Broderick and Rogan, and, after a warm discussion, a vote of confidence in the Countess was proposed by H. Broderick, seconded by P. J. Fox, and carried by seven votes to six.

It was then moved that the Secretary be called upon to tender an apology to Countess Markievicz, and to this the meeting apparently agreed.

The Secretary said he could not apologise for saying what he believed to be the truth, and wrote out his resignation, which was accepted at a Council meeting held a few days following.

The Commandant, Jim Larkin, was anxious to avoid all appearances of disunion, and he called a general meeting of members to consider the whole question, which meeting was held in the Concert Room, Liberty Hall, which was filled with the members of the Army.

Jim explained the whole circumstances of the attack made upon the Countess, and sincerely deprecated it. He appealed to the Secretary to withdraw anything he had said, and allow everything in the army to proceed smoothly without friction or unnecessary contention.

The Secretary briefly said he was sorry he could not do as Jim suggested, and that his decision was definite and final.

After some warm remonstrance on the part of the Commandant towards those whom he said evidently lacked the broadmindedness one would expect from them, the meeting harmoniously concluded by all of those present, excepting two members, taking the pledge to only serve and obey in a military capacity the officers of an Irish Republic.

Chapter IX

Some Incidents, and Larkin's Departure

Slan as ceud on dtaoibh seo uaim,
Cois Maige na gcaor, na gcraobh, na gcruach,
Na staid, na seud, na saor, na sluagh,
Na ndan, na ndreacha,[5] na dtreun gan gruaim![6]

MaGrath

Events began to follow each other in rapid succession. The
Citizen Army was watching anxiously the trend of revolutionary thought in the ranks of the Volunteers, and were delighted
when the facts became known that the Provisional Committee
were returning to first principles, and had overthrown their
original acceptance of nomination to the Committee, and had
determined to submit the election of the governing Executive
to a democratically-elected Convention, which it was proposed
to hold in the near future.

The Irish Citizen Army had undergone a great change in
the personnel of its Army Council, which now had a new Secretary, J. Connolly, and afterwards Sean Shelly, Michael Mallon,
W. Halpin and M. Nolan were included on the Executive, and
all the members were mentally disturbed by the rumours that
were gathering fast about the contemplated departure of their
Commandant, Jim Larkin, for America.

On Saturday, October the 10th, a stop press edition of
The Worker announced that the Parnell anniversary would be
observed by the Volunteers the following day, and a procession
would take place to Glasnevin, after which a public meeting
would be held in Parnell Square.

[5] A misprint in the original text. The word should be "ndréacht."
[6] A hundred farewells to you beside the fruitful Maigue,
Whose banks are berry-laden, wooded, rich in corn,
Home of steeds, of workers skilled in gems, and in conclave
Poets sing to happy heroes stalwart-born!

Burning interest was manifested by the workers and the Citizen Army in this event, for it became generally known that Jim Larkin had received an invitation to speak at the meeting. This was something unprecedented in the history of the National and Labour Movement in Ireland. That the leaders of the National Movement should not only allow, but actually invite, the Labour Leader to participate in a meeting organised by them opened up a possibility of definite unity and progress undreamt of a few short months before. The Citizen Army jubilantly hailed this overture as a certain indication of a desire on the part of the Volunteers to recognise the aims and aspirations of the Irish working class.

There is still a good deal of mystery surrounding this invitation. Whence it came no one seemed to know. It was afterwards generally believed that Jim, through perhaps a natural misunderstanding, took a general invitation to Labour to participate for a particular invitation to himself to speak at the meeting on behalf of the Citizen Army and the Labour Movement generally.

Some thought that the invitation was purposely issued by the more militant section of the Irish Volunteer Executive with a view of fixing an unbreakable bond on militant Nationalism and Labour.

That Jim Larkin received some kind of an invitation is certain, and that he mistook the full tenour of its meaning is very probable.

However, when the meeting was opened in Parnell Square, under the chairmanship of Mr. John MacNeill, it became clearly evident, when the Labour Leader approached the platform, that his presence was undesirable.

A most unhappy and embarrassing situation was immediately created, for an open and irremediable rupture between Labour and Nationalism was at once threatened. This unfor-

Q

tunate assurance was, happily, averted by the prompt and
determined action of Tom Clarke and Sean MacDermott, who
took measures to hold an independent meeting themselves, at
which Jim Larkin and other Labour leaders spoke.

During the course of the meeting an exciting incident
occurred which for a time threatened to have a tragic ending.
A strong contingent of National Volunteers, returning from the
march to Glasnevin, attempted to break through the crowd
surrounding the speakers, and, by Jim Larkin's orders, the
members of the Citizen Army deployed across the road and prepared to resist the attempt. These were shortly after joined by
a strong force of Irish Volunteers under the command of Captains Monteith and Fahy, and for more than half an hour it
seemed inevitable that a serious collision would take place between the united forces of the Volunteer and Citizen Army and
the National Volunteers, who appeared for a time to be determined to force an issue.

Fortunately wiser counsels prevailed, and the National
Volunteers faced right about and marched away in the opposite
direction, followed by a cheer from the opposing party, which
was instantly suppressed by the various officers, who deprecated
strongly any indication of triumph at the discomfiture of
brother Irishmen.

This day was memorable for the fact that it was the first
time that the Irish Citizen Army and the Irish Volunteers had
officially united in action and had unmistakably demonstrated
the affinity of thought and ideal that existed between the two
organisations.

A short time after these exciting incidents happened, the
time came for Jim Larkin to say farewell to the Citizen Army
and to Ireland, to undertake a tour in America for the purpose,
as he declared himself, of benefiting the Union of which he was

Secretary, and to explain to American Labour the aims and aspirations of the Irish Proletariat.

In the *Irish Worker* of October the 24th, 1914, appeared Jim Larkin's farewell message to the members of the Citizen Army:

> To My Comrades of the Irish Citizen Army:
>
> In my absence Jim Connolly will take command. Bear yourselves before all men according to your past.
>
> Remember your constitution and your oath—Ireland first, last, and all the time. Sobriety, unquestioned obedience, and keenness for drill be your motto.

And then this fiery human comet passed from the orbit of Irish life, to be attracted back again by the power of its heat—when? Ah! who can say?

Chapter X

Jim Connolly Assumes the Leadership

> My country claims me all, claims every passion;
> Her liberty henceforth be all my thought!
> Though with a brother's life yet cheaply-bought;
> For her my own I'd willingly resign,
> And say, with transport, that the gain was mine.
>
> Martyn

Under Jim Connolly's leadership an appreciable change began to appear in the attitude of the Citizen Army Council towards the Volunteers. The attitude of passive sympathy began to be gradually replaced by an attitude of active unity and co-operation. In their break-away from the control of the Parliamentarian Party the Volunteers had built a bridge over the stream of thought that separated the two forces from each other, and speculation became common as to whether the Volunteers would absorb the Citizen Army or that body's influence would sway the councils of the Volunteers. Jim Connolly had never associated himself with any of the attacks made upon the Volunteers during their earlier history—indeed, whenever he had previously interested himself in the affairs of the Citizen Army, which was seldom, his influence had been invariably exerted to moderate the mutual hostility that smouldered, and occasionally flamed, into passionate recriminations—and, consequently, the relations between him and the militant members of the Volunteer Council soon became cordial. It is difficult to understand the almost revolutionary change that was manifesting itself in Connolly's nature. The Labour movement seemed to be regarded by him as a decrescent force, while the essence of Nationalism began to assume the finest elements of his nature. His articles that now appeared in the *Workers' Republic* with consistent regularity, the speeches that he delivered at various demonstrations and assemblies, all proclaimed that Jim Connolly had stepped from the narrow byway of Irish Socialism on to the broad and crowded highway of Irish Nationalism. The vision of the suffering world's humanity was shadowed by the nearer oppression of his own people, and in a few brief months pressed into a hidden corner of his soul the accumulated thoughts of a lifetime and opened his broad heart to ideas that altered the entire trend of his being. The high creed of Irish Nationalism became his daily rosary, while the higher creed of international humanity that had so long bubbled from his eloquent lips was silent for ever, and Irish Labour lost a Leader.

A well-known author has declared that Connolly was the first martyr for Irish Socialism; but Connolly was no more an Irish Socialist martyr than Robert Emmet, P. H. Pearse, or Theobald Wolfe Tone.

But as this little work is intended to be historical rather

than critical, we must take up again the simple and concise narration of the facts as they occurred.

The Constitution of the Irish Volunteers was radically altered on Sunday, October 25th, 1914, at the first Convention held by that organisation in the Abbey Theatre, Dublin. The Convention was called after the original Provisional Executive had definitely repudiated the government of the nominees which Mr. J. E. Redmond had selected to ensure that the Irish Volunteer movement would be always subsidiary to the Constitutional agitation carried on by the Parliamentary Party in favour of self-government for Ireland. The Volunteer movement had been riven in sunder and two distinct branches now called upon the people of Ireland for support and allegiance: the National Volunteers under the patronage of the Parliamentarians, and the Irish Volunteers under the government of the original Executive Committee.

Force of circumstances compelled the Irish Volunteers and the Citizen Army to link forces together on many occasions. Their sympathies at least became identical in hostility to everything connected with the Parliamentarian Party. The members of the two movements began to fraternise together, and on the day of the Convention the members of the Citizen Army helped to line the roads leading to the Abbey Theatre, in which the Volunteer Convention was held, and gave many indications of their feeling of exultation at the formation of a Volunteer Association which had been largely purged of what they considered to be reactionary elements, and which had formulated a Constitution which evoked their sympathies and commanded their support. To all that carefully reflected upon passing events it was apparent that the Citizen Army was really becoming the militant Left Wing of the Irish Volunteers.

Referring to the Convention, the *Irish Worker,* October 31st, 1914, said: "We congratulate the Volunteers on the success they have achieved. It is a significant sign, and should give Irishmen here at home reason to pause to see Volunteer delegates from London, Glasgow and Liverpool taking part in the proceedings and standing side by side with the true men in the movement. They have not forgotten the hellish system which forced them to seek a living in the land of the stranger."

At a great Emmet Anniversary held on Sunday, October the 25th, organised by the Irish Volunteers, the Irish Citizen Army attended in full strength, and the following notice in the *Irish Worker* indicated the desire of the Volunteers to enlist on their side the power and influence of Labour:

IRISH VOLUNTEERS' FIRST ANNUAL CONVENTION
SUNDAY, OCTOBER 25th
GREAT DEMONSTRATION
AND TORCHLIGHT PROCESSION
Around places in this city sacred to the memory of the
United Irishmen and other patriots who died for Ireland.
To be concluded by a
MEETING IN STEPHEN'S GREEN
at which a declaration of the policy adopted by this
Convention will be made.
All Nationalist and Labour Bodies and Bands are invited
to co-operate.
Procession will assemble in Beresford Place at 6:30 prompt.
Mr. Eoin MacNeill will speak.

It became quite obvious now to all that the Irish Volunteers and the Citizen Army were essentially one in ideal, and would eventually be one in action. Things were hurrying towards a bloody climax, but as yet the cloud in the sky was no larger than a man's hand, and no one realised that in a few weeks it would have enveloped the whole of the City of Dublin in smoke and blood and fire.

The drilling of the Volunteers and the Citizen Army daily became more pointed and practical; and in the manoeuvres practised by both organisations, it became apparent that everything possible was being done to prepare their members to make the most of their limited numbers and circumscribed powers.

A further indication of the singular change in Jim Connolly's ideas, and of his determined attachment to the principles enunciated by Sinn Fein and the Irish Volunteers, which were, in many instances, directly contrary to his life-long teaching of Socialism, was the fixing on the frontage of Liberty Hall a scroll on which was written the inscription: "We serve neither King nor Kaiser—but Ireland." His speeches and his writings had long indicated his new trend of thought, and his actions now proclaimed trumpet-tongued that the appeal of Caitlin Ni hUllachain[7]—"If anyone would give me help, he must give me himself, he must give me all"—was in his ears a louder cry than the appeal of the Internationale, which years of contemplative thought had almost written in letters of fire upon his broad and noble soul.

Liberty Hall was now no longer the Headquarters of the Irish Labour movement, but the centre of Irish National disaffection. Activities redoubled; preparations went forward with feverish haste, and the night was made joint labourer with the day. Route marches were organised, and carried out at every conceivable hour with order, and disciplined enthusiasm, and no member of the Citizen Army knew when he retired to bed how long he might be allowed to repose there, for frequent summonses were issued to members to join their units at an hour's notice to go they knew not where, and do they knew not what.

One day everyone entering Liberty Hall was startled to read on the notice-board that that night the Irish Citizen Army was to make an attack upon Dublin Castle, and many a con-

[7]Kathleen ni Houlihan.

jecture was framed as to the seriousness of the purpose indicated on the notice-board. At midnight out marched the Citizen Army under their leaders, through a heavy fog that enveloped the city, the mist-shaded electric street lamps blinking at this body of armed men marching by, like watchful eyes eagerly endeavouring to discover the reason of this unusual and singular sight in the streets of Dublin at such an hour.

But it was only a test, and these practices continued making the members used to sudden calls, and generally preparing them for the heavy struggle that was soon to break the gentle and happy sleepiness of Dublin City.

A definite union had now been formed between the Irish Citizen Army and the Irish Volunteers, and on the Sunday before Easter Day, 1916, an outward and visible sign of the inward union was given by the dramatic hoisting of the Irish Tricolour, of Orange, Green and White, over the most conspicuous part of Liberty Hall.

On the evening of the ceremonial, thousands thronged the square in front of the Hall, and as the ball of bunting flew up the flagstaff, shook itself free on the breeze, and contrasted its lines of Green, White and Orange with a dull grey sky, there was a thunderclap of cheering which proclaimed unmistakably that the union of Labour and Militant Nationalism was a popular one, though many in the assembled crowd merely came to feast their souls on a novel pageant, which event is always a sweet luxury to the uneducated Irish nature.

Labour had laid its precious gift of Independence on the altar of Irish Nationalism, and this display was a sign to the governing classes to at least consider the dumb wish of an aspiring people.

It was followed by fire and bloodshed, and, as the great Englishman, Carlyle, says: "The governors who wait for these to instruct them are surely getting into the fatallest courses—

proving themselves sons of Nox and Chaos, for Insurrection is
a mere announcement of the disease—visible now even to the
Sons of Night . . . the falsehood of it alone will be conquered,
will be abolished as it ought to be; but the truth of it is part of
Nature's own laws, co-operates with the world's eternal tenden-
cies and cannot be conquered."

Chapter XI

The Rising

When the dark world seems all too desperate,
A hopeless, hideous struggle without cease,
When hope is gone what left but seek release
In one mad grapple with the thing you hate;
Flinging all counsel to the whirlwind, send
Defiant challenge to the world; and so
Recklessly facing your triumphant foe,
Pray that some welcome bullet bring the end.

Yours was this grim resolve that nerves the will
When faith and hope are fled beyond recall,
As it was theirs who died at Bunker Hill,
'And those mad boys who held the Roman Wall;
Your dreams, maybe, were madmen's dreams; but still
You gave your lives for them—God rest you all!
W. N. Ewen, "The Five Souls"

From the blue skies was falling a golden curtain of shimmering sunshine, clothing buildings in its filmy cloth of gold,
and veiling their naked ugliness in beauty, or adding a richer
appearance to their classic grace and strength.

It was a day on which to make merry, and crowded streets
proclaimed that the influences of the sun's geniality was making
melody in the hearts of man. Many were climbing joyously onto
the trams to seek in Nature's bosom a place that would hide
them for a few hours "far from the madding crowd's ignoble

strife," while distinct gatherings of people stood by near Nelson Pillar and found happy moments in the contemplation of the passing activities of human life. Curious glances were flung at passing vehicles, burdened with hopeful crews, flashing swiftly by on their way to Fairyhouse Races, and the pulse of human anxiety was scarcely felt besides the quick-beating pulse of human enjoyment.

Now the holiday seekers were disregarded for an additional novelty; the cars for Fairyhouse went speeding by unnoticed, and a semi-lazy but curious concentration of attention was fixed on an approaching body of marching men.

Passengers on the tram cars leisurely approached the sides and looked down on the armed force, and wondered vaguely at the sharp order to halt, as they came in front of the General Post Office. "Those there," said someone, "dressed in the dark-green uniforms, with the slouch hats, are the Citizen Army, and the others in the green-grey are Irish Volunteers."

The curiosity displayed in the proceedings gave place now to bewildered astonishment as the ring of falling glass echoed from the direction of the Post Office. Astonishment was followed by stupefaction as faint echoes of rifle shots penetrated from a distance to where the people were gathered together, and all things were forgotten as the news spread from mouth to mouth that the Volunteers and the Citizen Army were taking Dublin, that a Provisional Government had been established and an Irish Republic proclaimed.

At three o'clock P.M. on Easter Monday the General Post Office was occupied by the united forces, and separate detachments of the Citizen Army were marching on Stephen's Green and on Dublin Castle.

The contingent that took possession of Stephen's Green was in command of Michael Mallon. Countess Markievicz was second in command, and detachments were hastily sent to hold the advanced positions of Harcourt Street Station and Ranelagh Bridge till the Green could be advantageously arranged for occupation by the main body of the Citizen Army. Owing to the fewness of the contingent that operated in this district, it was found to be impossible to take possession of the surrounding buildings, and, consequently, the position became untenable, and it was abandoned on Tuesday morning, the Citizen Army retreating under heavy machine-gun fire to the College of Surgeons, which they immediately fortified as best they could, and where they were reinforced by a detachment of Volunteers from Jacob's biscuit factory.

The company which attacked the Castle was under the command of Shaun Connolly, who was fatally wounded in the *melee*. For hours a bitter struggle raged in the Castle Yard, in Henry and James', Parliament Street, and in the *Mail* offices, during which this little band, contending against hopeless odds, suffered severely, and were finally forced to gradually withdraw to stronger positions nearer the Headquarters of the Republican Army.

On Thursday morning the attack on the Republican Headquarters commenced. Field Artillery had cleared away many of the intervening buildings, and incendiary bombs were dropped in regular order on the roof of the Post Office. Blazing buildings surrounded them on every side. Most of their faces were blood-stained; the skin was chipped from their cheeks by flying fragments of stone and mortar, and occasionally, the bright flame of the burning Post Office would be stabbed by the dark shadow of a falling man. Connolly, who had been wounded twice, was carried, by his orders, from the room that was being used as an hospital to superintend the withdrawal from the front defences, and it became clear that if the little band was not to be buried in the tottering masses of timber and stone, an immediate retreat was inevitable.

On Friday night, between 8:30 and 9:30, the retreat began from the side entrance of the Post Office, into Moore Lane, where a party held a cottage facing Glass Marble Alley, up which, from behind a barricade, a contingent of soldiers were firing rapidly at the passing Volunteers and Citizen Army.

A plan had been determined upon which was to break through the houses in Moore Street towards Parnell Street, in which there was a strong force of soldiers. These were to be attacked and driven back by a picked company of Volunteers, and the main body was then to seize the premises of Williams and Woods, link up with the detachments fighting in North King Street, and beat a fighting retreat towards the north in order to make an effort to arouse the companies of Volunteers and sympathisers, who, it was thought, only waited a definite opportunity to throw in their lot with the Irish Republicans.

It was discovered that, owing to the superiority of the Royal troops, this attack, arranged to take place at dawn, could not possibly succeed, and it was accordingly postponed till the dusk of the evening, so that the element of surprise might, conceivably, make up for the numerical weakness of the Republican attacking force, and orders were given to the men to take such rest as might be possible under the circumstances that surrounded them.

A few hours after rumours were circulated that communications had been commenced with the General Commanding to ascertain the best possible conditions which would be given to the Republican forces should a surrender be decided upon, the rumour being shortly confirmed by an order that no shots should be fired pending the discussion that was then taking place between the leaders of the opposing armies.

At 8:30 on Sáturday night, April the 29th, the men were definitely told that surrender had been decided upon, and Sean MacDermott, his whole frame shaking with emotion, in

the yard of a house in Moore Street, spoke to the silent gathering of dust-covered men, gloomily sharing the half-suppressed
agony of their leader, and told them "that their Republican
Army had surrendered, not because they were beaten, but
because they wanted to save their women and children and their
beloved city of Dublin. They would march out with their arms
through Moore Street, Henry Street, to O'Connell Street, where
they would lay down arms."

In the gathering shadows of a spring evening the small band
of men, who had passed through such a terrible experience,
marched in order of company column to the statue of Parnell,
where, in the centre of O'Connell Street, they deposited their
arms and accoutrements, which step was shortly augmented by
the arms of the different contingents arriving from the various
parts of the city.

Afterword

Iram indeed is gone with all its Rose,
And Jamshyd's Seven-ring'd Cup where no one knows;
But still the Vine her ancient Ruby yields,
And still a Garden by the Water blows.

OMAR KHAYYAM

The breath of Death which had swept over poor Dublin
carried with it the seeds of a new life, which, falling in different
parts of Ireland, began to appear as green blades of new thought
and new activities. The bonfires of Sinn Fein began to blaze on
every Irish hillside, and thousands of the Irish people danced
around the blaze of Sinn Fein, as if they warmed themselves at
the fire of life. Parliamentarianism was a sinking fire, and, now,
not all the united breath of a united party could ever again
succeed in blowing it into an inspiring flame. The new wine of

new thoughts and new activities was everywhere bursting the old bottles, but though the new wine was a Sinn Fein label it certainly has not an absolutely Sinn Fein flavour, for Labour has tinged it with a brighter colour and strengthened it with a stimulating cordial.

In this new wine a lowly life, like a pearl, had been dissolved; a life untarnished by worldly ambition, or selfish perception; a life of mourning struggle and valorous effort sacrificed humbly and fearlessly for the general good; sacrificed under circumstances that stripped the offering of all the impressive draperies of martyrdom. Unwept, except by a few, unhonoured and unsung—for no National Society or Club has gratefully deigned to be called by his name—yet the ideals of Sheehy-Skeffington, like the tiny mustard seed to-day, will possibly grow into a tree that will afford shade and rest to many souls overheated with the stress and toil of barren politics. He was the living antithesis of the Easter Insurrection: a spirit of peace enveloped in the flame and rage and hatred of the contending elements, absolutely free from all its terrifying madness; and yet he was the purified soul of revolt against not only one nation's injustice to another, but he was also the soul of revolt against man's inhumanity to man. And in this blazing pyre of national differences his beautiful nature, as far as this world is concerned, was consumed, leaving behind a hallowed and inspiring memory of the perfect love that casteth out fear, against which there can be no law.

In Sheehy-Skeffington, and not in Connolly, fell the first martyr to Irish Socialism, for he linked Ireland not only with the little nations struggling for self-expression, but with the world's Humanity struggling for a higher life.

He indeed was the ripest ear of corn that fell in Easter Week, and as it is true that when an ear of corn falls into the ground and dies it bringeth forth much fruit, so will the sown body of Sheehy-Skeffington bring forth, ultimately, in the hearts of his beloved people, the rich crop of goodly thoughts which shall strengthen us all in our onward march towards the fuller development of our National and Social Life.

One of the most gratifying and encouraging indications of the broader and kindlier vision of human nature was the earnest sympathy expressed towards the Irish people by many of the leaders of thought among the English people, subsequent to the sad events of Easter Week. Nowhere in England, among the working classes, was manifested that insensate outburst of rage and malice that invariably characterised the attitude of England's workers towards Irish people during previous Irish declarations of revolt towards the English domination. It has certainly demonstrated that even the English workers have been potently influenced by the change of thought that has enwrapped man in a new and better social environment. Sympathy and kindly feeling towards Ireland were manfully expressed in many places in England during this period of sorrow and sacrifice, which ought to convince even the most bigoted of Sinn Feiners of the truth testified to by Boyle O'Reilly and John Mitchel in the fundamental unity of man.

George Lansbury, speaking at a great meeting held in Albert Hall, to commemorate the Russian Revolution, said: "We English people have to clear our own doorstep. I stood here just about three years ago; almost where Williams is sitting sat James Connolly (cheers). He and his dead colleagues of a year ago were just too soon, that is all; and, friends, we British people have got to clear that Irish question up, because until we do it, it is not for us to celebrate other people's triumphs over reaction." And in many English Labour papers the writings of Jim Connolly have been quoted, and his Labour songs published, so that these and many other indications conclusively prove that the mind of the English working class has undergone a revolutionary change, and that "the unbought section of the English Labour movement"—to quote from *Nationality*—is seriously anxious to stretch forth the hand of true comradeship towards their Irish fellow-workers.

We laugh, frequently, at the efforts of English Governments and English journalists to understand us, and our amusement is invariably justified; but let us at least make an effort to acquaint ourselves with the new trend of thought passing like a pillar of illuminating fire over England's workers, that we may know them as they are, before we unjustly and foolishly relegate this all-powerful element in England's political and social life among the irreconcilable enemies of Inisfail.[8]

While the ultimate destiny of Ireland will be in the hands of Labour, it would be foolish to deny that the present is practically in the hands of the Sinn Fein Organisation. Its activities are spreading over the land, and Labour comes halting very much behind. This is explained by two reasons: Sinn Fein is not yet democratic, though Irish; while Labour, though fundamentally democratic, is far from being National. As Parliamentarianism was a poor copy of English Liberalism, so is Irish Labour a poorer reflex of English Trades Unionism. Its boasted Irish characteristics are far from being apparent, and its pretended love for the Irish language is very superficial indeed. It has done nothing to ensure that Irish shall be the language of the future nation; its propaganda literature is practically written from an English point of view, and the Irish Labour leaders are all painfully ignorant of their country's history, language and literature. It is because of these self-evident facts that Sinn Fein possesses a tremendous advantage over the Labour movement. Persecution has deepened our sympathies with our Irish origin, and the Irish Labour leaders, sooner or later, will be forced to realise that they must become Irish if they expect to win the confidence and support of the Irish working-class. Sinn

[8]Ireland.

Fein, too, will have to cope with the greatest of all difficulties
—success. Here now, like tares and wheat, the good and evil
will grow up together. It will roughly be composed of two
classes of thought: those who love themselves so well that they
have none left for Ireland, and those who love Ireland so well
that they have none left for themselves. The first love is selfish;
the second is foolish.

It is from these elements that Labour must build the future
state, democratising the national movement and Irishising itself.
Labour will probably have to fight Sinn Fein—indeed the challenge seems to have been thrown down already—but the Labour
leaders must become wiser and more broadminded than they
at present seem to be; they must remove the beam from their
own eye that they may clearly see to remove the mote from the
eye of Sinn Fein, and then they will find in that organisation
elements that will readily yield to its penetrating forces; then
the leaders of Labour in Ireland will be able to glean grapes
from a tree that hitherto brought forth only wild grapes, because Labour, through the Citizen Army, has broken down the
first trenches of national prejudice, and has left a deep impression on the bloody seal of Irish Republicanism.

R

Stories

O'CASEY has written occasional short stories all his life. Most of them were published in and never resurrected from the pages of various journals. Some of them O'Casey has later incorporated in a play or an autobiography. Four of them he published in *Windfalls* (1934) and republished in *The Green Crow* (1956). He has considered his stories the by-products of his art, but if they were collected they would add up to a substantial and entertaining volume.

Reprinted here are four of his earliest tales. "The Seamless Coat of Kathleen" is a political allegory that satirizes the efforts of various groups to control the Irish Free State in 1922, and that foreshadows the phantasy of "Kathleen Listens In" and of his recent plays. "The Corncrake" is a loose translation of a traditional Irish tale. (O'Casey was later to take an occasional suggestion for a plot in this manner.) But the tone of the story seems entirely O'Casey's; and the comical characters and the wild arguments of Ginger and Lanky are the kind of characters and arguments that inhabit O'Casey's plays from "Nannie's Night Out" to *The Drums of Father Ned*. "Gulls and Bobbin Testers" was suggested by a holiday jaunt with a cousin and her friend to the Hill of Howth. The story is further proof that, regardless of what Irish critics have said, O'Casey was never a literal transcriber of fact. As artist, he performed the function of the artist—to transform fact. The dream phantasy that concludes this story is as magical a transformation as the remarkable third-act dream phantasy of *Red Roses for Me*. O'Casey had always more sympathy for Strindberg's dream plays than for Ibsen's factual realism. "Irish in the Schools" may initially seem more a vehicle for opinion than a story, but it holds its own as story. When it ends we know more than Jack's, and O'Casey's, opinion of the compulsory teaching of Gaelic. We have had dramatised the grinding hopelessness of unrelieved poverty; and the story's concluding sentence is a perfect dying fall to bring home sharply, implicitly, and artistically the miserable futility of the dismal lives of those Dublin workers.

The Seamless Coat of Kathleen,
A Parable of the Ard Fheis

The unity seamless coat of Kathleen has always been a little tight for the colleen. But it has been in the family now for a long time, and tradition has made it sacred. She is not always happy when she discards it, but she is never happy when she is wearing it; its close-fitting tightness hampers the free movements of her body, and the pressure of blood to the head makes original and independent thought impossible.

Indeed, dressed in the coat, her natural activity is so restricted that she can no longer stray along the banks of the Shannon, wander through the wild glen of Imaal, or watch the lashing sea or hear the crashing winds of Connaught shouting their tumultuous song of Liberty.

Neither can she climb, as she sometimes does in mad moments, the perilous slopes of Cave Hill, from which journey she often returned blood-stained and weary, to receive the reproaches of her older and more sensible relatives, and suitable punishment from her anxious and benevolent guardian, who had shaped her mother's destiny in the past, and was now equally anxious to shape the daughter's in the future.

And most sensible children would be satisfied with the well-ordered loveliness of the garden specially arranged for her enjoyment by the confederation of Kilkenny, well fertilized by Castlereagh, strongly walled by the gardening Parliamentary Party who were so eager to preserve the symmetry of the original that, when their head gardener tried to make the view more extensive, they stoned him, and buried him in a deep grave in a place called Glasnevin.

Poor little Kathleen never dons the garment willingly; she has outgrown it, and her vigorous body is always resisting its pressure. But at times all the Irish family think it necessary that she should wear it, and then the whole of them, down to cousins of every degree, seize the unhappy colleen, and, in spite of her struggles, dress her in the cramping coat of Unity.

Occasionally, however, some of her younger relatives become aware of the stifling dangers of the garment to the growing limbs of their sister, and, rebelling against all the traditions of the family, endeavour to help Kathleen in her efforts to become free. Then angry words are exchanged and blows struck; but, usually, the larger part of the family succeeds in yoking the coat on Kathleen, and then the family divides itself into those who are determined to keep the coat on and those who are determined to take the coat off.

The poor little coat is beginning to show unmistakable signs of many and many a struggle, torn by those trying to keep it on and rent by those trying to take it off.

The wearing of the garment is always an evil, and it only becomes a necessary evil when it is worn to prevent an outside force from clothing her with a garment, laced with iron, intended to crush the very heart out of her; for, old-fashioned and ill-fitting as the coat may be, it bears at all events, the marks of "98," "67," and "16," mingled with the finger-marks of Charles Stewart Parnell.

And now, once again Kathleen was bound up in the coat of Unity for a while at least. All the family had a hand in it this time, and, for fear of any mistake, three thousand buttons have been used to fasten the coat—in fact, you can scarcely see the coat for the buttons. And there, in her little garden, the colleen sits from morning till night, and from night till morning. A short time ago it was a terrible scene of desolation and disorder. The walls had been broken down, crowds of men had trampled the pretty plants and flowers to pieces, and here and there were patches of bloodstains; but all these signs of tumult have been cleared away, and now the garden is neater and newer and fresher, and ever so little bigger than before.

Leading up to her residence, "The Castle," is a fine avenue of British oak, elm, and beech trees. Trespassers have spoiled some of them by carving deeply in the bark such unseemly phrases as "Tom Clarke-Pearse," "MacDermott-Independent-Connolly," "Kevin Barry-MacSwiney"; but these vandals have been driven away by the police, with permission to write these things on the sands of the seashore, where they will be soon destroyed, and not in places where they would be a permanence and a disfigurement. And in little out-of-the-way corners the gardeners are planting little plumtrees for their own future enjoyment.

The place always presents an animated appearance; crowds are continually strolling about, some of them with happy faces, murmuring "Everything in the garden looks lovely"; others preserving a mystified silence, and a few—a good few—declaring that "you are sowing in joy, but we tell you, you shall reap in sorrow."

Above all the various murmurs shall be heard the voices telling Kathleen why she must wear her coat for ever and ever, either by itself or over any garment that may be purchased for her—the symbol of the "ultra-fraternal cohesion of our people"; a symbol of their "singleness of purpose," their faith in themselves and each other, their concepts and their country. Sometimes a man, hurrying nervously by, will stop for a moment to whisper, "You're getting too big for it, Kathleen, but it'll stretch"; and another, "You'll feel a lot better when you get your new under-skirt of Downing Street nainsook, with its alluring Canadian lace trimming; I hope to heaven it won't burst your little coat; but, sure, if you're not free, you'll feel free; and even if you don't feel free, you will be free: so it's all the same."

In the mystical stillness of the glooming a man, short of stature, silent and self-absorbed, will stop to look at the quiet, pensive figure, and about to pass, will determinedly pat the dear, dark head, and say, "Be of good cheer, my girl; I rocked you in your cradle, and if needs be I will lower you into your grave." Not a nice thing, really, to say to a young girl, full of latent life and full of potential vigour.

The twilight sky deepened into a darker shade; the Evening Star on the rim of the distant horizon showed the exquisitely delicate gleam of her silver glow. Kathleen watched star after star add to the heavens their symbols of indifference and cosmic serenity—watched them with those eyes in whose depths and shadows and lights could be seen the scorn of Shane the Proud, the perseverance of Tone, the enthusiasm of Emmet, the fire of Mitchel, the patience of Stephens, the strength of Parnell, the determination of Clarke, the humour of MacDermott, and gentle fervour of Pearse, the age of Cuchullain, and the youth of Kevin Barry.

The outlines of the garden began to grow faint and indistinct, and finally vanished. The talk of the crowd became a lulling murmur like the drone of a passing bee, that assumed a gentle cadence of sound so alluring and so exquisite to the inner consciousness of Kathleen that her lips moved in rhythmic correlation: "Not merely free, but Gaelic as well; not merely Gaelic, but free as well. What doth it profit a nation to gain the shame of an Empire and lose its own soul? Not merely Gaelic, but free as well—free as well—what doth it profit a nation—what doth profit a nation—what—"

And Kathleen fell asleep.

Poblacht Na H-Eireann, March 29, 1922

The Corncrake

(Translated from the Irish by Sean O Cathasaigh)

It was raining heavily and, though the business of the market was almost over, there were still a few standing in the square of Ballycoolin with a fading hope in their hearts that someone would come to relieve them of their vigil and the pig or the cow they had to sell.

Ginger Gilligan, with his shoulder leaning lovingly against the doorframe of the little village tavern, dreamily watched the little group lingering in the narrow street, eager to seek shelter from the fast-falling rain, but yet determined to endure it till fortune should take their wares and give them a fair exchange.

Ginger was enjoying the exquisite sensation of a complex joy; the failure of the others gave the contemplation of his own successful sale a richer satisfaction; the consciousness of being safe in shelter while others were being beaten by the driving rain was a sensual source of pleasure; and Ginger smoked his pipe—for life patted him on the back, and Ginger smiled at life—for the time being.

Ginger, with his short perky body, his sallow cheeks, his aggressive way of talking, his self-conscious display of conceit when he was arguing the point—which was very often indeed—was a celebrated unit in the life of Ballycoolin. Indeed, there was only one man who dared to oppose Ginger in an argument, and that was Lanky Lonergan, a long, thin, spare, stick of a man, with a thin pipe-like neck, supporting a heavy head, large-eyed and lantern-jawed, with an indescribably comical look of melancholy on his immovable face.

Whenever Lanky met Ginger, or Ginger encountered Lanky, there was an end of harmony and good fellowship. It was considered impossible, and it was never expected by the people of Ballycoolin, that Lanky and Ginger could ever agree, in this world or the next, upon any subject that interested the sons of men. Lanky's scorn for Ginger's opinion was only equalled by Ginger's contempt for the opinions of Lanky.

Ponderous and difficult were the questions they discussed, from why a dog turned three times before he lay down, to the settlement of the question whether the hen came before the egg, or the egg came before the hen.

Well, free from care, Ginger was blissfully smoking, when who should come along but Lanky, anxious to have a drink, with a pig's cheek under his arm.

"God save us," said Lanky, with an ominous gleam in his eye that was nearest to Ginger, "isn't it terrible weather we're havin'?"

"Oh, it's fine an' soft, anyhow, thanks be to God," replied Ginger, with an equally ominous gleam in his eye that was nearest to Lanky.

"Come in out o' the rain, anyhow," said Lanky, and accompanied by six or seven others who had been at the fair, they entered the pub, and soon began to drink each other's health with anxious sincerity, while they were waiting for the weather to clear.

But the rain continued to fall steadily, and the dreary prospect of drearier walk home that confronted most of them, induced them to continue their mellow expressions of fellowship, which expressions were expanded and developed with additional drinks.

Everybody was waiting for the coming dispute between Lanky and Ginger; how it was to commence nobody knew, but that it was an ultimate certainty everyone was convinced.

"I heard the corncrake this mornin' for the first time this season," said a little man, as he thoughtfully took a drink from his tumbler of stout; "it's a curious bird with a curious call; I don't mind if anybody ever seen it."

"I seen it," said Ginger, "not once but hundreds of times."

"I wonder what way does he be when he gives out that comical call o' his," said the little man again.

Lanky's eyes held an expression of pity as he answered: "That's the simplest thing in the world for anyone to tell who has kept his eyes open. Sure everyone ought to know that the corncrake makes the comical noise when he calls by sticking his bake in the ground."

"Well," said Ginger, as he carefully deposited on the counter the glass from which he was drinking, "I don't mind what everybody knows, for they mostly know wrong; it's sickenin' the foolish things some people say; his bake stuck in the ground! Anyone who has ever seen the corncrake knows that when the bird is givin' its call it does be stretched on the broad of its back with its legs kickin' in the air."

Then the battle started, Lanky trying to convince Ginger, and Ginger determined to convince Lanky, and you may be sure they got all the help they needed from the surrounding company.

One minute you would hear, "I knew Lanky would see that point, an' it puts the kybosh on you, Ginger"; and the next minute, "You took them words out o' me mouth, Ginger; sure I often seen the corncrake doin' it meself, an' he's got the kinch on you there, Lanky."

More and more animated the discussion grew; graphic descriptions were recklessly whirled around the corncrake's habits, customs, manners, legs, wings, beak and plumage. Ginger exhausted all the local science of ornithology concerning every known bird, and vigorously applied it all to the corncrake. Lanky recounted all he had ever read, and a good deal he had never read—nor anybody else—about the corncrake till the shades of evening fell upon them, and the time came for the reluctant master of the tavern to bid farewell to his guests.

And the worthy landlord ushered them out—"themselves and their corncrake"—telling them that the question would have to be settled elsewhere, and reminding them the good people at home would be wondering what was keeping them.

It's a singular thing, by the way, how anxious the owners of taverns become about the people at home when the time arrives for the closing of the shop.

The assembly, still disputing about the corncrake, poured themselves out into the street, and gradually, for it was still raining heavily, departed, some this way, some that, till nobody was left in the now lonely vicinity of the public-house but Ginger and Lanky, still arguing about the call of the corncrake.

The melancholy moon began to peer through thinning clouds, and the rain began to fall more timidly as the pair at last began to move slowly and tentatively homewards—Lanky with the pig's cheek still under his arm.

It was painfully puzzling to Ginger and Lanky that the width—or rather the narrowness—of the road put more difficulties in their way than its length. The hedges, too, seemed to be in a playful mood, continually leaping around them, and bumping into them in a way that was far from reassuring. The very road, as well, seemed to be packed with hills and hollows in a way that never troubled them before, or, let us hope, never will again; but through it all they still continued to discuss the evolution of the corncrake's call.

"Arrah, look here," said Lanky, "you can talk till the tongue falls out of your head, but you'll have to admit that she sticks her gob in the ground."

"Whisht, whisht, man," responded Ginger, "and don't let anybody hear you talkin' that way; how could the creature stick his gob in—look out, here's the hedge again—supposin' she was standin' on a rock how could she—mind that hole there

—stick her bake in the ground? It's on her back she does be, I'm tellin' you."

"Now, listen to me," said Lanky, "I don't like to be arguin', but if you have the least bit of sense in your thick head" —suddenly both of them stopped dead in the middle of the road and began to listen intently, wearing an expression of awe that was comical to behold.

"Creek, crawk, creek, crawk," came with startling insistence from the middle of a field on the side of the road.

"The b----y bird itself," ejaculated Lanky.

"There, now, what did I tell you," said Ginger, in a tone of dogmatic scorn. "Maybe you're satisfied at last."

Lanky made no rejoinder, but softly murmured to himself: "Blessin' o' God on me eyesight; look now where's his gob?"

"Man," rejoined Ginger fiercely, "don't you see her legs?"

"What are you tryin' to say," retorted Lanky. "Is it blindness that's on you or what?" And the two of them glared at each other in a menacing manner.

"It's my opinion," said Ginger, slowly and decisively, "that you never seen a corncrake in your life."

"The gentleman that's talkin'," rejoined Lanky, "wouldn't know a corncrake from a hen."

"Here," said Ginger, with a vicious decision, "I'll bring you to the bird an' show you him makin' his call lyin' on the broad of his back with his legs stickin' up in the air."

"An' I'll show you him," said Lanky, "with his bake stuck down in the ground."

As the little corncrake continued to lustily give forth her cry, the pair excitedly crossed the hedge, and began to steal towards the place from which the call came. But the certainty of their ears was a fallible guide, for a difference quickly arose about the right locality. "This way, man, this way," muttered Lanky.

"Over here, man, over here," responded Ginger, as they stood in the centre of the field, disputing violently, their noses almost touching each other.

The corncrake evidently heard the disturbances, for her call suddenly ceased, and the two stood trembling to fear that they had frightened her away.

"Why couldn't you keep quiet for a minute?" remonstrated Lanky; "your row would wake a dead man out o' the grave."

"Yourself ye mean," retorted Ginger. "Sure, anything wud see that ugly face o' yours on your long pole of a neck stuck up among the clouds."

Just as Lanky was about to retort, they heard the "creek, crawk" of the bird coming from another part of the field.

Away they went again; and so as not to be seen, as they thought, they began the journey on their hands and knees. The corn was more than a foot and a half high, dripping with moisture as well from the recent rains, so that before very long they were as wet as the saturated corn.

But they didn't care a pin; there was a question to be settled, and settle it they would, even at the imminent peril of their lives.

Now there were two mischievous gossoons in Ballycoolin, named Shawn Beag and Sheumas Ruadh, who by some chance, good or bad, were always in the place where they were least expected. If a person was quietly gathering a few heads of cabbage from a neighbour's garden, or a few sods of turf from a heap that was not his own, it was as certain as the sun was in the heavens that the young devils should be near, and the whole story bruited about the village before you could have time to bless yourself, and it was the great and irreparable misfortune that Ginger and Lanky should be seen by these two young rascals. Wondering what could be going on in the field in the middle of the night, they crept to the hedge and watched the antics of the pair who were chasing the corncrake. But they no longer wondered when they saw that Ginger and Lanky always crept towards the place from which they thought the call of the corncrake came.

"Bedad, we'll have a bit o' fun now," said Shawn to Sheumas, and away he went to the end of the field furthest from where were Lanky and Ginger, while Sheumas remained where he was.

Inside were the benighted pair, creeping carefully on their hands and knees through the dripping corn, Lanky leading, his long head and neck lifted above the surrounding corn, murmuring softly: "We're not a mile from her now"; when suddenly the call ceased again. They stopped, listened, looked at each other, and were about to launch into mutual abuse again, when they heard the "creek, crawk" more distinctly than ever before, from the other end of the field. Away with them again towards the place from which the call came, moving now as rapidly as they could go on their hands and knees, for, becoming excited in the chase, each was anxious to be the first to catch a glimpse of the corncrake.

But it wasn't long befor Shawn ceased his mimicking cry, and Sheumas took up the cry far away behind them, and turning swiftly, Ginger and Lanky moved madly in the opposite direction.

Back and forth, from left to right, from right to left, went the now frantic couple, ay, till the whole cornfield had been traversed on hands and knees for more than fifty times. Exhausted and teeming with sweat from their exertions, they still continued to creep at a mad miniature gallop towards any place in which they heard the cry of the mysterious bird.

At last, as they paused together in the middle of the field

waiting to hear the call again, the two birds began to cry together. This was puzzling, and Ginger and Lanky were immediately in a state of mental disorder. Each chose a different corncrake to follow, and then the dispute arose in an effort of each to persuade the other to follow the bird of his choice.

"The one over forninst us," said Lanky.

"The one that's right behind us," said Ginger.

But Lanky refused to go up the field, and Ginger was equally determined not to go down. The difficulty was at last overcome by each following, in a burst of anger, his own particular corncrake.

Down the field went Lanky, and who should the corncrake be but my bould Sheumas Ruadh. When Lanky came near to him he stopped the call, but he didn't stop Lanky; and away fled Sheumas to the other side of the field, and, unfortunately for Lanky, he recommenced the call. Over the hedge jumped Lanky into the adjoining potato field, stumbling through the ridges and splashing through the water that had gathered in the hollows between the ridges, till, reaching the centre of the field exhausted and half dead, he lay down in one of the hollows, and the vigorous cries of the corncrake failed to arouse him again, for Lanky was dead to the world.

Meanwhile Ginger was in hot pursuit of his own bird. When he came to the ditch he heard the call out in the bog. With the heedlessness of a madman he went over the ditch in one bound and raced towards the bog. He was on a hot scent now, and gathering together all his remaining energy, he rushed forward and plunged headlong into a cold and brimming bog-hole, giving vent to an agonizing yell as he disappeared beneath the surface.

Shawn Beag ran to his assistance, and, catching hold of him by the collar, tried to pull him out, but his effort was in vain. So he had to bellow for Sheumas, who, running up, lent

s

a hand, and their united efforts withdrew poor Ginger from his perilous position. Poor Ginger never let a whimper out of him. All the corncrakes in the world might call their loudest, but Ginger wouldn't pay the slightest attention to them. Like Lanky, he was dead to the world.

Sheumas and Shawn, each catching hold of an arm, half carried, half dragged him to the door of his house. After knocking loudly at the door, they left Ginger standing stupidly before it and fled. The wife of Ginger came and opened the door, and astonishment was writ large on the face of Ginger when he saw the wonder on the face of his wife.

"Oh," said he, "is it asleep you were?"

"Ay," said she, "the sleep of the corncrake," and stretching out her hand, she gripped Ginger by the collar, and the poor man passed away from the world's ken.

"Where did you leave Lanky?" inquired Shawn, as they were returning to the scene of the hunt for the corncrake.

"Asleep in Peg's potato field, and the last trump wouldn't waken him," responded Sheumas. "We'll have to go and waken him, too; but he's too heavy to carry."

They thought of the problem for a few moments, and at last decided to commandeer old Farmer Dermody's yellow mule cart. Having secured the cart, they brought it to the potato field, and put in Lanky, with his two long legs streeling out from the back of the cart, and in this manner conveyed the unconscious man home. They kicked violently at the door, and hearing the approach of Lanky's wife, they fled, and left Lanky to explain as best he could what he was doing in Farmer Dermody's yellow mule cart.

"Well, well," said old Mihaul to his friends in the little pub of Ballycoolin a few days later, "you should have seen the state o' me corn, an' all the roads destroyed, an' the curiousest thing about it all was that the divil a sign of anyone or anything I ever found there, save a pig's cheek an' it wrapped in paper."

The Gael, June, 1922

Gulls and Bobbin Testers

"Here's a nice grassy place," said Olive. "Shall we sit down here, for a little, for I'm nearly played out after the stiff climb." And, without waiting for a yea or nay, Olive glided down in a restful posture on the grass that displayed here and there in its folds a sprig of purple heather.

Maisie and I sat down beside her, on the rugged lap of the Hill of Howth, our faces turned towards a sea, that in its quiet calm, seemed to be the mirror of the indifference of the gods. I watched Maisie and Olive carefully placing in their handbags little treasures that they had gathered on the way; sprigs of heather, beautiful with a purple, lovelier than the purple of the robe of Caesar; cornflowers with the tint of the sky in them, and gorse agleam with gold finer than the fine gold that shone from the Cherubims in Solomon's Temple.

Olive and Maisie were Bobbin Testers, over from Lancashire on a week's holiday. Both of them were very young—nineteen years—and both of them were pretty; Maisie dark and thoughtful, and Olive fair and vivacious. Maisie was pale; but in the cheeks of Olive shone the bloom that an Irish poet would write of as "sneachta geal gan ealuing go geur i geath le dath an róis,"[1] and, indeed, it would be hard to say where the whiteness of the lily ended and the red of the rose began.

"It is strange," said I, "that a girl like you, Olive, working in a factory, should have such a red bloom lingering in your cheeks."

"Everybody wonders at it," said Olive, "but they aren't as red as they used to be."

"A good deal of us were like Olive at first," said Maisie, "but it won't be long till Olive is like the rest of us."

[1]Bright snow stealing away to war with the colour of the rose.

"Ah," said I, "the lily always conquers the rose, for lilies are for the dead, and roses for the living."

"Look at the mowter bowt! look at the mowter bowt!" suddenly said Olive, pointing to the little vessel cleaving the waters, apparently miles and miles below us, containing a solitary man stretched out on the bottom, with his eye fixed on the sky.

"That must be a selfish blowke," said Olive, "or he'd have a girl with him."

"Maybe he's a married man," said Maisie.

"I never thought of that," said Olive.

"How do you like your work?" asked I, as my wandering eyes halted to gaze on the Baily lighthouse, standing on the edge of the promontory, like a mail-clad figure on guard, with a gridded helmet on his head.

"Ow, none of us like it," said Olive, "especially when some mill or other asks for red bobbins. After you've been looking for hours at the bobbins whirling on the spindles, it does give you a headache, and you long for the buzzer that tells you to knock off. Often your eyes do be dancing out of your head."

"They're the worst," said Maisie, "the brown, or the green or the white aren't so bad, but the red make you dizzy."

The three of us remained silent for some moments, looking at the gulls as they circled round and round the cliffs, with heads bent and beaks stretching out towards the sea below.

"And your hours, are they long?" I asked, as I watched the graceful, sweeping glide of a gull, just brushing the diamonded breast of the sea, and then rising with a bold and vigorous movement of her lovely wings.

"The hours are nothing to grouse about now," responded Olive; "we're on three-quarter time at present, and, starting at eight, we finish at half-past five."

"And get only nineteen shillings a week for it," said Maisie.

"Full time," explained Olive, "we'd start at six, and get twenty-four bob a week."

"Six o'clock's a terrible time to be getting up in the winter," said I.

"I've done it for three years," said Olive, "and I don't mind it now."

"And I," added Maisie, "since I was fourteen; besides it means five bob in the week more, and that's not to be sneezed at."

"Sometimes," said Olive, "it's a bit of a rush, when you sleep it out, and be pulling on your blouse when you're skipping to the factory as fast as you can run."

"An' if the Foreman sees you coming in half-dressed," added Maisie, "back you go for the rest of the day."

Again there fell a silence, decorated with the plaintive, sometimes challenging cries of the flying gulls, echoing in our hearts plaintive and challenging cries against enveloping injustice, and the sway of its apparent immutability.

> For if you but listen closely to their crying
> You'll hear them calling out to one another
> With human voices.

"How would you like to be a gull?" suddenly said I to Olive.

"And have to lie all night on the hard rocks of the cliffs, and fly all day over the cold sea, and never to have a dance, or to have a boy's arm around you—no thank you," said Olive, "I wouldn't like to be a gull!"

"Nor me, either," said Maisie.

And again there fell a brooding silence; and a warm haze spread over the sky, and the cries of the gulls diminished to a droning murmur.

And suddenly I beheld a great flock of gulls, so great that

no man could number them, and they slowly lighted on the cliff not very far away. And, like the penguins of Anatole France, they began to grow bigger and bigger till they assumed the stature of living men and women. And over beyond them I saw thousands and thousands of Bobbin Testers growing smaller and smaller, till they assumed the proportions of birds, and as the gulls were like unto living men and living women, so were the Bobbin Testers like unto gulls with wings and beaks; and with loud cries they rose in the air, and flew around the cliffs or glided over the bosom of the sea.

And the gulls that had become living men and living women gathered round one bigger than them all, whose voice was like to the sound of many waters, and whose eyes flamed with a great passion.

And he that was bigger than all the gulls that had become like unto living men and living women, spoke unto all that were gathered around him, and said:

Come, I will make the continent indissoluble,
I will make the most splendid race the sun ever shone upon,
I will make divine magnetic lands,
    With the love of comrades,
        With the life-long love of comrades.[2]

And he shook out in his hand and held aloft a banner that was like unto the flaming colour of the setting sun, and the rest answered him with a mighty shout that shook the hills and moved the sea to restlessness.

And they all followed him in a great multitude; and as they marched along they sang, and their voices were like the storm of the sea when it shaketh itself in anger, and the noise of many trees bowing before a mighty wind.

[2]Walt Whitman, "For You, O Democracy."

And this is what they sang:

All the past we leave behind,
We debouch upon a newer, mightier world, varied world,
Fresh and strong the world we seize, world of labour and
          the march,
Pioneers! O Pioneers![3]

                              * * *

"Jack, Jack! wake up; you've been asleep for the last hour
or so, and we're thinking of being on the move."

It was the voice of Olive, and she was shaking me by the
arm.

And I rose up, and beheld that the gulls that had become
living men and living women had changed to gulls again; and
those that had become gulls were changed again to Bobbin
Testers.

And I could not find it in my heart to blame the gulls.

                              The Irish Statesman, September 6, 1924

Irish in the Schools

Through the slowly rising, heavy wreaths of tobacco
smoke Jack could faintly see the coveted space in front of Hatch
67, where he was to get the Talisman entitling him to a sum
of fifteen shillings. He had been standing in the queue for more
than an hour, yet, for every step he took forward, the damned
Hatch, like a receding tide, seemed to retreat a step backward.
Another half-hour, and the demon behind the grille would murmur snappily, "Closed till after dinner!" and the ordeal of
merging oneself into the slowly moving, tightly-packed queue,
with its occasional surge of half a step forward, its nerve-racking
medley of murmurs about claims lodged, claims ignored, mo-

[3]Walt Whitman, "Pioneers! O Pioneers!"

mentarily silenced by the forcible comments of some clamorous claimant against the hardness of the hearts that animated the bodies of the busy devils moving with the stealthy steps of tigers behind the grilles, would have to be repeated.

"One, two, three—" Jack was counting the heads in front of him, when he felt a sharp dig of an elbow in his right side.

"Where in the name of God are you shovin'?" said Jack; but the angry menace in his voice died down, as he looked upon the face of a young carpenter with whom he had often worked.

"Hello, Jim," went on Jack, "sorry to see you here; how's the missus an' the three kids?"

"I have five o' them, now," said Jim grimly; "all well, so far; the two that are goin' to school are the hope o' the family: they are able to say their prayers in Irish, and a teacher of sixty is learnin' them how to dance a jig!"

"Thanks be to God," said a big builder's labourer in front, "that we've won th' right to speak our own languidge, anyway."

"D'ye hear that?" said Jack to his mate; "an' the only thought in his head is subsistence if he gets the dole, and destruction if he doesn't!"

"Ah, well," said Jim, "it does us no harm to honour the old tongue."

"Like the paper the other day," said Jack, "that wrote 'The Gardai were attacked with stones and other missiles by the mob.' By calling the Civic Guards 'The Gardai' we're honouring the old tongue. What's the use of saying it's essential to the nation when our whole life proves that if we want to say anything, or do anything, we must forget all about it? It is like the balloons the jazz dancers carry through the whirl of their movements: the Government Officials are flicking it from one Department to another; the clergy have a half hour's play with it on each St. Patrick's Day; the Labour Leaders have fixed it to the Red Flag, and even the Protestants carry one in their pockets, to be blown out on particular occasions. It's not so bad so long as it remains a pastime for those who have all the necessities of life and many of its comforts, but when they start to make the language an additional torture and an additional strain to the children of the workers, it is time to snap the balloon from the hands of the fanatics and burst the thing, for it is an imposition of torture upon the little ones, that their pain may change to a semblance of reality a gigantic sham of their elders."

Jim was silent for a moment, then he murmured softly, "Still, Jack, we ought to have an Ireland not only free, but Gaelic as well; the first thought towards our children is to make them Irish."

"The first thought towards our children," responded Jack, "is their life, rather than their language; to see that the tissues of life get every necessary nourishment, and every possible protection, to provide them with clothes that will leave them cool in the Summer, and clothes that will keep them warm in the Winter. And you know, as well as I do, Jim, that the sparrows on the housetops are better fed, and the dolls that are born for Christmas are better clothed than the children of the workers. I was readin' lately in one o' the daily papers a menu for small incomes; I'll just mention two: 'Monday—roast forequarter o' lamb, mint sauce, tapioca puddin' an' lemon jelly. Tuesday— cold lamb, mint sauce, potato cake, cucumber salad, rhubarb tart an' custard.' Not by any means a gluttonous diet for a worker an' his family, but as easy for the workers to reach as it is for a traveller to get to the North Pole. When we were workin' a few months ago, where they were dishin' out meals to the school children, what did we see them gettin'? Greasy cocoa in horrible enamel tins; an' chunks o' bread painted with a delicate coat o' margarine. The Government, through the Corporation, allowin' tuppence-ha'penny per nipper that he may be stuffed with a Government plenitude of food; an' the same Government givin' a pound a day to teachers to enable the same nipper to be stuffed with Irish idiom!"

"For God's sake, thry to keep movin'," said an anxious voice behind; "if I'm not back with th' dough be three o'clock, it's out on th' street me an' the mot'll[4] be flung!"

"Nothin' more for me to get!" roared a voice beside the grill of Hatch 67; "nothin' more for me to get! An' how th' hell d'ye make that out?"

"You've got all that's comin' to you," said the cold, incisive voice of the Demi-gorgon behind the grille, "so get a move on out o' the way, an' give some one else a chance."

"If yous think yous can do me a dot," roared the voice again, "yous are damn well mistaken; only for the likes of us yous wouldn't be here; no more comin' to me! Be God, we'll see about that!"

"What's th' use of blamin' that man?" commented several voices in the vicinity. "'Tisn't his fault, is it?"

"Well," roared the voice, as it was pushed and elbowed away to the farther end of the hall, "I'll let them see they won't swindle me out o' me stamps. Sure as God, if I ever hear one o' the chiselers at home use as much as one word o' Irish, I'll knock Ireland a notion out o' them in quick time, I'm tellin' yous!"

"Another poor devil," murmured Jim, "up to his neck in the stream of Cocytus—well; it's one head less in front of us, anyhow."

"Ay," said Jack, "an' if a job doesn't come quick, we'll shortly be plungin' in after him. The problem of havin' enough food to eat is of more importance than that of havin' a little Irish to speak. The Gaelic spoken by the Ard-Breitheamh[5] for the first time in Dublin Castle is very different to the Gaelic

⁴Wife.
⁵The High Judge.

spoken in the Labour Exchange. It makes me mad to think of those who are shoutin' we've nothin' to do but learn Irish if we want to enter into the joy of the Lord. And then, to think of our over-crowded schools, over-worked teachers, underfed children, hardly one of whom is sound in body, everyone of whom is the child of an anxious father and a harassed mother, indifferent as to whether the school will prove to be to their children a means of intellectual grace, through which, as they grow in years, they will grow in wisdom, or a place in which their children suffer the pains of stupefying torments. Teachers that have never been able to teach (generally through lack of time and opportunity) our children one language are now wiping the sweat from their brows trying to teach them two. Children, who are rickety on their legs, are to be told of Cuchulain's hero leap over walls as high as Nelson's Pillar. Children who are fed on tea and margarine, are to be told of the wine and venison feasts of the Fianna.[6] Children told in the schools of the beauties of Tara and of Emain Macha are to spend their leisure hours peering in through the railings of Mountjoy and Merrion Square watching the divinities within playing tennis on the sward."

"Still," murmured Jim, thoughtfully, "the soul of Ireland—"

"Ah, the soul of Ireland," interrupted Jack, irritably, "is as apparent here as it is at a meeting of the Fainne. It speaks just as truly in the wild words of a drunken spunker as it does in the jubilant cooing of President Cosgrave at a banquet in the Metropole; or the innocent babbling of President de Valera on a platform in Ennis. It gleams vividly from the brilliant realism of Joyce as it sparkles radiantly from the lovely imagery of Yeats. The Soul—"

"No more till after dinner," snapped out the clerk behind the grille.

[6] A warrior caste of the second and third centuries A.D., whose greatest leader was the legendary bard, Finn Mac Cool.

"Ah, Mother o' God," said Jim, "an' only three in front of us. It's the last thing to have to come to a place like this."

And with the rest of the murmuring crowd, they silently moved towards the exit door, down the stone stairs and out into the street.

The Irish Statesman, November 29, 1924

Plays

Before W. B. Yeats, Lady Gregory, and Lennox Robinson rejected *The Silver Tassie* in 1928 and precipitated O'Casey's break with the Abbey Theatre, the theatre had produced five of O'Casey's plays. Three of these plays—*The Shadow of a Gunman, Juno and the Paycock,* and *The Plough and the Stars*—established O'Casey's international reputation as a major dramatist. The two other plays—"Kathleen Listens In" and "Nannie's Night Out"—are here printed for the first time. Both plays are one-acts: the former is a satiric phantasy which foreshadows the method of O'Casey's recent work, and the latter is a tragi-comedy similar in manner to the three famous early plays.

The Shadow of a Gunman was the first play O'Casey had accepted by the Abbey. It was produced in April, 1923, when O'Casey was forty-three years old, and it had a resounding success. No alterations were made in the script except that the title was changed from *On the Run.*

It does not detract from the accomplishment of the *Gunman* to note that O Cathasaigh the labourer had done some arduous apprentice play-writing before O'Casey the master dramatist erupted onto the Abbey stage and into the modern repertoire. He had written four or, possibly, five one-act plays that were unproduced. The names of these earlier plays were "The Robe of Rosheen," "The Frost in the Flower," "Nipped in the Bud," "The Harvest Festival," and "The Crimson in the Tri-Colour." None of them has as yet come to light.

Of "The Robe of Rosheen," O'Casey wrote in *Inishfallen, Fare Thee Well:*

> Well, he had done his best to get a word in edgeways. He had written a one-act play, satirising the contesting parties and putting official Labour against the wall for its stupid and selfish pursuit of jobs, instead of flinging themselves between the opposing guns, calling out the question of which of you will fire first! Sean could never hear a word about his little play, though he had sent it to *The Plain People,* and though he asked many who were connected with the distribution of the journal. It was ten years after, when he was living in London, that a priest from Kerry visited him, and reminded him of his play, *The Robe of Rosheen,* which had appeared so long ago in the Republican paper, though ne'er another soul, apparently, had ever noticed it.

In *The Green Crow* O'Casey speaks of *"Roisin's Robe* . . . printed in *The*

Plain People" and says that the play, "His first play ever to appear in print was in his later manner."

O'Casey next wrote "The Frost in the Flower." As the paragraph describing the play in *Inishfallen, Fare Thee Well* also contains the sentence, "Instead of trying to form Ireland's life, he would shape his own," the play probably was written after O'Casey's resignation as secretary of the Citizen Army in 1914. The play was a satire on Frank Cahill, the founder of the St. Lawrence O'Toole Gaelic Club and an early friend of O'Casey. (With Cahill, O'Casey had founded the club's Pipers' Band.) The play was refused by the group, and about 1919 O'Casey sent it off to the Abbey. In *Sean O'Casey, the Man and his Work,* David Krause relates the trouble O'Casey had in preparing the manuscript. "Since he had no money for paper and ink, he had to improvise. Several of his friends who worked in offices made off with batches of odd-sized sheets of paper and a box of indelible lead pencils; and by boiling the purple lead in water he concocted a pot of home-made ink." In her Journals Lady Gregory writes that O'Casey told her the play had been rejected with the comment, "Not far from being a good play." In *Inishfallen, Fare Thee Well* O'Casey tells us more about the note which had said:

> how interested they were in the play, which was promising, but one of the main characters had been too critical, reminding them of various characters in Abbey plays, a characteristic that tended to become tiresome and irritating.
>
> Sean guessed that this comment was wrong, and a little ridiculous, since he had been in the theater but twice, . . .

Although the play has not come to light, O'Casey in *Inishfallen* has given us a summary of it:

> The play dealt with a young man, a lay teacher in a Christian Brothers' school who, though full of confidence on gigantic questions he was never called upon to touch, was timid as a new-born mouse over simple questions concerning himself. He got a very small salary from the Brothers, paid to him quarterly, mostly in sixpenny pieces and threepenny bits. A teachership in elementary mathematics and elementary English fell vacant in a Technical School, the gift of a Dublin Council Committee, and Sean's timid friend, certain he hadn't a chance of getting it, applied for the job. To his frightened dismay, he was elected by a fine vote, and everyone in the parish brought him all kinds of books to help in preparing him for the work he would

have to do. Though he had the ability, he hadn't the will-power; and the play ended in the midst of a party given in his honour, at which it became known that he had resigned from the job, to become the scorn of his family and the joke of the parish.

In *Sean O'Casey as a Poetic Dramatist,* an unpublished doctoral dissertation at Dublin University, Robert W. Caswell mentions that O'Casey wrote a sequel to "The Frost in the Flower" called "Nipped in the Bud." O'Casey nowhere refers to this play, and Caswell's authority is P. T. MacDonnell who, with O'Casey, started an amateur acting group within the O'Toole Club.

O'Casey's next play, "The Harvest Festival," seems to have contained the germ for his most recent long play, *The Drums of Father Ned.* "The Harvest Festival," O'Casey tells us, "dealt with the efforts of militant members of the unskilled unions to put more of the fibre of resistance to evil conditions of pay and life into the hearts and minds of the members of the craft unions whose gospel was that what was good enough for the fathers was good enough for the sons. The action took place in the busy preparations made by a church for holding the annual harvest festival, which the Anglo-catholics sneeringly called the Feast of Saint Pumpkin and all Vegetables."

The play was partially suggested by the fate of Father Michael O'Flanagan, a parish priest in Sligo who, when he saw that his parishioners had no money for winter fuel, sent them to a privately-owned peatbog and told them to help themselves, and who was relieved subsequently of his parish. Father O'Flanagan is mentioned in the prefatory note to *The Drums of Father Ned* as well as in the discussion of "The Harvest Festival" in *Inishfallen, Fare Thee Well.* The tostal festival of the later play is akin to the harvest festival of the first, and the theme and situation of both plays seem the same.

Caswell suggests that the play may have been written for the amateur dramatic group at Liberty Hall, as it was not intended for the O'Toole Club. However, this play was also rejected by the Abbey, and it "brought back to Sean a letter saying that the work was well conceived, but badly executed; with an added note from Mr. Lennox Robinson, then the Manager of the Abbey Theatre, saying that he liked very much the character of the clergyman in the play, which was something, though not enough for Sean."

The next play, "The Crimson in the Tri-Colour," was almost accepted by the Abbey. Lady Gregory was especially impressed and wanted

T

to produce it, but Yeats, although it reminded him of Tolstoy, refused. The ultimate refusal did not come immediately, however. O'Casey was first told that he must have the manuscript typed. "At that time," O'Casey later told Lady Gregory, "it was hard for me to afford even the paper it was written on."

Then Lennox Robinson lost the manuscript and asked O'Casey for a new copy. For a man of less determination this might well have been the *coup de grâce*. ". . . Sean had clenched his teeth, for there was no copy; not even notes from which a copy might be built." A year later O'Casey heard that the play had been found and typed and reread by the Directors and finally refused.

That was the last that O'Casey saw of the play. Lennox Robinson told O'Casey that he still had the manuscript and promised both O'Casey and his wife at various times to return it; but he never did, and Robinson's executors have found no trace of the play in Robinson's papers.

The suspense and the reiterated disappointments over "The Crimson in the Tri-Colour" must have been at the time staggering. Remembering the events, O'Casey later wrote:

> There was nothing to do but forget, and go on; forget, and go on. He had made up his mind years ago that the Abbey Theatre curtain would go up on a play of his; and up it would go, sooner or later. First decide slowly and deeply whether it is in you to do a thing; if you decide that you can, then do it, even though it kept you busy till the very last hour of life.

A year later he had completed *The Shadow of a Gunman* and the belated refusal of the earlier play became more bearable when the new one was accepted. Still Lady Gregory reports that O'Casey told her, "I will tell you that it was a bitter disappointment for I had not only thought at the time it was the best thing I had written but I had thought that no one in the world had ever written anything so fine." Later he came to believe that some of these early plays were better than ones the Abbey was producing; a glance at the plays the theatre was producing in these years suggests that he was quite correct.

O'Casey had to fight to get his plays upon the stage. The enormous odds and the painful setbacks, coupled with what we know of O'Casey's life, and tossed against his ultimate triumph, must stand as a tribute to the man's unconquerable determination.

*   *   *

"Kathleen Listens In" was first produced on October 1, 1923, at
the Abbey Theatre. The play was directed by Lennox Robinson and
had the following cast:

MICEAWL O'HOULIHAN	F. J. McCormick
SHEELA O'HOULIHAN	Maureen Delany
KATHLEEN	Eileen Crowe
TOMAUS THORNTON	Barry Fitzgerald
JIMMY	Michael J. Dolan
THE MAN IN THE KILTS	Gabriel J. Fallon
THE FREE STATER	Arthur Shields
THE REPUBLICAN	Tony Quinn
THE BUSINESS MAN	U. Wright
THE FARMER	Maurice Esmonde
THE DOCTOR	Eric Gorman
THE MAN WITH THE BIG DRUM	Peter Nolan
TWO MEN	Walter Dillon, P. J. Carolan

In *Inishfallen, Fare Thee Well*, O'Casey describes the play as:

a jovial, sardonic sketch on the various parties in conflict over Irish
politics—Sinn Fein, Free State, and Labour. It was a short one-act
work, and was performed after a major play had ended. Another
experience for Sean! The audience received the little play in dead
silence, in a silence that seemed to have a point of shock in its centre.
Not even a cold clap of a hand anywhere. They all got up from their
seats, and silently filed out of the theatre. He was the one and only
playwright to have had a play received in silence by an Abbey
audience; the only one to be deprived of even a single timid hand-
clap. Indeed, it did look as if his talent, too, would have to perish in
silence and with malice of afterthought. What would he do, for he
was vexed, and a sense of humiliation discouraged him; what would
he do? Go on, go on! Forever he would go on seeing through his own
eyes, hearing with his own ears, speaking with his own tongue. No
power of influence, no seduction of wealth, no affection for friend,
nor would any love for woman draw him away from his own integrity. Let that integrity be right or wrong, it would be a true reflection of what he felt in his nature from the things he saw and the
things he heard around him.

Reviews of the play do not report such a stonily apathetic reception,
but they may well have glossed matters over, as newspaper criticism frequently does. At any rate, a reading between the lines of the following

sympathetic account from *The Evening Telegraph* of October 2, suggests that the play had a far from happy reception.

> The first production of a new one-act phantasy by Sean O'Casey, "Cathleen Listens In," an event eagerly looked forward to by all who had seen this author's previous tragedy, "The Shadow of a Gunman," took place last night at the Abbey Theatre. All expectations as to the wittiness of the play and its aptness and interest were more than fulfilled; but it was a play to slightly puzzle a first-night audience. To begin with, utter phantasy, however direct of meaning, is not gathered in completely at first to the mind of any audience unless they have been extraordinarily well prepared for it. "Cathleen Listens In" is utter fantasy, in which Cathleen of Ireland is a modern young woman in the Free State house, for which her father has sold the family cow; and around and about all this the author has made glancing dialogue, with many a sharp truth revealed or subtly-half-hidden. . . .
>
> The play is hilarious throughout in the manner intended, marvellously acute in its irony. . . .
>
> "Cathleen Listens In" was most appreciatively received.

A few days later, on October 6, the paper reported that:

> Sean O'Casey's new play at the Abbey Theatre this week has been a success—though the first night it seemed to show the fault of being above the heads of its audience. As soon as the latter had realised its type, however, and as the week went on, they expressed their approval warmly. Of course it is a somewhat unorthodox kind of trifle; just a fantsy [*sic*] packed full of witticisms—but it has breadth and depth and vitality enough for its scope, and enough to show us that something is being done here. We long to see our author in a new style of comedy—of tragedy—for he is as much as ever a person whose work we must await with interest.

Other reports were less favourable. The *Irish Independent* commented on October 1, that "The Audience was rather amused at the idea, obscured as it was by some irrelevant talk at the outset." Joseph Holloway wrote in his journal, *A Dublin Playgoer's Impressions* for October 1, that "The audience was eager to laugh with him but couldn't, only by fits and starts!" and for October 2, that, "I again saw 'Cathleen Listens In'— clever and all as it is as a satire, it misses fire as a play." Such attitudes were amplified by the unfavourable review in the *Evening Herald* for October 2:

There was subtle inspiration in the idea of presenting to us last night at the Abbey Theatre Mr. Sean O'Casey's new play, "Cathleen Listens In," considering the fact that about the same time Mr. Cosgrave was introducing Ireland to the Imperial Conference. Right about there the subtlety ended, for Mr. O'Casey's play is not a play at all, but a quip, a whimsicality, a safety valve for some funny opinions he holds on present-day Ireland.

His new work will neither add to, nor detract from, the reputation he gained over his first play "The Shadow of a Gunman," but it is in itself clear proof that Mr. O'Casey, while having a good sense of the essentials of stage atmosphere, has very little dramatic technique, and that his work is inclined to be of the jester, ephemeral, type rather than that of real comedy or tragedy. Perhaps it is that Mr. O'Casey has not yet found himself and just cannot quite decide upon which is the better way of saying that which he has got to say, but producing topical tit-bits such as this play of Cathleen, the daughter of Mr. Meehawl O'Houlihan, will rather spoil the possibilities of his doing serious and better work and give his plays a quality of facetiousness which is deceptive.

The play should not have seemed so baffling, and one may attribute much of the uneasy reaction to the nature of the audience. The two most frequent criticisms of the Abbey were that the plays too often were trivial knock-about farces and that the audience only wanted to laugh and would frequently spoil a serious moment by what one commentator has called "the repeated bellows of stupid and prolonged mirth . . . bovine merriment . . . brainless laughter." These criticisms are, of course, mutually dependent, and they suggest a central problem of every theatre. The Abbey was perhaps criticised more than other theatres because the Abbey at one time set a higher standard and actually forced good drama upon the stage despite threat, censorship, and riot.

That an intelligent viewer could easily take "Kathleen" in stride is suggested by the review in the *Irish Statesman* for October 6, signed by "S. L. M." (probably Susan L. Mitchell):

The new play at the Abbey Theatre, "Cathleen Listens In," calls itself a Phantasy, and is not, we imagine, taking itself very seriously as a play; but it invites some serious consideration as an allegory, or perhaps we might say a rough-and-tumble morality play. In spite of the distraction of mind caused by the commotion of the acting, necessary, we admit, to the idea, the audience emerges from the tumult and the shouting a little breathless, but quite coherent. We have no fault to find with the obviousness of the play, there is a comfort to the playgoer often bewildered by subtleties, to find himself quite clear as to the idea the playwright had in mind; it puts him in good humour with himself, and satisfaction in the audience reacts on the players, establishing their morale, giving them confidence. In "Cathleen Listens In" this is an important point, as the slight breathlessness in the witty dialogue when the stage is full hints at a team that is new at pulling together. This will, of course, disappear after a few performances. It is unnecessary to explain a play where the heroine is Cathleen, the daughter of Houlihan, and the characters are a Free Stater, a Republican, a business man, a farmer, a labourer. The mordant idea of the play is found in the spectral Gaelic League, under the figure of a feeble old man in kilts—who receives solemn homage from the actors, whenever he appears, but is voted a nuisance and a lunatic when his back is turned. The climax of comedy is reached when at the height of the shouting of the claimants for Cathleen's suffrages the Boundary Question stalks by outside playing on a big drum the appropriate air. Casey is not Shaw, but he has a lively mind and no bitterness, and though a guffaw so near tragedy as we are just now may offend the taste of some, others will find it salutary.

O'Casey described "Kathleen" as a "jovial, sardonic sketch," a "Political Phantasy," a "little play." These descriptions are quite apt, and I should only want to add that it is a good sketch and a successful little play. Its subject matter is mainly national and topical, and some of its barbs have perhaps had their points a bit blunted by time. But the play retains its high spirits and all of the flavour of its language. It is hard to see how a perceptive Irishman in the 1920's would not have been fairly tickled and delighted by it.

Beyond its merits as play, "Kathleen" has another importance, for it proves again that, even at the beginning of his career in the theatre, O'Casey was interested in other dramatic manners than the so-called realism of *Juno and the Paycock* and *The Plough and the Stars*. It is instructive, and depressing, to note that the adverse criticism of "Kathleen" is precisely the same kind of stuff with which the Irish critics would greet O'Casey's mature phantasies like *The Bishop's Bonfire* and *Cock-a-Doodle Dandy*.

Since the ruckus in the middle twenties over *The Silver Tassie,* a chorus of Irish critics has lifted tremulous trebles to the strains of "Come Back to Erin," all pleading to O'Casey to "write plays like you used to, nice plays with lots of laughs like *The New Gossoon,* not these wild things we can't understand."

O'Casey has pretty well weathered the criticism floating across the Irish Sea that his plays since *The Plough and the Stars* are terrible, but it took about twenty years to do so. Once the seed of a literary opinion has been sown, it easily sprouts up into that hardy weed, the critical cliché.

The text of the play is based on O'Casey's original typescript, which contains many later marginal and interlinear changes, some evidently added after the play's production. As the typescript is a draft never intended for the printer, I have attempted to bring its format into line with that of O'Casey's printed plays. If ever format clashed with content, I have, of course, not sacrificed content. I have collated this version with a copy of a slightly different version lent me by Ronald Ayling.

Kathleen Listens In
A Political Phantasy in One Act

CHARACTERS

MICEAWL[1] O HOULIHAN, *the man of the house*
SHEELA O HOULIHAN, *the woman of the house*
KATHLEEN, *their daughter*
TOMAUS THORNTON, *a neighbour*
JIMMY, *a workman*
THE MAN IN THE KILTS
THE FREE STATER
THE REPUBLICAN
THE BUSINESS MAN
THE FARMER
THE DOCTOR
THE MAN WITH THE BIG DRUM
JOEY AND JOHNNY, THE NATIONAL PARTY

[1]Pronounced Meehaul.

SCENE: The Garden before the house of the O Houlihan Family.
TIME: The Present.

*The garden beside the house of the O Houlihan family. To
the Right the front part of the house is seen. A door leads into
the house; above the door are two windows, resembling church
windows, in which the panes are broken. A low wall runs along
Back; a gate in wall on Left. Outside the wall, partly hidden by
the house, is a tree. In the Centre of the garden is a flagstaff from
which flies a small Tricolour.*

*When the curtain rises the stage is empty. Loud and angry
voices are heard inside the house.*

Miceawl's Voice. If yous want to kick up a row, go outside an'
kick it up; the house can well do without yous—since yous
came into it, yous have done nothin' but make a noise.

1st Man's Voice. Poppies in a pot in th' centre o' th' table! The
next thing yous'll be puttin' a crown o' roses an' thistles
round th' head o' Henry Grattan. Yous'll grow shamrocks
or yous'll grow nothin'!

[*The door opens and 1st and 2nd Man appear with Miceawl
behind ready to close the door.*]

1st Man. Spendin' seven hundhred years of our life shovin' half o'
th' strangers out o' th' front door, an' now we're to let you
bring in t'other half th' back way—If you go on as you're
goin', we'll not leave a Saint or a Scholar in your Jazz Band
Government.

2nd Man. Are you goin' to take them poppies out o' th' pot, or
are you not? Are you goin' to pull down that Lion an'
Unicorn that's hangin' over th' fireplace, jeerin' at
everybody?

1st Man. Are you goin' to sing Th' Soldier's Song before an'
after meals, an' read a chapther o' Mitchel's Jail Journal
every night before goin' to bed?

Miceawl. I'm busy now with th' plans for th' electhrification of the Shannon an' Suck, th' Lee an' th' Liffey, th' Bann an' th' Boyne an' th' Tolka, so I'll have to say tooraloo.

1st Man. We think what we thought, we say what we said, we stand where we stood seven hundhred years ago; the world may change but Ireland'll never alther.

2nd Man. As it was in th' beginnin', is now an' ever will be, world without end, amen.

Miceawl. Yous are keepin' me from me work; I've a bit o' paintin' to do—so cheerio to th' pair o' yous. [*Singing as he closes the door*]:

> It aint gonna rain no more, no more,
> It aint gonna rain no more;

[*he closes the door and continues inside*]

> But how th' hell can anybody tell
> That it aint gonna rain no more!

1st Man. Saints an' Scholars dead an' gone, ghost o' Malachy that wore th' golden collar an' he a nipper, d'ye hear that! Oh! that's what comes a steppin' off th' steppin' stone.

2nd Man. Lions, Unicorns an' Poppies; cheerios an' tooraloos, Oh Paddy, Paddy, Paddy, none but righteous men can make our land a Nation once again!

1st Man. Oh, Joey, Joey, Joey, an' me afther me keepin' th' house in repairs for years without assin' a make, an' yestherday he had a man mendin' th' roof that wouldn't do a tap for him a few weeks ago—oh, Joey, Joey, wasn't I th' right mug!

2nd Man. An' Johnny, Johnny, look a th' years I spent there paintin' life size pictures for him, without takin' even time to run home for me meals—Sarsfield in th' kitchen, Robert Emmet in th' drawin'-room, an' Wolfe Tone on th' ceilin's —Oh, wasn't I th' right mug too!

[*Jimmy the Workman crosses wheeling a barrow.*]

Jimmy. I'll not stick this much longer, so I won't. Th' hardest worked an' th' worst fed in th' house—I'll emigrate to Russia, so I will! [*Exits.*]

1st Man. We're not goin' to take this lyin' down, min' you. We'll form a National Group an' demand to see Kathleen; if she knew we were driven out like this she'd raise hell. We'll demand to see her. [*Taking a green flag from his pocket, handing it to 2nd Man and singing*]:

> Wrap th' green flag round me, Joe,
> To die 'twere far more sweet,
> Than to be sacked out o' me job,
> An' sent to walk th' street.

2nd Man. You knock at th' door an' I'll shout in at th' window; we'll have to get back into th' house some way or another— be God, I'm beginnin' to feel very cold out here.

[*1st Man knocks at the door; 2nd Man goes to the window.*]

1st Man. Ay, Mick, open th' door for a minute; Mick, ay Mick!

2nd Man. Kathleen, Kathleen, ar'yin, ar'yin? Mrs. Houlihan, ar'yin? Ay, Mick, ar'yin, ar'yin?

1st Man. Oh, isn't he the cute oul' codger! He's turnin' th' bothered ear to us, now, you know.

2nd Man. I'll soon waken him up a bit, be sendin' a stone through th' window. [*He does so. Miceawl and the Man in the Kilts thrust their heads out of the window.*]

The Man in the Kilts. What th' hell are yous doin'? An inch nearer, an' yous ud cut the eye out o' me!

Miceawl. Ay, dhraw it mild there; there's enough o' damage done to th' house without yous startin'.

The Man in the Kilts. Who are yous, anyhow—what's your names?

1st Man, 2nd Man [*together*]. A chara, sir, agus is misheh lay mass more.[2]

---

[2]This does not mean a great deal. "A Chara" (friend), is the salutation of a letter; the rest (I remain repectfully yours) is the complimentary close.

The Man in the Kilts. Well, there's some o' th' Civic Guards down in th' cellar lookin' for poteen, an', if yous done behave yourselves, I'll send them up on top o' yous, an' then maybe yous'll give over your throwin' o' stones. [*He withdraws.*]

Miceawl. Well, what do th' pair o' yous want, now?

1st and 2nd Man. We want to see Kathleen; we must see Kathleen; we'll not go away till we see Kathleen.

Miceawl. Yous can't see her; it's young men she's lookin' for, not oul' fossils like yous. Yous can't see her—she's listenin' in! [*He goes to withdraw.*]

The Two Men. Mick, ay, Mick, hello Mick!

Miceawl. For God's sake, don't be callin' me Mick. What ud th' neighbours say if they heard yous callin' me Mick? I'm Miceawl—Mr. Miceawl O Houlihan.

1st Man. Mr. Miceawl O Houlihan, we're not goin' to be sacked be you; we've wrapped th' green flag round us an' we want to see Kathleen. We've formed ourselves into a National Group.

Miceawl. When yous were in yous wanted to get out; an' now, when yous are out yous want to get in—d'ye think I've nothin' to do but to be openin' an' shuttin' doors?

1st Man. The pair of us went to school with Kathleen; we learned our first lesson together in Easther Week.

Miceawl. Yous all went to school with Kathleen; people that don't know how to read an' write went to school with Kathleen! You learned your first lesson in Easther Week! Well, she's learned a lot since then. She's studyin' mathematics now; she can't be always stuck at her A B C.

Kathleen [*sticking her head out of the window*]. What do yous want with Kathleen?

2nd Man [*sings*].

> Oh, Kathleen, th' two only things that can save us,
> That are betther than bacon, than butter an' bread—
> Are th' life o' Wolfe Tone an' th' poetry of Davis,
> While you read th' hymnbook o' Churchill—nuff said.

1st Man [*sings*].

> Mavourneen, mavourneen, take heed to they warnin',
> That Johnny an' Joey are shoutin' at thee!
> If you want to be up to th' top o' th' mornin',
> Is misheh lay mass more, acushle ma chree!

Kathleen. Oh, for God's sake go away, an' done be annoyin' me. I have to practice me Fox Trots and Jazzin' so as to be lady-like when I make me deboo into the League o' Nations. [*She goes away.*]

Miceawl [*sharply*]. Off yous pop, now, th' pair o' yous. Throwin' stones is bad enough, but if I hear another note o' Kathleen Mavourneen, I'll send for th' Civic Guards. [*He goes.*]

Jimmy [*crossing the stage with a barrow*]. There's not a bone in me body that's not achin'; champagne an' oysthers for them, an' I'm to live on air, but I'll not stick it, so I won't. [*Exits.*]

1st Man. Oh, Joey, Joey, Joey, it's nothin', now, but a nest o' jobbery, jobbery, jobbery.

2nd Man. It'll have to be put down, Johnny, it'll have to be put down.

> [*They go out slowly, following each other step by step, singing dolorously.*]

> > The harp that once through Tara's hall,
> > The soul of music shed,
> > Now hangs as mute on Tara's wall,
> > As if that soul were fled.

> [*Miceawl enters the garden by the door. He is carrying a pot of green paint and a paint brush. He begins to paint the door.*]

Miceawl. A, ah, it's a dangerous thing to get on any way well in this world; when I was down everybody was tryin' to lift me up, an', now that I'm a little bit up, everybody's tryin' to knock me down! A, a, ah, I was a damn sight easier in me min' when I had nothin'!

[*By the gate Tomaus Thornton enters; he is a middle-aged man. His countenance is one of quiet cunning serenity; he tries to take the world as easily as the world will allow him. He is fond of talk but not of discussion, which he endeavours to avoid by passing it off. He is dressed in working clothes, which bear no marks of work.*]

Tomaus [*singing*].

Soldiers are we, whose lives are pledged to Ireland;
Some have come from a land beyond the sea—God
bless them!

God save all here, an' bless the work!

Miceawl. You too, you too, Tomaus . . . you too.

Tomaus. What's wrong with you, Mick; are you not well, or what? You're not lookin' very hilarious!

Miceawl. For God's sake, Tomaus, don't be callin' me Mick! You know as well as I do the kind o' people that's livin' in the Fawinne district; an' what would they say if they heard you callin' me Mick?

Tomaus. Ah, I wouldn't be mindin' that crowd. Even if you can't speak as they want you to, sure they can't put you out of the house, can they? A couple o' them kem to me t'other day—I heard afther that they wanted me to change me name from Thornton to Drineen dhoun,[3] or somethin'; they kep talkin' an' talkin' for hours an' hours, an' divil a bit o' me knew a word they were sayin'—ah, I wouldn't be botherin' me head about them at all.

[3]Irish for Thornton.

Miceawl. I have to keep up appearances now, I have to keep up appearances.

Tomaus. Ah, sure you've a nice little house of your own now, an' you needn't care for anybody.

Miceawl. Ah, the house is hardly worth livin' in, Tomaus; hardly worth livin' in. The inside's in a shockin' state! That rowdy Dawn o' Liberty Fife an' Drum Band is afther puttin' the finishin' touch on it.

Tomaus. I always had me own opinion about that same band. There's too many bandmasters in it! Playin' an' playin' the one tune, till everybody was fed up with it. Howsomever, nobody'll be able to hear much of them now since you've got your Brass Band.

Miceawl. Ah, I dunno, I dunno; me heart's bruk tryin' to keep them together. T'other band'll only play the one tune, but every member in ours wants to play a defferen' tune, an' the big drummer only wants to hear himself.

Mrs. O Houlihan [*popping her head out of the window. She has a worn and harassed look; her sleeves are tucked up indicating that she is busy. If her entire body could be seen, she would appear in a rough skirt, wearing heavy boots, but she is wearing a fancy Crepe de Chine blouse.*] Will the pair o' yous not be talkin' so much Bayurla![4] If yous don't mind, the Irish speakin' lodger'll hear yous! [*She withdraws.*]

Tomaus. A lodger! Have yous got a lodger now?

Miceawl. Oh, the fella that was always in the house—he was born in it, an' I suppose he'll die in it. The Man in the Kilts, you know. You could hardly get him to speak before the house was me own, an' now, he'll hardly let anyone else speak! I don't think he's right in the head. "I'll never give yous a bit o' peace," says he, "till yous all talk Irish."

[4]English.

Tomaus. He was always a bit queer; I'd let it run off me like wather off a duck's back—I wouldn't be botherin' me head about him.

Miceawl. Ah, you have to bother your head about him. Isn't the PP[5] an' the Schoolteacher afraid o' their lives o' him? Were you ever up in his room, Tomaus?

Tomaus. No; I don't want to be alone with a fella like that.

Miceawl. It's the curiousest room you ever seen! You'd lose your way in it, the way he has it filled with passages goin' in an' out, an' round about—taken he says from the Book o' the Yella Cow, or somethin'.

Tomaus. I never heard tell o' that book—ah, I suppose it's a book somethin' like Oul' Moore's Almanac.

Miceawl. An' he has all the walls destroyed with comical figaries that he calls fibulas, turks an' crosses o' cong; an' he won't let Kathleen read anythin' but the Book o' Kells—he says anythin' else ud be bad for her morals.

Tomaus. Sure, I wouldn't let him stop in the house at all, at all; the Book o' Kells! God, I'd rather even read The Lives o' th' Saints—an' that's bad enough—was he always as bad as he is now?

Miceawl. He's gettin' worse; he's a dangerous man right enough to have about the house. Such outlandish things as he does say: "Knock the house down," says he, "an' build it on the Hill o' Tara." "All round here," says he, "used to be the homes o' the people that came out o' the Ark."

Tomaus. For God's sake! What Ark; Noah's Ark?

Miceawl. Yis, the first Gaels.—An' of a queen that used to shake a wand an' the waves o' the sea ud come into the shore an' start to play dulcimers.

Tomaus. Some kind of a band in oul' gods' time that used to play on the seashore like them that do be in Bray.

[5]Parish Priest.

Miceawl. An' he's always blatherin' about the harp, an' he
couldn't play as much as a note o' Home Sweet Home on a
tin whistle. Ah, he's had everybody plagued, for he's a very
freemakin' fella, interferin' with everyone that comes into
the house, an' forcin' them to sit on an oul' stone that he
says was the throne of the oul' kings of Ireland.

Tomaus. A, ah, we're too far advanced now to be thinkin' o'
kings—I wouldn't be botherin' me head about him.

[*The Man in the Kilts enters the garden by the porch. He
is a very old and feeble man; he carries a stick, and walks
with an effort. Miceawl and Tomaus at once stand to
attention, and wear a reverential look.*]

The Man in the Kilts [*singing*].

> Key kirheh thoo lesh eg cassoo nah mo,
> Eg cassoo nah mo, eg cassoo nah mo,
> Key kirheh thoo lesh eg cassoo nah mo,
> Mar dulsey dolsey dayro![6]

Go on, sing it out, th' pair o' yous!

Miceawl and Tomaus [*together*].

> Key kirheh thoo lesh eg cassoo nah mo,
> Eg cassoo nah mo, eg cassoo nah mo,
> Key kirheh thoo lesh eg cassoo nah mo,
> Mar dulsey dolsey dayro!

The Man in the Kilts [*sighing*]. Government Irish, Government
Irish! . . . Ah, I'm not meself at all; I feel rotten—I'm
afraid I'm not long for this world!

Tomaus. Ah, I wouldn't say that, I wouldn't say that now;
you've a long spell in front of you yet, with the help o' God.

---

[6]"Who will you put with me tending the cattle Tending the cattle, tending the cattle/Who will you put with me tending the cattle . . ." The last line
is a somewhat meaningless refrain like "Hey nonny nonny."

The Man in the Kilts. Ah, I dunno, I dunno; I think I'm dyin'
on me feet—the doctors all say I haven't much longer to
live.

Tomaus. Ah, the doctors is the last I'd mind; they're oftener
wrong than right. If that's all you have to fret you, you
needn't mind—I wouldn't be botherin' me head about the
doctors.

The Man in the Kilts [*suddenly*]. Yous betther try that again.

Miceawl and Tomaus [*together*].

> Key kirheh thoo lesh eg cassoo nah mo,
> Eg cassoo nah mo eg cassoo nah mo;
> Key kirheh thoo lesh eg cassoo nah mo,
> Mar dulsey dolsey dayro!

[*When the verse ends the Man in the Kilts goes off Left.*]

The Man in the Kilts [*as he goes off*]. It could be a lot betther,
it could be a lot betther.

Tomaus. That oul cod's crocked; it won't be long till he snuffs it!

Miceawl. May it come soon an' suddent! Isn't it a shockin' thing
to have to be puttin' up with the like o' that—himself an'
his dulsey dolsey dayro!

Tomaus. Sure I wouldn't be doin' it for him; haven't you somethin' else to do besides dulsey dolsey dayroin'? I'd let him
say what he likes or think what he likes—I wouldn't be
botherin' me head about him.

Miceawl. Ah, you don't know, man, half o' what I have to do to
keep him quiet; he's goin' out of his mind—there's no
doubt about it. One minute he'll tell you he's a Roman, an'
the next that he's a Gael. D'ye know what he said yesterday?
Spell cup, says he; C, U, P, says I, astonished like; no, it's
not, no it's not, says he, in a rage, it's K, U, P—that's the
simplified spellin'—what's anyone to think of a man like
that?

U

Tomaus [*tapping his head significantly*] That's enough—I wouldn't bother me head about him, any more.

[*Sheela enters through the porch, carrying a stool which she places in the garden.*]

Tomaus. God save you, Mrs. Houlihan.

Sheela. You too, you too, Tomaus.

[*Sheela returns to the house.*]

Tomaus. I'm afraid the missus is doin' too much.

Miceawl. The pair of us is doin' too much. It's terrible the way we're kep' goin', an', along with that we have to stick that dulsey dolsey gazebo.

Tomaus. Doesn't Kathleen give yous a han?

Miceawl. Ay, tidyin' the ornamints on the chimney-piece—or the few that's left o' them. I don't know what's comin' over her —she won't do a han's turn since she started that bloody listenin' in!

[*Sheela returns, carrying a tub containing clothes which she commences to wash, having placed the tub on the stool.*]

Tomaus. There's a power o' washin' to be done about a house, Mrs. Houlihan.

Sheela. I don't think there's a house in the whole wide world that there's so much washin' to be done as there is in this house.

Tomaus. Ah, I wouldn't say that, now, I wouldn't say that; when you get used to it it'll be as easy as kiss han's.

Sheela. We'll all get our death o' cold if the windows isn't put in soon. We thought that because they were like church windows they'd respect them, but they didn't leave one that they didn't put in.

Tomaus. Ah, no matter where you go you'll get blaguards, Mrs. Houlihan.

Sheela. Indeed I thought the childer about here were betther reared; servin' at the altar an' a minute afther firin' a stone at you—I have a lump on me head yet as big as a duck egg from a skelp I got.

Miceawl. All along o' sellin' the family cow, as who'd have a betther right to sell it than us? What'll I sell it for, says I. Ass all you can, says they; but it's a bit ould now an' a little shaky, an' you'd betther take whatever you'll get, says they, or you might get nothin'. Twenty pouns, now, wouldn't be a bad price, says they. An' because I sold the cow for 19, 19 an' 11½ with a postidge stamp thrun in, they want to make out that I gave the beast away.

Sheela. We'll make them swally their words one o' these days, for there's one thing they can't deny, that we kem into the house with our heads up!

Tomaus [*to Sheela*]. Sure you're worse yourselves to be takin' any notice o' them; I simply wouldn't be botherin' me head about them.

Sheela. I wouldn't min' so much if Kathleen was all right. All that listenin' in is turnin' her brain; I hope to God that Doctor Feverwell'll come today, because I'm terrible anxious about her.

Miceawl. He's to come today in his gig.

Sheela. I hope he'll not forget to come.—An' there's Jimmy, the general labourer, commencin' to grouse as well; sayin' he has as much right to the house as anyone—an' more.

Miceawl. An' we afther sellin' the only cow we had to buy it.

Sheela. Sure he can't expect to get as good grub as we get.

Miceawl. If the house wasn't here he wouldn't get any at all.

Sheela. What ud the pair o' yous do without me, says he.

Miceawl. If you don't like it you can go somewhere else, says I.

Sheela. From the sun down to the centre the place is me own, says he.

[*Jimmy enters at a gallop wheeling the barrow, stopping suddenly in the centre.*]

Jimmy. I'm not goin' to stick this no longer, I'm not goin' to stick this no longer—[*bawling*] I'm going to go on strike!

Sheela. Why d'ye rush in like that, Jimmy, frightenin' the life out of a body?

Miceawl. Ah, then if you go out on strike this time, me boyo, you can stop out!

Jimmy. I'm goin' out anyhow; I couldn't be any worse out than I am in.

Tomaus. Aw, Jimmy, be reasonable! I'm sure if you tell Mr. O Houlihan quietly what you want, he'll only be too happy to listen to you.

Jimmy. What's the good o' listenin'? Isn't Kathleen listenin' in from mornin' till night, an' what good is it doin' her?

Sheela. Fellas pretendin' to love Kathleen, an'—

Jimmy. What's the good o' lovin' Kathleen, when she won't take any notice o' you? Others can hold her hand for hours, an' bring her for walks, but whenever she sees me, she passes me by with her nose in the air—just because I can't play the bloody piano!

Miceawl. Maybe it's playin' the piano y'ought to be—is there anything else you'd like!

Tomaus. Aw, be reasonable, be reasonable, Jimmy; I'm sure Mr. O Houlihan ud do anything to satisfy you—bar playin' the piano.

Jimmy. I want the house painted red!

Sheela. Ah, then, if Miceawl attempts to paint it red, he can look for some one else as a housekeeper. The people that come to our Gawden Pawties don't want a Bolshie in th' house!

[*The Free Stater and the Republican enter quickly.*]

The Republican [*shaking the hand of Miceawl*]. Ah, the bould
Miceawl; where's Kathleen? I must see her; I've a little
present for her—a picture I painted of herself in 1916 in
everlastin' oils.

The Free Stater [*shaking Mrs. O Houlihan's hand*]. Good
evening, Mrs. O Houlihan; how are you, Mrs. O Houlihan?
Where's my little pet, Kathleen? I've a little present for
her—a Manual on the Government of a house accordin'
to a Constitution.

Sheela. Poor little Kathleen's not well at all; the doctor says
she's not to be excited in any way.
'[*The Business Man and the Farmer enter.*]

The Farmer [*shaking Miceawl's hand*]. Evenin' Mr. O Houlihan; where's Kathleen? I've a little present for her—a bag
o' self-raisin' flour.

The Business Man [*shaking Mrs. O Houlihan's hand*]. Good
afternoon, Mrs. O Houlihan; where's Kathleen? I've a
present for her—a little clockwork motor car that'll run
all around the room; think o' that, Mrs. O Houlihan—a
little clockwork motor car that'll run all around the room!

Jimmy. Yous'll all have to go away ou' o' this—there's a
sthrike on here!

Tomaus. Jimmy, Jimmy, conthrol yourself, man; remember th'
glories o' Brian th' Brave! If you're goin' to turn into a
Bolshie, I'm done with you—I wouldn't be botherin' me
head about you! These fellas'll dhrive her mad before
they're done.

Sheela. If I bring Kathleen out, yous'll have to behave yourselves; she's so low, that talk above a whisper sets her out
of her mind.

All. Never fear, Mrs. O Houlihan, never fear; we all love little
Kathleen too much to do anything that ud go agen her.

Sheela [*at window*]. Kathleen, love, here's four young gentlemen wantin' to see you.

[*Kathleen comes out, Mrs. O Houlihan holding her arm. They all bow.*]

The Republican. Me own sweet, little red little rose!

The Free Stater. Me own fair, little Drimin Donn Deehlish![7]

The Farmer. Me clusther o' little brown nuts, me heart's longin' for you.

The Business Man. I'll crown thee with gold an' I'll crown thee with silver, sweet little beautiful pulse o' me heart!

Jimmy. The people's flag is deepest red—

Tomaus. For God's sake, man!

The Free Stater [*singing*]. There's a dear little colleen that lives in our isle—

The Republican. She's as fresh an' as fair as a daisy—

The Farmer. An' she's bless'd with a tear an' she's bless'd with a smile—

Tomaus. Faith, some day, yous'll all dhrive her crazy!

The Business Man. An' we all, big an' small, lov'd her well thro' th' ages—

Jimmy. An' I'd love her more for an increase in wages!

All. An' it's dear little Kathleen, sweet little Kathleen, dear, little sweet, little Kathleen of Ireland!

Sheela. Oh Kathleen, aren't they a lovely lot o' gentlemen?

Kathleen. Oh, I've heard this too ofen, ma; I'm gettin' sick of it; . . . it's all codology!

Miceawl [*to Tomaus*]. Which o' them, now, would you vote for?

Tomaus. Which o' them would I vote for? . . . I wouldn't vote for one o' them . . . I wouldn't bother me head about any o' them!

Kathleen. Me legs is thremblin' under me.

Sheela. Get her a chair out o' th' house, one o' yous.

7"Little brown cow," another name for Ireland.

[*The Free Stater, the Republican, the Farmer, the Business Man and Jimmy rush into the house for a chair.*]

The Free Stater [*inside*]. Ay, leggo ou' o' that— I'm well able to carry it meself!

The Republican [*inside*]. Give it to me, or I'll smash it over your head, you gang o' hypocrites, perjurers an' job-hunthers!

The Business Man [*inside*]. You ignorant country boor, how dare you jostle me; how dare you, how dare you, sir!

[*Noise inside of furniture being knocked about, and the breaking of delph.*]

Sheela. God Almighty, what are they doin' now?

Tomaus. They're smashin' up th' little happy home inside.

Miceawl [*to Tomaus*]. Which o' them, now, would you vote for?

Tomaus. I wouldn't be lettin' them knock about at all. Haven't you an' th' missus enough to do without this kind of racket?

Miceawl. I wish to God they didn't love Kathleen as much as they do!

[*The Free Stater and the Republican come out carrying the chair, with the Farmer and the Business Man hanging on, with Jimmy following holding on to the coat tails of the Business Man; all are tossed looking.*]

The Business Man [*indignantly*]. Lemme go, lemme go, do you want to pull th' coat off me back, you scoundrel?

Jimmy. It wouldn't take much to make me take off me coat an' knock th' stuffin' out o' you!

Sheela. Gentlemen, gentlemen, remember th' weakness o' little Kathleen!

The Republican [*to the Free Stater*]. I'll settle you, me boyo, one o' these days. Sit down, Kathleen; sit down, me little pet.

The Free Stater [*to the Republican*]. You'll settle me, will you? You'll have to eat a few more spuds, me boy, before you'll be able to do that. Sit down me little girl, sit down.

Tomaus [*excitedly*]. Wisht, th' whole o' yous; here's th' oul cod in th' kilts comin' along—attention, boys, for God's sake.
[*As the Man in the Kilts crosses they all sing.*]

All.   Kay kirheh thoo lesh eg cassoo nah mo,
                Eg cassoo nah mo, eg cassoo nah mo;
                Kay kirheh thoo lesh eg cassoo nah mo,
                Mar dulsey dolsey dayro!

The Man in the Kilts. Oh, that's terrible Irish, terrible Irish. Well, if I can't ram it into yous, I'll ram it into th' chiselurs. Unless they learn their Irish, they're to get nothin' to eat, nothin' to eat, do yous hear? I'll ram it into th' chiselurs, I'll ram it into th' chiselurs. [*He goes off.*]

The Free Stater [*shouting*]. Give's a kiss, give's a kiss, Kathleen.

The Republican [*shouting*]. Don't be a fool, Kathleen, don't be a fool—it's th' kiss o' Judas, it's th' kiss o' Judas!

The Farmer. Let me put me arm round you, Kathleen, an' you'll feel all right.

The Business Man [*shouting*]. Come for a walk, Kathleen, an' we'll combine business with pleasure!

Tomaus [*looking down the road*]. Here's th' doctor comin' in his gig.

Kathleen. Mother, mother, I don't know what's comin' over me —I feel as if I was goin' to faint!
[*The doctor runs in and feels her pulse.*]

The Doctor. Put her to bed, put her to bed!
[*Kathleen is helped in by Mrs. Houlihan. The Crowd follows trying to hold Mrs. Houlihan back.*]

The Free Stater. Ay, houl on there, Mrs. Houlihan; one minute, one minute.

The Republican. One word about the Republic before you go, Kathleen—it'll only take me five or six hours to say it.

The Farmer. Ay, keep back there, keep back there; I've a message for Kathleen that can't wait.

Miceawl [*hooshing them back*]. Ay, will yous all go to hell ou' o' this, an' let th' little girl get a minute's peace?

Tomaus [*remonstratively to them*]. Can't yous thry to take things a little easier. . . . Yous are makin' a nice show of yourselves, an' th' whole world lookin' at yous. . . . Be God, yous are changin' th' proverb from united we stand, to united we fall, divided we stand! Can't yous be united if it was only for five minutes an' give little Kathleen a chance.

The Business Man. That's what we're all lookin' for—unity an' peace.

The Republican. That's what I've been fightin' for all along.

The Farmer. Let's talk things over quietly in th' corner o' th' garden; maybe we could form a kind o' coalition committee.

Jimmy. This is some other game to cod th' workin' man.

[*They gather together in a corner of the garden.*]

Miceawl [*shouting up at the window*]. Is she all right, doctor, is she all right?

The Doctor [*at window*]. She's very weak, but she'll pull round after a bit, if she gets perfect quietness: A whisper may prove fatal—she'll need perfect peace and quietness for the rest of her National life.

Tomaus. Oh, be heavens, she's sure to get it too! If peace came we'd all die a sudden death!

Sheela [*at window, to Miceawl*]. Come up here an' give me a han', man.

Miceawl [*to Tomaus*]. Here, do a bit o' this, Tom, while you're waitin'.

Tomaus. Certainly, Mick, certainly. [*He starts to paint.*] Now, I'm goin' to get nothin' for this. This is a thank you job. . . . Oh, I'm not goin' to be a mug for anybody. [*He leaves off painting, takes a paper from his pocket, and sings as he goes off.*]

> Let politics go an' be damned,
> It's a thing that desthroys an' debases;
> I'll just have a read for to find
> A winner for Fairyhouse Races.

The Free Stater. Now let us all thake a solemn an' sacred oath.

The Republican. I won't, I won't, I won't; I'll not take no oath for nobody, so help me God!

> [*The Free Stater, the Farmer, and the Business Man rush into the house; the Republican runs to the window; Jimmy stands at the door.*]

The Free Stater [*inside, shouting*]. Vote for me, Kathleen; a vote for the Free State is a vote for Ireland.

The Republican. He's a liar, Kathleen; vote for me, and the Irish Republic, one an' invisible, one an' invisible!

The Farmer. Don't listen to him, me girl, they're ramming it down our throats. The only thing they're fit for is th' turnin' o' their coats; your happiness depends upon me stock o' spuds an' oats, me little Kathleen Houlihan o' Ireland! . . . an' I'm the man to mind it for you! Speed the plough, Kathleen, speed the plough!

Jimmy [*shouting*]. Socialism's the only hope o' th' workers, socialism's th' only hope o' th' workers.

The Orangeman [*appears outside the garden beating a big drum and singing*].

> Come let us all with heart an' voice,
> Applaud our lives' defender;
> Who at th' Boyne his valour show'd,
> An' made his foes surrender.
> To God above th' praise we'll give,
> Both now an' ever after,
> An' bless th' glorious memory
> Of William that crossed th' water.

[*Noise, confusion and shouting.*]

. . . an' we can build houses for th' workin' class! How can you have trade without the harvest? Stick to me, Kathleen, and we'll have so many houses the workin' class'll be able to choose.

Miceawl [*appearing at the window*]. Holy God, are we not goin' to be let get even one night's sleep in peace!

CURTAIN

Wrap the Green Flag Round Me, Boys

Kathleen Mavourneen

The Harp that Once Through Tara's Halls

Key Kirheh Thoo Lyume

Soldiers' Song (Excerpt)

There's a Dear Little Colleen
(The Dear Little Shamrock)

Let Politics Go and Be Damned

The Orangeman's Song

* * *

"Nannie's Night Out" was first produced on September 29, 1924, at the Abbey Theatre. It was directed by Michael J. Dolan and had the following cast:

MRS. POLLY PENDER	Maureen Delany
OUL JOHNNY	Barry Fitzgerald
OUL JIMMY	Michael J, Dolan
OUL JOE	Gabriel J. Fallon
IRISH NANNIE	Sara Allgood
ROBERT	Gerald Breen
A BALLAD SINGER	F. J. McCormick
A YOUNG MAN	Arthur Shields
A YOUNG GIRL	Eileen Crowe

CROWD: Seaghan Barlow, F. Ellis, W. O'Hara, M. Judge

For October 6, 1924, Joseph Holloway recorded in his journal that the Abbey was thronged to see *Arms and the Man* and O'Casey's new one-act, "Nannie's Night Out." O'Casey, he wrote, "has caught the ear of the public in no uncertain fashion and the theatre is usually overcrowded to see his plays." Holloway spoke to O'Casey before the performance and learned that the playwright had seen the doll incident enacted in a shop and that he had based Polly and the three old boys on people whom he knew. "Oul' Jimmie," recounted Holloway, "often presented the real-life Polly with jewellery but begged it back on seeing other candidates in the field for her hand." Holloway also mentioned that O'Casey "doesn't much care for the farce himself, now that he sees it on the stage."

In *Inishfallen, Fare Thee Well* O'Casey gives nearly a page to "Kathleen" but dismisses in half a sentence "a one-act work called *Nannie's Night Out,* a play no-one liked, except A.E., otherwise known as George Russell, who thought it O'Casey's best work; an opinion that didn't bother Sean, for he knew A.E. knew nothing about the drama, and felt it a little less. . . ."

A.E.'s approving review was delivered Poloniusly with much pontifical muzziness. For instance, "I went away from the theatre hearing her [Nannie's] voice and remembering that learned Cardinal who spoke to John Inglesant about the virtue in passion released from all limits and how it followed in its motions a divinity than which there is none higher." Reading the review is like reading Chesterton on Shaw; you can scarcely see the subject for the commentator.

A second review appeared in A.E.'s *Irish Statesman* which more perceptively described an intelligent viewer's reaction. On October 18, Bertha Buggy wrote:

> If I go to a tragedy or an ordinary "straight" drama I likewise adjust my mentality to the prompting of the play-bill. But at a play of Mr. O'Casey's I am a thing without anchor—to be tossed from one side to the other at his strange behests.
>
> Take his latest play—*Nannie's Night Out*—a rocking, roaring comedy—Dublin accents; queer "characters"; window-smashing; burlesque love-making. Our sides ache, we laugh; we roar; we gasp—and then—a sudden feeling of discomfort, a queer, stupid feeling as if we wanted to cry. . . . He brings us to his plays and then he heaves life at us, with its sharp corners and its untidy jumble of laughter and tears. . . . And the worst of it is, that if we go on

allowing him to make us laugh and cry together in this hysterical manner, we may end by insisting that he is a genius.

Discussing "Nannie" and "Kathleen" with O'Casey, I learned that he still prefers "Kathleen" and thinks "Nannie" rather negligible. O'Casey is no longer interested in the kind of play that "Nannie" is; his later plays have been in the fantastic manner of "Kathleen." "Nannie" is of the same family as O'Casey's three great early dramas—the two-act *Shadow of a Gunman,* the three-act *Juno and the Paycock,* and the four-act *Plough and the Stars.* The one-act "Nannie" is the least of these plays, but it is cut from the same cloth. And, to this reader, within its narrower scope, it has the same excellences.

Although O'Casey preferred that a later one-act be chosen, he allowed a revival of the play for the Lafayette Little Theatre at Lafayette, Indiana, which had previously presented the first performance of *The Drums of Father Ned.* The second production of "Nannie" occurred thirty-seven years after the first, on March 13, 1961. The ending used was the second ending printed in this book. Gabriel Fallon wrote me, "I do recall a conversation in which Sean said there were *three* endings, the one he wanted, the one they wanted, and the compromise, which was the one we used."

A wave of illness in the cast prevented the Indiana production from being as sharp and incisive as it should have been, but it came close enough to reveal a play as rich in moving pathos as in brilliant comedy. The second ending, in which Nannie is dragged screaming to the police station is not so obviously pathetic as the version wherein she dies and the mourners chant a litany that foreshadows the brilliant chants of *The Silver Tassie* and *Within the Gates.* But when O'Casey juxtaposes Nannie's wild exit against the Ballad Singer's closing song on a darkened stage, he is manipulating the prisms of his kaleidoscope in the same way and with something of the same brilliance that he used in the endings of *Juno* and *The Plough.* Indeed, the whole play is eminently alive. It is packed with the song, the dancing, the wild rhetoric, and the verve that have become O'Casey's trademarks.

Most of the characters would appear in other guises in O'Casey's later plays, but a word must be given to Irish Nannie. She appears as Mild Millie in *Drums Under the Windows,* the third volume of O'Casey's autobiography; and Ronald Ayling has suggested to me, with considerable plausibility I think, that Jannice, the Young Whore in *Within the Gates,* owes much to Nannie. Although Jannice is more complex, there are similarities strong enough to show the relationship. Compare, for instance, Jannice's "I'll go the last few steps of the way rejoicing; I'll go, go game, and I'll die dancing." Also, on December 27, 1925, the *New York Times* printed a letter from O'Casey which said, "The Abbey directors finally allowed the author to withdraw the work because he felt the character of Nannie deserved the richer picture of a three-act play." I mention these facts as another example—if another still be needed—that O'Casey is scarcely a literal transcriber of reality. Nannie is one of the most demanding and exhausting and flamboyant parts that O'Casey has ever written for an actress. To my mind, she must surely take her place next to Juno Boyle and the Bessie Burgess of O'Casey's most brilliant early plays. Directing the play merely confirmed for me the conclusion I had reached after reading the manuscript and preparing it for the printer: "Nannie's Night Out" is one of the superb one-act plays of the modern stage, and it must take a place next to the great one-acts of O'Casey's colleagues—Strindberg, Synge, and Shaw.

The text of the play is a recension of four varying and incomplete versions—the original typescript and three Abbey typescripts—and two pages of added material. I have printed only two of the three endings to the play, for the third ending does not differ materially from the second, except for the excision of the gunman scene. I have retained an allusion to the teaching of Irish to the children in the schools, even though O'Casey indicated in a letter of 1929 that he would omit it in future performances (". . . as I'm no longer living in Ireland, it would be a bit of chique to criticise the cult"). The allusion occurred in the original performance and was evidently a telling line, for *Irish Truth,* on October 4, 1924, stated that "There was a loud round of applause when Polly Bender asked if it would not be 'betther to do something for the poor kids instead of teachin' them Irish?' " Elsewhere in this book, O'Casey has made the same point, and he has since made much stronger criticisms of Ireland. Finally, for a reason that quite eludes me, the line still drew laughter from an audience of Hoosiers.

Nannie's Night Out

A Comedy in One Act

CHARACTERS

MRS. POLLY PENDER, *proprietress of the Laburnum dairy*
SWEET ON POLLY:
> OUL JOHNNY, *a lodger*
> OUL JIMMY
> OUL JOE

IRISH NANNIE, *a young spunker*[1]
ROBERT, *Nannie's son*
A BALLAD SINGER AND HIS WIFE
A YOUNG MAN
A YOUNG GIRL
CROWD

SCENE: The Premises of the Laburnum Dairy.
TIME: The Present.

Two Ballad Singers—a Man and a Woman—are heard singing:

> For Ireland is Ireland thro' joy an' thro' tears.
> Hope never dies thro' they long weary years;
> Each age has seen countless, brave hearts pass away,
> But their spirit still lives on in they men of to-day!

The Curtain rises and shows:

A small dairy and provision shop in a working-class district. The shop is about as large as a fairly sized room; a small counter, on which are a crock of milk and a butter-weighing scales. At Back, a window filled with a medley of sweets, soap, penny toys, cigarettes, sauce, balloons, etc. At the end of counter, Right, is a railed-in till; on this is hanging a notice: "No Credit Given." Beside the notice is a price list, written with coloured chalks on

[1]Spunker: a drinker of methylated spirit.

black millboard. At Back, in a prominent position, are some small dressed dolls. The entrance from the street to the shop is on Right. On Left, a door leading to another part of the house. One electric bulb supplies the light. It is about eight o'clock, on a cold, wet, wintry evening.

Mrs. Pender, behind the counter, is weighing up sugar; she is a tall, straight, briskly moving woman, of about fifty; age hasn't yet taken all the friskiness of youth out of her. She is a widow, living alone—all her children being either married or dead—working from morning till night, the shop brings her in just enough to keep her going.

Johnny is standing beside Mrs. Pender, his hand on a newspaper, that is on the counter. Johnny is an elderly, stout, rubicund visaged man approaching sixty; his skin is tight on his body, like the tensely drawn head of a drum. His moustache is closely cropped. He is in his shirt sleeves, and is wearing a jerry hat. Beside him, on the counter, is a small cream jug.

Johnny [*looking up into Mrs. Pender's face*]. An' she hot you right between th' two eyes with it?

Mrs. Pender. How do I know you got th' egg here, or no, says I; d'ye doubt me word, says she; I don't doubt your word, says I, but I'm not goin' to take th' egg back. With that, she let it fly, an' hot me right between th' two eyes with it!

Johnny [*putting his arm around her neck*]. As long as they know you're a lone widda, they'll stop at nothin'. The sooner you get buckled, Polly, th' betther.

Mrs. Pender [*slyly*]. To you?

Johnny [*tightening his arm round her neck*]. Polly—

Mrs. Pender [*taking his arm away*]. Here, go on up, an' get your tea; I'll be wantin' you to take th' shop for a while in a few minutes.

Johnny [*taking up the paper and looking at it*]. Heated scene in th' Doyle:[2] Deputy Morrison moved that th' Doyle end at six, instead of twelve, as th' Deputies were gettin' tired. Deputy Doran said they were sent here to do th' Nation's business; an' they could, an' they would do it, if they stopped up all night. It was like th' Labour Party, thryin' to do as little as they could. Labour Deputies, leppin' to their feet: withdraw, withdraw!

Mrs. Pender. Right between th' eyes I got it—

Johnny. Th' Cann Come-early,[3] ordher, ordher!

Mrs. Pender. What's th' Cann Come-early?

Johnny. Th' Sword Bearer, of course.

Mrs. Pender. Why do they be usin' names no-body understands?

Johnny. Everybody undherstands it; you might as well say that no-one ud undherstand Dunnlockairy meant Kingstown. I don't like th' idea of them goin' to inthroduce this new Divorce Bill—a nice thing if we had Free Love in this counthry.

Mrs. Pender. I don't know what th' Doyle is doin' at all; ah, I suppose th' only thing to do, is to put our trust in God.

Johnny. I betther be goin' up, or th' tea'll be stewed.

> [*Taking the cream jug, he goes out by door on Left. Mrs. Pender resumes the weighing of the sugar.*]

Voices of the Ballad Singers.

> For Ireland is Ireland thro' joy an' thro' tears.
> Hope never dies thro' they long weary years.
> Each age has seen countless, brave hearts pass away,
> But their spirit still lives on in they men of to-day!

> [*A pause: then the Man Ballad Singer enters. The under life of his profession has soiled him a good deal; he has all*

[2]Dail Eireann, the Irish legislative body.
[3]Ceann Comhairle, the chief counsellor, the Speaker of the House.

the cuteness of his class; there is a week's growth of beard on his chin; he is sometimes deferential, sometimes defiant, timid and bold. He wears a heavy, tattered top coat. His battered hat is in his hand, and he stretches it out in a suggestive, imploring and expectant movement. The woman's voice can still be heard singing some distance away, For Ireland is Ireland, etc. There is a slight pause, which is broken by a gentle cough from the Ballad Singer. Mrs. Pender shakes her head. The Ballad Singer holds the hat a little nearer. Mrs. Pender shakes her head a little more vigorously. A pause.]

The Ballad Singer. It's a cowld night an' a wet wan . . . me an' th' Mot[4] is nearly drownded . . . God an' th' Holy Angels bless you, maam. . . . It's cruel—th' whole street to be able to spare only tuppence—it's cruel. [*A pause.*] Tuppence! Th' fourth part of th' price of a pint—it's cruel!

Mrs. Pender. This is a bad place to come; everythin' goin' out an' nothin' comin' in—when all is paid, I don't have what ud jingle on a tombstone.

The Ballad Singer [*coming nearer to her*]. Eleven o' them me an' me Mot has . . . eleven chiselurs[5] to keep . . . eleven livin' an' two dead . . . now if it was only two livin' an' eleven dead, I'd have an aysier conscience.

[*A clamour of voices heard outside, punctuated by shouts from Irish Nannie.*]

The Voice of Irish Nannie. This is Irish Nannie; out o' jail again an' lookin' for throuble; let them send along their Baton Men, Nannie's got a pair o' mits that'll give them gib!

Voices in Crowd. Up Irish Nannie; give us a song, give us a song, Nannie; let th' poor woman alone.

[4]Wife.
[5]Children.

The Voice of Irish Nannie [*singing*].

> She's an' oul' fashion'd lady with oul' fashion'd ways,
> An' a smile that says welcome to you.
> An oul' fashion'd bedside where she kneels an' prays,
> When th' toil of th' long day is through.

The Ballad Singer [*as Nannie is singing above*]. If it was th'
Summer, aself, it wouldn't be so bad. . . . It's no laughin'
matther to be singin' 'Kelly o' Killann,' an' the rain beatin'
into your dial. Cruel.

> [*Irish Nannie enters singing. She is about thirty years of age,
> well made, strong, and possibly was handsome before she
> began to drink. Her eyes flash with the light of semi-mad-
> ness; her hair is flying about her shoulders. Her blouse is
> open at the neck. A much damaged hat, containing flow-
> ers that once were brightly coloured, but are now faded,
> is on her head. Her manner, meant to be recklessly merry,
> is very near to hysterical tears; a shawl is hanging over
> one arm.*]

Irish Nannie [*singing*].

> Tho' she wears no fine clothes, nor no rich silken hose,
> Still there's something that makes her divine,
> For th' angels above, taught th' way how to love
> To that oul' fashion'd mother o' mine!

> Irish Nannie's out again, an' as fresh as a daisy; an' as full
> o' life, an' lookin' for throuble.

The Ballad Singer. I don't know how we're goin' to live out th'
winther. I wouldn't mind about meself, if it wasn't for th'
Mot an' th' chiselurs. I'm waitin' for th' first spring prim-
rose to beckon me back to th' counthry roads. . . . Th' Mot
an' chiselurs is too delicate for th' counthry, an' I'm too
sthrong for th' city. . . . Everythin' here—th' threes growin'

in th' streets; th' stars thryin' to shine in th' sky; th' rain fallin' and th' win' blowin'—they're all soiled with th' thrademark o' Dublin. . . . It's cruel.

Irish Nannie [*giving her shawl a defiant pull, and her voice a triumphant tone*]. I'm only afther comin' out o' the "Joy"—two months I done . . . assault an' batthery on a Polisman . . . me an' him had a hard sthruggle. . . . Th' same boyo'll think twiced before pullin' Irish Nannie again. . . . Be God, I didn't let him take me for nothin'—I bet him up in th' face!

Mrs. Pender. Wasn't that th' second time you were in Mountjoy, Nannie?

Irish Nannie. Second time me neck! Th' hundhred an' second time ud be nearer th' mark! Don't I know every stone in th' buildin'. Las' year ten months—it didn't take a feather out o' me—only a few o' th' wans in me hat!

Mrs. Pender [*to the Ballad Singer*]. There's no use o' you waitin', me poor man, I can't give it to everywan.

The Ballad Singer. You can't give it to everywan offen provides an excuse to give it to no-wan.

Mrs. Pender [*to Nannie*]. Young Doran hopped over this mornin' with a bad egg, an' because I wouldn't change it, she let me have it between th' two eyes.

Irish Nannie. I'm tellin' you th' Polis is makin' a mistake if they think they can tame Nannie; Nannie's not like some o' th' Judies that's knockin' about, that has as much gizz in them as if they war afther a hundhred days' hunger strike! Irish Nannie has gizz in her, gizz in her, gizz in her! [*Singing.*] For the angels above taught th' way how to love, to that oul' fashion'd mother o' mine! [*Slapping the Ballad Singer on the shoulder.*] A short life an' a merry wan, ay, oul' cock?

The Ballad Singer. Oh, it's cruel, it's cruel. Yis, yis, a short life an' a merry wan—oh, it's cruel, it's cruel.

Irish Nannie [*coughing, sits down*]. I'm dyin' on me feet . . . th'
spunk has me nearly done for. . . . Th' prison docthor told
me th' oul' heart was crocked, an' that I'd dhrop any minute. . . . I'm afire inside . . . no-one cares a curse about
Irish Nannie. . . . [*Screaming.*] I'll make a hole in th' river,
I'll make a hole in th' river!

The Ballad Singer. It's cruel, it's cruel.

Irish Nannie [*to the Ballad Singer*]. Never say die till you're
dead. . . . [*Singing.*] She's an oul' fashion'd lady with oul'
fashion'd ways, an' a smile that says welcome to you. . . . If
ever I meet that long-legged, counthry-faced bousey of a
bobby that got me pulled, th' Lord look down on him; I'll
batther th' helmet down over his head. . . . [*Going up to the
door and shouting to the street.*] I'll kick th' shins off him!
They're not bringin' a chiselur to school when they're
bringin' Nannie to th' Polis Station. Five o' them it took, an'
she sthrapped on a sthretcher, th' last time to bring her in!
Nannie can tear an' kick an' bite! I'll die game. [*Screaming.*] I'll die game, I'll die game!

The Ballad Singer. It's cruel, it's cruel.

Mrs. Pender. Go on home, now, Nannie, an' have a good lie
down; you need it badly; go on home, Nannie—there's a
good woman.

Irish Nannie [*coming back and sitting on the stool in front of
the counter*]. Nannie's no home. . . . Wan place is as good
as another to Nannie. When Nannie was a chiselur any oul'
hall she could find was Nannie's home—afther gettin',
maybe, a morguein' from her oul' wan. Sleep? What does
Irish Nannie want with sleep?

The Ballad Singer. It's cruel, it's cruel.

Irish Nannie. It's merriment Nannie wants . . . singin' an' dancin'
an' enjoyin' life. . . . What's the use o' bein' alive if you're
not merry? [*Screaming.*] Merriment, merriment, merri-

ment! [*Subsiding with a cough.*] We'll be long enough dead. [*To the singer.*] Nothin' like keepin' up th' oul' heart, ay?

The Ballad Singer. Ay, if you had anything to keep it up with. Afther singin' your fill in a dozen sthreets, an' gettin' nothin'; findin' that half o' th' people was blind, an' th' other half deaf, you'd say it was cruel, cruel!

Irish Nannie [*catching him in her arms*]. We'll be long enough dead, man. A short life an' a merry wan. [*Waltzing him round the shop, singing.*] She's an oul' fashion'd lady with oul' fashion'd ways, an' a smile that says welcome to you.

The Ballad Singer [*in vigorous protest*]. Ay, houl on there, houl on there. Me joints wasn't made for that gallivantin'; . . . will you houl on there, I'm tellin' you!

[*People gather at the door of the shop, amused at the sport; they offer encouragement with cries of, "Good man, Nannie; give him a good jazz; give him a balloon, Mrs. Pender."*]

Irish Nannie.

An oul' fashion'd bedside where she kneels an' prays,
When th' toil of th' long day is through.

[*She suddenly releases the Ballad Singer, and seizing one of the balloons hanging up in the shop, she goes out singing and dancing, and can be heard going along the street followed by the crowd.*]

The Ballad Singer [*leaning against the counter, exhausted*]. That's a wild animal, that wan.

Mrs. Pender. There's no use o' you waitin'. . . . Now an' again a coin comin' in between a finger an' thumb, an' people expectin' you to be givin' it back in handfuls.

The Ballad Singer [*with a little bitterness*]. Divil a much fear o' you givin' it back in handfuls.

Mrs. Pender [*briskly*]. Fear or no fear, there's no use o' you waitin'. . . . Wan comin' in assin' you to give them a penny stamp . . . another thumpin' th' counther when you're upstairs, an' when you're afther breakin' your neck rushin' down, they'll ass you, "What's th' right Time, Mrs. Pendher?" . . . an' someone'll folly them be a short head, assin' you for change of a threepenny bit!

The Ballad Singer [*fiercely*]. A penny won't break you, will it? If th' oul' spirit still lives on in th' men o' to-day, it doesn't look like as if it was livin' on in th' women!

[*Mrs. Pender takes a brush from the end of the shop, and with the handle knocks at the ceiling. After a few moments oul' Johnny White enters by door on Left. He has a habit of catching the lapels of his coat and pulling at them with a jerk, ejaculating, "ayee" as he does so. His coat is on now, and he is still wearing his hat. He looks from the Ballad Singer to Mrs. Pender.*]

Johnny. Ayee.

Mrs. Pender. Here, take th' shop, Johnny, for a few minutes till I wet a cup o' tea.

[*Mrs. Pender goes out by door on Left; Johnny takes off his coat, and goes behind the counter.*]

Johnny [*looking at the Ballad Singer*]. Well, sir?

The Ballad Singer [*derisively*]. Well, yourself, sir?

Johnny [*forcibly*]. If you want nothin', you betther clear ou' o' this.

The Ballad Singer. You don't own th' shop, do you?

Johnny. Own or no own, you clear ou' o' this.

The Ballad Singer. Oh . . . are you th' cock lodger?

Johnny. Cock lodger or hen lodger, you clear ou' o' this!

The Ballad Singer. Sure, isn't it all over th' neighbourhood, everybody talkin' about it . . . you an' oul' Joe an oul'

Y

Jimmy makin' a holy show o' themselves runnin' afther her.
. . . You're a nice lookin' thing to be lookin' for a woman to
be sittin' on your knee . . . an' you afther berryin' two o'
them.

Johnny. What is it to you if I berried a regiment o' them? Pop off
ou' o' this, now, or you'll go out quickern you come in, I'm
tellin' you!

The Ballad Singer. Name some o' th' deadly sins, says a clergyman to a kid he was examinin' for Confirmation; Pride is
wan, says th' youngster. Gwan, says th' priest, name another. Mathrimony, says th' chiselur—an' when I look at
you an' think o' her, I wouldn't say but th' chiselur was
right!

Johnny [*coming from behind the counter*]. Right or wrong, you
betther be gettin' out' o' this while you're safe.

The Ballad Singer. More than me's been havin' a good laugh at
yous; you that ud hardly be able to walk twiced round
Nelson's Pillar without sittin' down for a rest. Oul' Jimmy
that's so blind with age, that he wouldn't know a live bird
in a cage from a dead wan, unless he heard it singin'. An'
Oul' Joe so bent that he could pick a penny off th' ground
without stoopin'. [*Mrs. Pender appears at door in a flame of
indignation.*] Oh, it ud be hard to say which o' th' two
plagues is th' worse—youngsters that you can't force into
gettin' married even wanst, or oul' stagers that you can't
keep from gettin' married three or four times. It's cruel, it's
cruel.

Mrs. Pender [*going behind the counter*]. Here, clear on ou' o'
this y'oul' scandal-giver. If a body wants to marry aself,
we're not goin' to ass you for a special Dispensation. Buzz
off, now; if th' man won't deal with you, th' woman will. Be
off, now, an' take your spirit that still lives on in th' men o'
to-day with you.

The Ballad Singer [*to Johnny*]. Why don't you put your arms round her an' give her a birdie? Isn't she waitin' for wan? You'd find Oul' Joe or Oul' Jimmy ud do it if they got th' chance. . . . Oh, me love is like a red, red rose! Wanst it was th' man that had to pick out th' best o' th' women, but now, it's th' lassie that has to pick out th' handsomest o' th' men—I wouldn't like her job, for there's none o' yous nice lookin'. I think meself, it'll be Oul' Joe. [*To Johnny.*] Maybe you don't know she was at th' pixstures last night with him? Me an' th' Mot seen her hangin' on his arm, an' a bow in her hat as big as th' wings of an aeroplane! . . . Orange blossoms an' cypress trees. . . . [*He goes slowly to the shop door, lilting softly as he goes out.*]

Th' mountain brooks were rushin', Annie dear;
Th' Autumn eve was flushin', Annie dear;
But brighter was your blushin', when first, your murmurs hushin',
I told me love out-gushin', Annie—

Oh, it's cruel, it's cruel! [*He goes out.*]

Mrs. Pender [*to Johnny*]. You'll want to pull them up on you if you want your name over th' door. There's not much use of havin' a man like you about th' place, if any oul' thramp can come in an' say what he like in th' shop.

Johnny [*going to her behind the counter*]. Now, Polly, Polly, you didn't want me to go an' hit an oul' man, did you?

Mrs. Pender. An oul' man! Sure he wasn't any ouldher than yourself. I'm tellin' you if you're goin' to be in this shop, you'll have to be dealin' with more than cock-sparrows. A big fella like you to be afraid of a poor oul' scrawl that was thin to th' point of emancipation. If Oul' Joe had a been here, he'd ha soon sent him flyin'.

Johnny. Oul' Joe! I'd like to see him boxin' an' he half blind.
Sure if he was lookin' at an elephant a few yards away, he'd
think it was a fly! Oul' Joe, ayee! If you took Oul' Joe,
it wouldn't be long till there was no name over th' shop.

Mrs. Pender. Well, there's Oul' Jimmy left. Not a bad oul' skin,
now, since he's taken th' pledge.

Johnny. Ayee. He's a great teetotaler now—wild horses wouldn't
drag him into a pub, an' in a day or two, wild horses won't
be able to drag him out o' wan!

[*A commotion heard outside some distance away, and the
voice of Nannie shouting.*]

Irish Nannie [*outside*]. Irish Nannie's out again, out again . . .
she's not dead yet . . . kept her crippled oul' fella for two
years . . . a jib of a crane fell on his back workin' on th'
docks, an' smashed his spine; two weeks' half pay he got
from th' stevedore, an' then th' bastard went bankrupt . . .
an' Nannie kep him for two years an' he lyin' on his back.
. . . We'll all be long enough dead.

Mrs. Pender. She's full up o' methylated spirits again. She'll
start smashin' windows in a few minutes.

Irish Nannie [*outside*]. Nannie doesn't care a curse for anybody.
. . . Let them send down their Foot, an' their Calvary—
Nannie's waitin' for them; she'll give them somethin'
betther than cuttin' down th' Oul' Age Pensions . . . Republicans an' Free Staters—a lot of rubbidge, th' whole o'
yous! Th' poor Tommies was men!

[*Oul' Jimmy is seen peering in through the window, shading
his eyes with his hands; he presses his nose against the
pane till it is flattened, desperately endeavouring to discover if Mrs. Pender be alone. Johnny perceives him,
and moves to the end of the shop. Satisfied that a fair
field is before him, he enters by the shop door. Jimmy is
well over sixty, but he is hardy and lusty still. He carries*]

*himself with a jaunty air, but age has given a stiff and
jerky action to his comical sprightly movements. His voice
is a shaky treble. He carries a heavy walking stick under
his arm. He is wearing a fancy waistcoat, a frock coat
and a seal-skin cap, and has a flower in his buttonhole.
He is painfully near-sighted, and peers closely at everything. He comes in whistling, but only succeeds in hitting
a note of the tune here and there.]*

Jimmy [*taking a bunch of flowers from under his coat, he does
not see Johnny*]. Them's for you, Polly . . . though a flower
doesn't need a flower, sure it doesn't . . . I was afraid that
other Ibex ud be here, annoyin' us, an'—

Johnny [*viciously*]. Y'ought to open your eyes a little wider, for
th' Ibex happens to be here. Maybe you ought to be a little
more careful of what you're sayin', Mr. Jimmy Devanny,
Esquire! Ibex, uh, be God, that's a good wan!

Jimmy. I, I didn't think you'd be hangin' around here—

Johnny. Haven't I as much right to be hangin' round here as
you have? It's a dangerous thing for an oul' man to be
looking for throuble, for he might get enough of it. . . . Ibex,
be God, that's a good wan!

Mrs. Pender. Now, we want no fightin' here . . . Irish Nannie's
enough, without havin' yous at it . . . Jimmy didn't mean
any harm.

Johnny [*buttoning his coat, preparatory to going*]. Oh, if he's
your choice, I wish th' both of yous luck. But if I was you
I'd keep him from callin' people Ibexes. I'm tellin' you no
man is goin' to be let call me an Ibex! Flowers! Romeo an'
Juliet! [*He goes towards the street door.*] It's sickenin'
. . . Ibex, be God, that's a good wan! [*He goes out.*]

Jimmy. He doesn't like to hear th' truth. . . . He's lookin' terrible
bad. His face is puffed like a purple balloon. . . I wouldn't
wondher if he dhropped down sudden, some day. . . . A

woman ud be a fool to have anything to do with him.

[*Mrs. Pender takes the flowers with one hand, and Jimmy catches hold of the other.*]

Mrs. Pender. They're lovely, they're lovely, Jimmy.

Jimmy. Not half as lovely as little, little Polly herself.

Mrs. Pender. Young Doran hopped here this mornin' with a bad egg. How do I know you got th' egg here, says I; d'ye doubt me word says she; I don't says I, but I'll not change it; with that she let fly, an' hot me right between th' two eyes with it!

Jimmy. Oh, I wish I'd ha been here; you'll always have to put up with them things till you have a man about th' place.

Mrs. Pender. Here, let go me hand, Jimmy.

Jimmy [*slyly*]. Oh, be th' way you don't like me to be holdin' it. Isn't it th' business? Who was it said that a woman's no meant yis; an' a woman's yis meant no? When are you goin' to put another little ring on th' little third finger of th' little left hand—wouldn't it be th' business?

Mrs. Pender. Now, don't be naughty, Jimmy, don't be naughty.

Jimmy [*elated at the idea of being naughty*]. Naughty, ay; why not? Oh, women is cute, women is cute—isn't it th' business? We're not as ould as all that. [*Singing.*]

Ses herself to meself, you can court with th' rest o' them.
Ses meself to herself, sure I'm better than gold;
Ses herself to meself, you can court with th' rest o' them.
Ses meself to herself, sure we'll never grow ould!

[*He begins to cough with the singing.*] O, o, o, o, this cough has me nearly worn away!

[*A young girl enters. She is nicely dressed, and speaks in a gushing way.*]

The Young Girl. How much is them dolls there? A little sisther o' mine is always assin' me to brin' her home a doll.

Mrs. Pender [*smilingly*]. A shillin' each, me dear.

The Young Girl [*astonished*]. Only a shillin'! Would you please let me have a look at wan, maam?

[*Mrs. Pender hands her one of the dolls.*]

The Young Girl [*examining the doll*]. Oh, I'll have to take wan o' them. . . . Isn't it marvellous how they make them for a shillin'! [*Holding the doll flat.*] Closes its eyes, mind you, too. . . . [*Looking at the clothes.*] Everything perfect—tangerine undies an' all! . . . [*Turning towards the door and raising her voice.*] Maggie, look at this lovely doll—an' only a shillin'!

[*She moves rapidly to the door and passes out. A pause.*]

Mrs. Pender. What on earth's keepin' her?

Jimmy. Showin' it to th' other wan, I suppose.

[*A pause.*]

Mrs. Pender [*rapidly, her suspicions aroused*]. Have a look out, Jimmy, an' see what she's doin'.

Jimmy [*going to the door and looking up and down*]. God, I can see neither sign nor light of her.

[*Mrs. Pender runs to the door and looks up and down the street.*]

Mrs. Pender. Well, God Almighty, isn't that th' limit! An' no sign or light of a bobby, either. [*Comes back into the shop.*] Th' cool way that was done!

Jimmy. Now, would you put anything a past them, afther that?

Mrs. Pender. Who'd think a body ud be taken in with a body like that? Talkin' as if butther wouldn't melt in her mouth. . . . Everything perfect, says she, tangerine undies an' all!

Jimmy. Tangerine undies an' all. . . . It's marvellous how they make them for a shillin', says she.

Mrs. Pender. Please let me have a look at wan o' them, maam, says she.

Jimmy [*with a chuckle*]. Be God, an' she's havin' a long look at it!

Mrs. Pender [*angrily*]. It's very easy for some fools to be made to laugh. . . . It's no laughin' matther . . . a shillin' afther walkin' out o' th' shop. . . . It'll take a lot o' hoppin' about before I make a shillin' profit. . . . If you think it funny for divils like them to be comin' into th' shop, I can tell you I don't.

Jimmy. I wassen' laughin', I wassen' laughin' . . . but th' whole thing was done so cute like, an' th' two of us lookin' at her!

Mrs. Pender. It was you gassin' here, out o' you, that made me take me mind off her, an' I knowin' th' sort o' billickers that's goin' about here.

[*Oul' Joe enters; he is about sixty years of age, very much bent in the body; he is dressed up to the nines—fawn coat, grey trilby hat, fancy muffler, brown boots and leggings. He carries a bunch of flowers.*]

Joe [*to Jimmy, stiffly*]. Good evenin'.

Jimmy [*just as stiffly*]. Oh, good evenin'.

Joe [*going over to Mrs. Pender*]. There's a few flowers for another little flower.

Mrs. Pender [*irritably*]. Ah, I don't want to be bothered with flowers now.

Joe. Why, what's up?

Mrs. Pender. A man about th' place! Faith, as far as I can see, a mouse about th' place ud be betther than a man.

Joe. That all depends on th' kind th' man is. Why, is there anythin' wrong?

Mrs. Pender. A minute ago in sails a young whipster of a wan; let's look at wan o' tham dolls, says she; how much is it, says she; shillin', says I; Oh, Maggie, says she runnin' to th' door, look a' th' lovely doll for a shillin', an' out she goes with th' doll, an we're waitin' for her to come back ever since.

Joe. She did!

Jimmy. It was th' cleverest done thing I ever seen . . . marvellous value, says she . . . [*chuckling*] everythin' perfect, says she, tangerine undies an' all! It was th' business!

Mrs. Pender [*with cold dignity*]. Mr. James Devanny, if you want to make a laugh of it, I'd be thankful if you'd make a laugh of it somewhere else, an' not in this shop.

Joe. People ought to show a little feelin', right enough.

Jimmy [*huffily*]. Oh, I'll be off if I'm not wanted. . . . If yous settle anythin' between yous, maybe yous'll ass us to th' weddin'. . . . Dressed up to th' nines! . . . Puffed, powdhered an' shaved . . . oh, there's no fool like an oul' fool! [*He goes out.*]

Mrs. Pender. There now, that's what comes o' makin' too free with some people.

Joe [*looking after Jimmy*]. Imagine a poor thing like that thinkin' he's a great man with th' ladies! Isn't it outrageous! . . . Well, every cripple has his own way o' walkin'. . . . Maybe it's a wife he wants! Love's young dhream, an' he tottherin' to th' grave! It's sods'll be fallin' on him soon instead o' confetti. . . . Wife! . . . Oh, isn't he th' right oul' ram! [*Going behind the counter.*] Isn't it a wondher he can't see you're only havin' a laugh at him.

Mrs. Pender. Stop where y'are, now, jus' stop where y'are; I've had enough of that sort o' thing for wan night.

Joe. Sure, it isn't fair to be always keepin' a man's heart in a frenzy of a flutter. Well, are you goin' to give us an answer wan way or t'other? What's th' use o' goin' on, buoyin' up men with false fancies? Can't you thry to come to a decision like th' Doyle, an' say either 'ta or nil? [*Coaxingly.*] It's ten to wan on th' favourite, isn't it darlin'? [*Joe goes round the counter and with his arm round Polly, sings the following, his eyes fixed with fascination on her face.*]

Gie me a quiet hour at e'en, me arms about me dearie o,
An' worldly cares an' worldly men, may all gae tapsal-
teerie o,
For Nature swears the lovely dears, her noblest work she
classes o,
Her prentice han' she tried on man, ah then she made th'
lasses o.

Th' two of us nicely balanced, neither too ould nor too young. . . . Come now, isn't it soon goin' to be for betther an' worse, for richer and poorer, come, say either 'ta or nil, dar-blast these chiselurs!

[*Robert, Nannie's boy, enters. He is twelve years old, and a hunchback, due to a spinal disease; pale and fragile, a half cunning, half wistful look in his eyes. His clothes are tattered, and his boots badly broken.*]

Robert [*handing Mrs. Pender a docket and a shilling*]. Dandy Dinny sent me back with this—Gollywog didn't run. I couldn't come any sooner.

Mrs. Pender. Blast it! An' yestherday Kisser was beaten be a neck!

Robert. You can never depend on th' two year ouls.

Mrs. Pender. Have you anything good for to-morrow, Robert?

Robert. Well, now, it's a toss up between Noisy Oysther an' Batthery Smoke. I think Noisy Oysther'll about do it.

Irish Nannie [*in the street, some distance away*]. There's th' Dublin Bobbies for yous. . . . Th' minute he clapped eyes on Irish Nannie off he skeeted. . . . Irish Nannie put th' fear o' God in his heart!

Robert [*running out*]. God Almighty, here's me oul' wan, I'll have to skip!

Mrs. Pender. Poor little Robert . . . he's afraid of his life of her . . . she leathers hell out of him.

Joe. He's a crabby lookin' little youngster.

Mrs. Pender. He couldn't be anything else; he lives on th' streets. When he was three or four he fell down a stairs an' hurted his back. . . . It's a wondher they wouldn't do something for poor little kiddies like him, instead o' thryin' to teach them Irish.

Joe. Oh, we've bigger things than that to settle first; we have to put th' Army on a solid basis, an' then, th' Boundhary Question has to be settled too—in comparisement with things like them, a few cripples o' chiselurs is neither here nor there.

Nannie [*coming nearer, from Right to Left, till she is seen outside the window*]. She's an oul' fashion'd lady with oul' fashion'd ways, an' a smile that says welcome to you—Nannie kep' her oul' father for years, an' he lyin' stretched out not able to stir a hand or foot . . . good money she earned for him, when it was to be got; an' bad money when there was nothin' else knockin' about. . . . Th' Prison docthor says she'll dhrop any minute. . . . Well, we've only to die wanst, an' Nannie'll die game, die game, die game! [*She passes out of sight.*]

[*Jimmy and Johnny enter the shop from the Right; they stand for a moment at the door looking up the street. A crash of breaking glass is heard.*]

Johnny [*coming in followed by Jimmy*]. There, she must have afther puttin' in a window. She's outdoin' herself to-night. Ow, it's cowld to-night, mind you.

Joe [*coming from behind the counter*]. Cowld? Maybe it is. . . . I don't feel cold meself, anyway. I never mind th' winther at all . . . other people have to be wrapped up in flannels.

Jimmy. You don't look very warm, then. . . . I don't feel cold meself. Indeed, it's a warm night . . . only for th' rain, I wouldn't have this coat on.

Johnny. Oh, I don't feel cold meself. . . . I was only sayin' what everybody's sayin'—doin' what th' Government wants us to do—fallin' in with th' will o' th' majority.

Joe. Th' heat has a drooth on me.

Jimmy. Here's th' same as that.

Mrs. Pender. There's plenty o' milk here to cool yous, if yous want to be cooled.

Johnny. Give's a glass of it.

Jimmy. Ay, an' me too.

Joe. I'll not be wan odd—give us another.

    [*Mrs. Pender gives them the milk, and goes into the room Left. They take a drink in fear and trembling.*]

Joe. Oh, God, that's murdherin' cold!

Johnny. It's like ice goin' down!

Jimmy. It's not safe to be dhrinkin' milk in th' winther.

Johnny. It's not safe to be dhrinkin' it anytime. Didn't th' paper say there was only wan dhrink worse than milk, an' that was a dhrink o' th' Liffey wather at th' Butt Bridge. It's right enough for chiselurs.

Jimmy. I've had enough of it.

Joe. Same here.

Johnny. Me, too.

    [*Mrs. Pender returns.*]

Mrs. Pender. Why don't yous drink your milk? That's th' stuff'll put th' gizz into yous.

Joe. Divil a much gizz I want; I'm as soople, nearly, as ever I was.

Johnny. It ud be a good job, then, to show your soopleness when you're leppin' off thrams.

Joe. Leppin' off thrams! Who was leppin' off thrams?

Johnny. Didn't I see you t'other day, an' you doin' th' big fella, leppin' off a goin' thram. [*To the others*.] An' th' next thing I seen was me boul' boyo, an' he standin' on his ear!

Mrs. Pender. He'll have to be more careful—he'd be no use to poor Polly if he was a cripple.

Joe. If I was hurted aself, I wouldn't be long gettin' over it. [*Stretching out his hand*.] Look a' that, now; not as much as a sign, an' it was an ugly cut when I got it. U, u, u, ugh, says th' surgeon, that's a bad wan, as soon as he had a decko at it. Seven stitches, says he, I'll have to put you asleep. For what, says I? Th' pain, you wouldn't be able to stick it, says he. Gwan, says I, an' don't be keepin' me waitin'.

Jimmy. That's not th' story I heard from them that seen you runnin' like mad through th' streets to th' hospital; or Micky Mannin, that was there when you came beltin' in, an' th' eyes leppin' out o' your head with fright, an' you kickin' like a divil at th' first door you met, an' shoutin'— where's th' doctor, where's th' doctor; am I goin' to be kep' waitin' till there'll be no use o' waitin' any longer; is there none o' yous gives a God's curse whether a man bleeds to death or no? [*He imitates the fright of Joe by clasping his left hand tightly with his right, as if it were badly cut, and kicking frantically at the counter*.]

Mrs. Pender. Aw, we don't mind Micky Mannin; he was jealous o' Joe, that's what it was.

Jimmy. Whether or no, a cut on th' hand isn't much to be blowin' about. It's not long ago since I was opened meself all around here [*his hand draws a circle round the middle of his body*]: an' everything inside o' me was as visible as th' works of a clock; there was only wan arthery that they didn't cut through—touch an' go, touch an' go, for days; an' here I am to-day, as sound as a bell.

Mrs. Pender. An' lookin' for a wife.

Joe. Ay, lookin' for a wife.

Jimmy. An', maybe'll get wan, too; ey, Polly?

Mrs. Pender. Faith is able to remove mountains, Jimmy.

Johnny. Well, thanks be to God, I can say my inside was never out of ordher—I never took a spoonful o' medicine in me life. I believe in keepin' fit be exercise.

Joe. Exercise; walkin'?

Jimmy. Leppin' off o' thrams?

Johnny. Leppin' off o' thrams! Swedish Dhrill exercises; I'm that fit, now, that I'd tackle any young fella, an' more than hold me own with him.

Mrs. Pender. Unless he had a gun, Johnny.

Johnny. Gun or no gun, I'd chance it.

Jimmy. That wouldn't be much to do; th' most o' th' gunmen goin' now, are afraid to use their guns.

Joe. Go for them straight; tackle them, tackle them, an' divil a much fight any of them'll show.

Johnny. Not bendin' me knees, I can tip me toes twenty times without stoppin'.

Joe [*scornfully*]. Oh, sure, anywan could do that.

Jimmy. Tcha, sure, you could keep that up all night, without feelin' tired.

Johnny [*challengingly*]. Would either o' yous do it?

Jimmy and Joe. Of course we'd do it.

Johnny. Twenty times?

Joe. Ay, fifty times.

Johnny. Here, I bet yous anything yous like, yous won't do it twenty times.

Joe. Let's see you doin' it first.

Mrs. Pender [*interested, and seeing some fun in front of her*]. The three of yous to-gether; gwan, I'll keep count; gwan, let's see which of yous is th' best man!

Johnny. All right; mind you, yous aren't to bend your knees.

Mrs. Pender. When I say wan, yous are all to start to-gether.

[*They form up, stretch their arms above their heads, and stiffly perform the exercises.*]

Mrs. Pender [*counting*]. Wan, two, three, four—you're bendin' your knees, Joe—five, six—tip your toes, Jimmy—seven, eight, nine.

Irish Nannie [*appearing at the window*]. Irish Nannie wants nothin' from anybody, Free State or Republic. . . . Th' sharks hasn't left much for anybody to get. . . . As long as Nannie has her pair o' mits, she'll fight her own corner. . . . [*Passing.*] For th' angels above taught th' way how to love . . . to that oul' fashion'd mother . . . o' . . . mine.

[*A young man in a light coat, and a cap pulled down over his eyes, enters; he looks at the exercising men for a moment.*]

The Young Man. Are t'ould goin' mad as well as th' young?

[*Joe, Jimmy and Johnny rise, and stand together, a little embarrassed.*]

Mrs. Pender [*to the Young Man*]. What d'ye want, sir?

The Young Man [*quietly, drawing a gun*]. I want all th' money you have in th' shop, quick!

Mrs. Pender [*appealingly*]. I'm a poor lone widow woman, sir; you wouldn't rob a widow, would you?

The Young Man [*snappily*]. Come on, come on; I've no time to waste arguin'.

Jimmy. You'd betther, Polly, you'd betther.

Joe. Take him quietly, Polly, take him quietly.

Johnny. Oh, what's th' use o' thryin' to argue with a gun?

Mrs. Pender. I'm not goin' to let meself be robbed, I'll not let meself be robbed!

The Young Man [*viciously, to Joe*]. Here, you, go behind, an' hand out th' cash. [*As Joe hesitates.*] Go on, y'oul' so an' so! [*Joe goes behind the counter, and Mrs. Pender bars the way to the till.*]

Joe [*imploringly, to Mrs. Pender*]. Polly, what's th' use o' goin' again Providence! Sure, when it can't be helped, it can't be helped.

Jimmy. For God's sake, Joe, get th' money, an' let th' man go about his business!

Johnny. If y'ass me, she's lookin' for throuble!

[*Nannie rushes in like a whirlwind, carrying the balloon in her hand. Knocking against the Young Man, she catches him in her arms, and pulls him around the shop. Joe, Jimmy and Johnny duck behind the counter.*]

Irish Nannie. A short life an' a merry wan. . . . She's an oul' fashion'd—

The Young Man [*struggling fiercely*]. Blast you, you dhrunked oul' rip! Let me go, let me go, d'ye hear, or I'll—

[*He breaks away and runs precipitantly out of the shop.*]

Mrs. Pender [*enthusiastically*]. Good man, Nannie; well done, Nannie. Bravo, girl, Nannie!

Irish Nannie [*wildly elated at realising dazedly, that she has done something remarkable, catching Joe in her arms, and dancing with him*].

An' a smile that says welcome to you;
An oul' fashion'd bedside where she kneels an' prays,
When th' toil of th' long day is through—

Joe [*savagely, in degrees of crescendo*]. Ey, ey, ey, ey, ey!

Irish Nannie [*releasing Joe, and seizing Jimmy*].

Tho' she wears no fine clothes, nor no rich silken hose—

Jimmy [*frantically*]. Ey, houl' on there, damn you, houl' on there; d'ye want to shake th' little life I have in me out o' me!

Irish Nannie [*releasing Jimmy and catching Johnny*].

Still there's something that makes her divine;
For th' angels above taught the way how to love,
To that oul' fashioned mother o' mine!

Johnny [*breathlessly*]. Ey, houl' on, there, houl' on there; leggo ou' o' that! I'm not able to be leppin' about like this if you are—leggo ou' o' that, I'm tellin' you!

Irish Nannie.

She's an oul' fashion'd lady with oul' fashion'd ways,
An' a smile that says welcome to you.
An oul' fashion'd bedside where—

[*She suddenly stops singing; her body assumes a statuesque rigidity; a look of fear and terror flashes into her eyes; after the passage of a few moments, her body sways tremblingly, her arms are outstretched, and her hands paw the air as if feeling for support, and the realization of something terrible about to happen to her deepens in her face.*]

Irish Nannie. Christ Almighty! What ails me! Me head is whirlin', me heart is stoppin'. . . . Get me brought to th' hospital, quick. [*She grips the counter convulsively.*] I'll die game . . . I'll die game, I'll die game! . . . Will none o' yous go for a docthor . . . I'm dyin', I tell yous, dyin', dyin', dyin'.

[*She sinks down to the floor, and lies with her head and shoulders supported by the counter.*]

z

Mrs. Pender [*running over to her*]. What's wrong, Nannie; what ails you?

Irish Nannie. For God's sake, some o' yous go for a priest. . . . I stuck be me oul' fella th' whole time he was crippled, till he died, till he died, till he died. [*Screaming feebly.*] I don't care, I don't care, I'll die game, I'll die game!

[*A crowd has gathered at the door, which includes the Ballad Singer and Robert, Nannie's child.*]

Robert [*running over to Nannie*]. What ails you, mother, what ails you?

The Ballad Singer. Aw, she's goin' right enough; I'm afraid this is th' end o' Nannie.

Irish Nannie [*feebly*]. Tho' she wears no fine clothes, nor no rich . . . silken hose . . . still there's . . . something . . . that makes . . . her . . . di . . . vine . . . Jesus, I feel me heart stoppin'. . . . Is there ne'er a wan to go for a docthor? . . . Th' priest, th' priest. . . . God'll not be too hard on poor Irish Nannie . . . poor Irish Nannie. . . . Say a prayer, will you . . . some o' yous . . . Nannie's goin' . . . she's goin' . . . . She'll die game, she'll . . . die . . . game.

Robert [*in anguish*]. Mother, mother!

Joe [*to Mrs. Pender*]. Say a prayer, you, Polly.

Mrs. Pender. My prayers ud be no good, I only know Protestan' prayers.

The Ballad Singer [*taking off his hat*]. Look at her eyes, she's goin' fast; I'll say all I can remember. Lord have mercy on her.

The Rest. Christ have mercy on her.

The Ballad Singer. Holy Mother o' God.

The Rest. Pray for her.

The Ballad Singer. Virgin Most Merciful—

The Rest. Pray for her.

The Ballad Singer. Health of the Weak—

The Rest. Pray for her.

The Ballad Singer. Refuge of sinners—

The Rest. Pray for her.

The Ballad Singer. May God look down on th' spirit of our poor sisther, that, feelin' th' wind, maybe got no message from it; that, lookin' up at th' sky, maybe seen no stars; that, lookin' down at th' earth, maybe, seen no flowers. Rememberin' th' bittherness of th' shocks her poor body got, may God give th' soul of our sisther th' sweetness of eternal rest!

The Rest. Amen!

[*The sound of an approaching motor is heard, stopping near the shop. Nannie is lying very still.*]

Johnny. Here's th' ambulance comin'.

[*Two Ambulance Men enter; they carry a stretcher. One of them goes over to Nannie, and, bending down, gently places his hand on her breast.*]

The Ambulance Man. Aw, gone west! They all go like the snuff of a candle. She'll sleep in th' Morgue to-night. . . . I suppose it's as good as any o' th' places she ever slep' in. . . . Catch a hold of her, Tom.

[*They swing Nannie on to the stretcher, and carry her out followed by Robert and the rest, except Mrs. Pender, Joe, Jimmy, and Johnny. The Ballad Singer lingers at the door.*]

Joe. Whoever ud a thought that she'd a dhropped so sudden?

Jimmy. It's very hard to have any sympathy for that class o' people.

The Ballad Singer [*turning round, and speaking passionately*]. Yous gang o' hypocrites! What was it made Nannie what she was? Was it havin' too much money? Who gave a damn about her? It was only when she was dhrunk an' mad that anywan took any notice of her! What can th' like o' them do, only live any way they can? Th' Poorhouse, th' Prison an' th' morgue—them is our palaces! I suppose yous want us to sing "Home Sweet Home," about our tenements? D'ye think th' blasted kips o' tenement houses we live in 'll breed Saints an' Scholars? . . . It's a long time, but th' day's comin' . . . th' day's comin' . . . Oh, it's cruel, it's cruel! [*He goes out.*]

Mrs. Pender [*going over to the shop door, and standing at it*]. Here, I'm goin' to shut th' shop; I've had enough for wan night. Addin' two an' two together, I think th' best thing Polly Pender can do, is to remain a bird alone.

Joe [*going out*]. Good night, all.

Jimmy [*to Johnny*]. Well, so long, Johnny. [*Going out.*] Everything perfect, says she; [*with a chuckle*] tangerine undies, an' all! It was th' business!

> [*Mrs. Pender closes and locks the door with a vicious movement.*]

Johnny. Give us a penny candle, an' I'll g'up an' go to bed.

> [*Without a word, Mrs. Pender gives him the candle, and he goes out by door on Left.*]

Voices of Ballad Singers [*some distance up the street*].

> For Ireland is Ireland thro' joy an' thro' tears.
> Hope never dies thro' they long weary years;

> [*Mrs. Pender extinguishes the light and leaves the shop. The rain has ceased, and the stars in the sky seem to be peering through the window into the darkened shop.*]

Voices of Ballad Singers.

> Each age has seen countless, brave hearts pass away,
> But their spirits still live on in they men of to-day.

THE CURTAIN SLOWLY FALLS

Another Ending

Irish Nannie [*releasing Joe, and seizing Jimmy*].

Tho' she wears no fine clothes, nor no rich silken hose—

Jimmy [*frantically*]. Ey, houl' on there, damn you, houl' on there; d'ye want to shake th' little life I have in me out o' me!

Irish Nannie [*releasing Jimmy and catching Johnny*].

Still there's something that makes her divine;
For th' angels above taught the way how to love,
To that oul' fashion'd mother o' mine!

Johnny [*breathlessly*]. Ey, houl' on there, houl' on there; leggo ou' o' that! I'm not able to be leppin' about like this if you are—leggo ou' o' that, I'm tellin' you!

Irish Nannie. Nannie'll put gizz into you [*Singing.*]

She's an oul' fashion'd lady with oul' fashion'd ways,
An' a smile that says welcome to you.
An oul' fashion'd bedside where she kneels and prays,
When the toil of th' long day is through.

[*She releases Johnny who sinks exhausted against the counter. Nannie catches up Jimmy's walking stick, dances round the shop and out into the street singing.*]

Tho' she wears no fine clothes nor no rich silken hose,
Still there's something that makes her divine,
For th' angels above taught th' way how to love,
To that oul' fashion'd mother o' mine!

Johnny [*with a gasp*]. Every bone in me body's shook asundher!

Jimmy. Me heart's thumpin' yet like a piston rod; an' I'll never see me walkin' stick again, either.

Mrs. Pender. What does a frisky youngsther like you want with a walkin' stick?

Joe [*going to the shop door and looking up the street*]. The like
o' them shouldn't be let out o' jail at all. . . . There she goes
whirlin' th' stick. [*A crash of glass is heard.*] O, o, oh, she's
afther puttin' in th' window o' Doyle's! If you seen th' way
she done it! [*Enthusiastically.*] Drew back her fist with th'
walkin' stick, let it fly an' gave it a larrup! It was th'
business!

Irish Nannie [*up the street*]. Nannie'll show yous whether she
cares about yous or no . . . she'll make some o' yous put up
your shutthers. . . . Nannie'll put th' fear o' God in some o'
your hearts!

Joe. Aw, be th' holy, there's three Bobbies down on top of her!
There's kickin' an' bitin' an' plungin'! God, it's th'
business!

[*Jimmy and Johnny come to the door. Mrs. Pender looks
out of the window.*]

Irish Nannie [*shouting outside*]. Yous'll bring down Nannie, will
yous? It'll take more than th' three of yous to pull her!
Three agen' wan . . . three agen' wan! . . . Yous gang o'
silver button'd bouseys! Th' poor Tommies was men, th'
poor Tommies was men!

The Voice of the Ballad Singer [*evidently to the Police*]. Have
yous ne'er a bit o' spiritual or corporal charity left in yous?
Don't be twistin' th' woman's arm!

The Voice of a Policeman. If I lay me hans on you, me bucko,
I'll twist your neck!

Irish Nannie [*in the distance as she is being brought away*].
Drag me down, drag me down. It's takin' three o' th' biggest
Bouseys in th' Force to take Nannie. . . . I'll swing for wan
o' yous yet . . . I'll swing for wan o' yous yet!

[*The clamour of bringing Nannie to the Station dies
away, and Jimmy, Joe and Johnny leave the door and
return to the shop.*]

Johnny. It ud be a God's charity if that wan got about ten years!

Joe. I'm not over th' rattlin' she gave me yet. There's wan consolation—they'll knock hell out of her when they get her to th' Station!

Mrs. Pender. They'll hammer hell out o' Nannie; but they weren't here to hammer hell out o' the gunman!

Jimmy [*half to himself*]. Closes its eyes, an' all, too, says she; an' only a shillin'—it was th' business.

Mrs. Pender [*going over to the door and standing at it*]. Comparin' Nannie with some o' yous is like comparin' a flywheel to a trouser's button—Here, I'm goin' to shut th' shop. I've had enough for wan night. Maybe there'd be another hold up, an' I don't want yous to be riskin' your lives. Yez are a nice gang of guardian angels for any poor woman to have hangin' round her. So th' whole of yous ud better buzz off ou' o' this. I suppose when yous go out yous'll be sayin' Nannie got in the way; only for Nannie yous ud have stretched him out: that Nannie saved his life!

Joe [*going out*]. I was jus' thinkin' o' goin' meself—good night all.

Jimmy. Well, so long. [*Going out.*] Everything perfect, says she; [*with a chuckle*] tangerine undies an' all — it was th' business!

[*Mrs. Pender closes and locks the door with a vicious bang.*]

Johnny [*meekly*]. Give us a penny candle, an' I'll g'up an' go to bed.

[*Without a word Mrs. Pender gives him the candle, and he goes slowly out by door on Left.*]

The Voices of the Ballad Singers [*some distance up the street*].

> For Ireland is Ireland thro' joy an' thro' tears.
> Hope never dies thro' they long weary years.

Mrs. Pender [*extinguishing the light and going out by door on Left*]. Addin' two an' two together, I think th' best thing Polly Pender can do is to remain a bird alone.

[*The rain has ceased; the sky has brightened, and the stars seem to be peering through the window into the darkened shop.*]

The Ballad Singers.

Each age has seen countless, brave hearts pass away,
But her spirit still lives on in they men of to-day!

The Curtain Slowly Falls

That Old-Fashioned Mother of Mine[6]

When Shall the Day Break in Erin

Words by Denis Downing   *Music by Aynsley Fox*

Annie Dear

Herself and Meself

Oul Joe's Song

Biographical Notes

To keep these notes within reasonable bounds, I have limited them to the major historical figures and the major contemporary figures whom O'Casey refers to in this book. I have omitted, in addition to minor figures, individuals like Yeats and Parnell for whom a gloss would be superfluous for anyone with an interest in Ireland.

A.E., see Russell, George William.

BIRRELL, AUGUSTINE (1850-1933), English essayist, barrister, and statesman. He was Secretary for Ireland in the British Cabinet from 1907 to 1916. During his term of office Parliament passed the Irish Universities Act, the Irish Land Act, and the Home Rule Act.

CARSON, LORD EDWARD (1854-1935), English politician and lawyer. Carson successfully defended the naval cadet in the famous Archer-Shee case of 1910 which later became the basis of Terence Rattigan's play, *The Winslow Boy*. He was bitterly opposed to Home Rule and organised in Ulster the military force called Carson's Volunteers, which may partially have suggested the idea of the Irish Citizen Army. Carson was largely instrumental in keeping the six counties as part of the United Kingdom.

CHILDERS, ERSKINE (1870-1922), Irish patriot and author of the remarkable thriller, *The Riddle of the Sands*. From 1910 to 1914 Childers engaged in political work and writing for Home Rule. He was elected to Dail Eireann in 1921, opposed the Anglo-Irish Treaty of 1922, supported de Valera and joined the Republicans in the Civil War. He was captured in 1922 and executed by the British.

CONNOLLY, JAMES (1870-1916), Irish labour leader and Republican. After Larkin's departure for America, Connolly was the leader of the Irish Citizen Army and the editor of *The Irish Worker*. Deciding that Socialism could not come to Ireland until the country was independent, he joined with the Irish Republican Brotherhood and the Irish Volunteers in the Rising of Easter Week. He was in charge of the fighting at the Post Office, and he was subsequently executed.

COSGRAVE, WILLIAM THOMAS (1880——), Irish politician. Cosgrave fought with Pearse in Easter Week, and was a member of de Valera's Republican ministry. He was later President of the Irish Free State after the deaths of Arthur Griffith and Michael Collins.

DAVIS, THOMAS (1814-1845), Irish poet and nationalist. Davis helped found *The Nation* in 1842. He was the chief writer for this journal, and in it he preached the gospel of nationalism. *The Nation* attracted a group of Irish intellectuals and revolutionists who became known as the Young Irelanders. The song, "Annie Dear," which the Ballad Singer sings in "Nannie's Night Out," is by Davis.

DE VALERA, EAMON (1882——), Irish politician. As a member of the Irish Volunteers, de Valera fought in Easter Week and was subsequently imprisoned. Upon his release, he worked for Republicanism, and after the secession of Sinn Fein from Parliament, he was made president of the Sinn Fein government. De Valera refused to accept the Treaty of 1922 and resisted the Free State government. After being imprisoned by the Government and released, he resumed leadership of Sinn Fein, but refused to participate in the Dail. He later took the oath of allegiance to the British king "as an empty political formula" and entered the Dail. Subsequently, de Valera became President of the Free State, Prime Minister of The Republic of Ireland, and at present he is President of Ireland.

DUFFY, CHARLES GAVAN (1816-1903), Irish Nationalist. Duffy was a founder of *The Nation* and a leader of the Young Irelanders. Advocating a more militant struggle against England, Duffy was tried for treason and acquitted in 1848. Convinced he could not improve the lot of Ireland, he migrated in 1855 to Australia where he had a distinguished political career. In 1880 he returned to Europe and spent the remainder of his life in literary work.

EMMET, ROBERT (1778-1803), Irish patriot and rebel. In 1800 Emmet journeyed to the Continent and became associated with the revolutionary society, the United Irishmen. In 1802 Emmet gained assurance of assistance from Napoleon in the fight for Irish independence, and returned to Ireland, where he organised an armed rebellion that miscarried. In 1803, at the head of an undisciplined force of 150 men with pikes, Emmet led an attack upon Dublin Castle which also miscarried, as his men dispersed along the way. He was captured and executed by the British. Emmet has been celebrated in literature by

Thomas Moore, Washington Irving, and others; he appears as the hero of Denis Johnston's remarkable play "The Old Lady Says 'No!' "

GRATTAN, HENRY (1746-1820), Irish statesman and orator. As the leader of the National party, Grattan petitioned successfully that the Irish Parliament be free from domination by the English Privy Council. However, the new Parliament still had no control over the executive appointees from England, and was, consequently, not notably effective. Grattan worked for Catholic enfranchisement and other reforms which were defeated. After his retirement came the uprising of 1798. O'Casey in his Nationalist period usually referred to Grattan contemptuously for working ineffectually for reform through parliamentary methods.

GRIFFITH, ARTHUR (1872-1922), Irish politician and journalist. In 1899 Griffith became editor of *The United Irishman* in which he preached a policy of strong nationalism. In 1902 he enunciated the policy of Sinn Fein (";We Ourselves"), or Ireland for the Irish. Sinn Fein refused to pay taxes to England and worked for an Irish Parliament which would have no ties to England except a formal submission to the Crown. Griffith supported the Irish Volunteers, and although he was not active in the 1916 Rising, he was imprisoned. In 1918 he was elected Vice-President of the Irish Republic. In 1921 he led the delegation to negotiate the treaty recognizing the Irish Free State. Although the Treaty established the Free State, it also established the division of Ulster, and Griffith and Michael Collins are usually thought to have been duped. Griffith was the first president of Dail Eireann, in 1922.

HOBSON, BULMER. Hobson was general Secretary and Quartermaster of the Irish Volunteers. He published in 1918, the same year in which O'Casey published *The Story of the Irish Citizen Army,* his *History of the Irish Volunteers.*

LALOR, JOHN FINTAN (?-1849), Irish revolutionary writer. Lalor was one of the Young Ireland Party who wrote for *The Nation.* Advocating physical force, his letters to *The Nation* were "marvels of passionate, persuasive rhetoric." After *The Nation* was suppressed, Lalor practically edited its successor, *The Irish Felon.* Imprisoned until his health was impaired, Lalor planned new conspiracies until his death. A quotation from Lalor appeared on the banner of Larkin's *Irish Worker:* "The principle I state and mean to stand upon is:—that the entire ownership of Ireland, moral and material, up to the sun and down to the centre is vested of right in the people of Ireland."

LARKIN, JIM (1877?-1947), Labour leader and orator. Larkin organised the Irish Transport and General Workers' Union, was the Labour leader during the 1913 Lockout, the editor of *The Irish Worker,* and one of the founders of the Communist Party in the United States. He was an enormously effective orator and inspired great devotion among the Dublin workers. He appears as Red Jim in O'Casey's play "The Star Turns Red."

MACNEILL, JOHN (EOIN) (1849-1926). MacNeill was Vice-President of the Gaelic League and a professor of Early Irish History at University College, Dublin. He helped organise the Irish Volunteers. C. C. Tansill, in *America and the Fight for Irish Freedom* (New York, 1957), says that when the I.R.B. began to infiltrate the Volunteers in preparation for an armed rising, Patrick Pearse and others were able to "assume powers which really belonged to Eoin MacNeill, who was Chief of Staff but whose natural indolence made it easy for more enterprising spirits to adopt a program with which he was in decided disagreement."

MARKIEVICZ, COUNTESS CONSTANCE (1868-1927), Irish patriot and Republican. Countess Markievicz, the daughter of Sir Henry Gore-Booth, married a Pole in the Russian consular service. Prominent in the social life of Dublin around 1910, she became thereafter active in labour and Republican circles. She was on the councils of the Irish Volunteers and the Irish Citizen Army, and she was second in command of the Stephen's Green detachment during the Rising. Subsequently she was condemned to death, reprieved to life imprisonment, and finally released in 1917. She was active in Republican circles until her death. In *The Story of the Irish Citizen Army,* O'Casey tells of the quarrel with Madame Markievicz which caused him to resign from the Army Council. In his autobiography O'Casey contrasts the motives and character of Madame Markievicz with that of Captain White (see below). See also Yeats's irritating but beautiful poem "In Memory of Eva Gore-Booth and Con Markievicz."

MITCHEL, JOHN (1815-1875), Irish patriot. Mitchel was a founder of and a writer for *The Nation* and a prominent member of the Young Irelanders. He was transported by the British to Bermuda and then to Australia in 1847. O Casey was much moved by Mitchel's *Jail Journal.*

O'CONNELL, DANIEL (1775-1847), Irish national leader and orator. O'Connell revived the Irish Catholic Committee to oppose British rule through constant nonviolent and legal agitation. Later he organised the Catholic Association. When elected to the British Parliament, he refused to serve until the anti-Catholic oath was repealed, and his refusal was a force in causing the Catholic Emancipation Act of 1829. He worked for repeal of the Act of Union in the English House of Commons, and though he made many inflammatory speeches, he was ever against violence.

O'GRADY, STANDISH (1846-1928), Irish man of letters. O'Grady was a pioneer in the Celtic Renaissance and published many volumes of romantic history, retelling the stories of the traditional Irish heroes.

O'NEILL, SHANE (called by the Irish "Shane an Diomais" or Shane the Proud), was the son of Conn Bacach O'Neill, Earl of Tyrone. He was constantly in rebellion against the English in Ireland, but he was killed with fifty of his followers by the Scots of Antrim at Cushendun in 1567. Of him Edmund Curtis writes: "Thus perished the greatest O'Neill that the old Gaelic order had produced."

O'REILLY, BOYLE (1844-1890), Irish-American politician and journalist. O'Reilly joined the Irish Republican Brotherhood and then enlisted in a British cavalry regiment to spread dissension and discontent among Irish soldiers. In 1866 he was court-martialled and transported to Australia, from where he escaped later to the United States.

PEARSE, PATRICK (1879-1916), Irish patriot, poet, and Gaelic Leaguer. The editor of *Claidheamh Soluis* and the founder of St. Enda's School for the teaching of Irish, Pearse joined the Irish Volunteers and was one of the principal planners of the 1916 Rising. He signed the Proclamation of the Republic, and he was Commander in Chief of the Republican forces during Easter Week. He was executed on May 3, 1916.

REDMOND, JOHN (1856-1918), Irish politician. Redmond was chairman of the Irish Nationalist Party after the death of Parnell. He worked for Home Rule through parliamentary methods. He did not believe in violence and was shocked by the Rising of 1916.

RUSSELL, GEORGE WILLIAM (A.E.) (1867-1925), Irish poet, mystic, and agricultural reformer. From 1923 Russell was the editor of *The Irish Statesman* in which several significant O'Casey documents were published.

SARSFIELD, PATRICK (?-1693), Irish Jacobite and soldier. Sarsfield was a major general after the Battle of the Boyne and the retreat of James II to France. He gallantly opposed the forces of William of Orange, and his stand at Limerick made him a popular hero.

SHEEHY-SKEFFINGTON, FRANCIS, who in his student days had published a dual pamphlet that also contained James Joyce's "The Day of the Rabblement," was killed during Easter Week while trying to prevent looting.

TONE, THEOBALD WOLFE (1763-1798), Irish Republican and patriot. Wolfe Tone helped organise the United Irishmen, attempted to persuade France to invade Ireland, and held a command in such an abortive invasion expedition. He was captured in 1798 and condemned, but cut his throat in prison before he could be executed.

WHITE, CAPTAIN J. R. (1879-?) was the son of a high-ranking British officer. He served in Africa and received the D.S.O. Later he served in India; then he retired and became for a while active in Irish politics. He trained and drilled the Irish Citizen Army. Later he offered to deliver two companies of the army to the Irish Volunteers. This extraordinary overture was made entirely on his own initiative and without sanction from the Citizen Army Council. Resigning from the Citizen Army, Captain White was for a brief time active in the Irish Volunteers. Both in *The Story of the Irish Citizen Army* and in his autobiography, O'Casey treats White with considerable magnanimity —with much more, in fact, than White treats O'Casey in his *Misfit* (London, 1930). In that book White gives the impression of being a naive and irresponsible romantic of considerable intelligence, considerable egotism, and little staying power. There is much information in the book about the Lockout of 1913. There are also a number of wild statements and some suppression of fact. White, for instance, attributes to himself the idea of creating a citizen army, and he also says nothing about offering to turn two companies of the Citizen Army over to the Irish Volunteers. His resignation from the army is worth quoting:

> I have already forecasted my resignation from command of the Citizen Army. When the strike was over, the Transport Union had leisure to realize that an uncontrolled military dictator in its midst needed a check. A committee was appointed to assist, advise, and shepherd me. I am not easy to shepherd yet; then I was impossible. After a few meetings of the committee the storm

broke. I don't remember even what the particular point of rupture was, very likely something affecting my personal vanity. If it had been an important point of principle, I would have remembered.

I turned to Connolly saying: "All you'll do will be to destroy my work," and to Sean O'Cathasaigh, who was secretary of the committee, saying: "And it's all your fault"; what I alleged to be his fault I forget. Then I marched out of the room, a free man, to spread myself with the rapidly spreading Irish National Volunteers; say rather a swollen-headed young ass looking for lime-light in a movement with which spiritually I had little or nothing in common. Perhaps I am too hard on myself. I was looking for scope for my abounding energy. . . .

White's actions and his book suggest to this reader a harsher judgment than O'Casey's. Indeed, it is hard to disagree with this conversation which White reports with James Connolly:

What Connolly said to me one day, when I remonstrated about my army being taken off to a political meeting without my being notified, was true enough, "You're nothing but a great boy," said he.

WILSON, ANDREW PATRICK, the columnist who wrote under the pseudonym of "Euchan" for *The Irish Worker,* later became an actor at the Abbey Theatre and, after Lennox Robinson's resignation in 1914, the manager of the theatre. During his management, the Abbey produced two of his own plays, *The Cobbler* and *The Slough,* the latter being the first Abbey play to treat of the Dublin slums. In 1915, on a visit of the Abbey to London, Wilson refused to rehearse *Deirdre of the Sorrows,* and resigned. He became for a short while the manager of Arthur Sinclair's Irish Players, and in 1921 he became director of the Scottish National Players. In his Irish period, Wilson referred to himself as A. Patrick Wilson; in his Scottish period as Andrew P. Wilson.

Printed in Great Britain by Lowe & Brydone (Printers) Ltd., London